To: My
Gayle

Your
Fabulous
Fifties

With Love

From:
"Auntie" Eloise Louis
July   2007

Your Fabulous Fifties

Mike Yorkey

Victor is an imprint of
Cook Communications Ministries, Colorado Springs, CO 80918
Cook Communications, Paris, Ontario, Canada
Kingsway Communications, Eastbourne, England

Cover Design: Smith/Lane Associates
Cover Photos: *Couple*: Don Klumpp/Image Bank; *Golfer*: Image Bank;
Trumpeter: Jeff Lane
Interior Layout: Pat Miller
Copyediting: Barbara Williams

Library of Congress Cataloging-in-Publication Data

Your fabulous fifties / Mike Yorkey.
       p. cm.
       ISBN 1-564-76729-9
       1. Middle aged persons--Religious life. 2. Baby boom generation--Religious
life. I. Yorkey, Mike.

BV4579.5 .Y68 2000   99-042496
248.8'4--dc21   CIP

---

2 3 4 5 6 7 8 9 10 Printing/Year 03 02 01 00

CONTENTS

2—YOU AND YOUR FAMILY

3—YOU AND YOUR GOD

4—YOU AND YOUR OLDER CHILDREN

6—YOU AND YOUR WORLD

7—YOU AND YOUR RETIREMENT FINANCES

8—YOU AND YOUR OLDER PARENTS

9—YOU AND YOUR TOUGH TIMES

10—ENDING NOTE

FOREWORD

by David & Claudia Arp

The second half of life can be a time of incredible fulfillment, no matter what challenges you previously faced. It can be a time of learning about God's long-term plans for your life—a time for dreaming, for making commitments, and for enjoying your marriage, family, and life in a new fresh way.

We still remember when we hit the fifties. Dave's big Five-O was fast approaching. Our last teenager, Jonathan, was graduating from high school and leaving soon for college. With the long-awaited empty nest looming, I (Claudia) concocted a birthday surprise for Dave. Without his knowledge, I arranged for our older two sons and spouses (who lived in other states) to join the fun.

On Dave's actual birthday, Jonathan and I surprised him by taking him to the place where our last family picture had been snapped. Waiting for us was our favorite photographer. When Dave wondered why, we explained that our fiftieth birthday present was an official empty nest picture. As the photographer snapped away, our other two sons and wives walked up as if they beamed down in Star Trek!

Was Dave surprised? Of course! And you may also be surprised as well at all the amazing discoveries that await you as you hit the fifties. Everything will change. Your marriage will transition from a child-focused to a partner-focused relationship. You will have the opportunity to reinvent your relationship, build a more personal, intimate friendship with your spouse, and deepen your love for each other.

Your family dynamics will change, even if your kids aren't immediately leaving the nest. For certain, your relationship with them will be different as they grow toward adulthood. And in your fifties, you'll probably meet your first grandchild.

Wonderful! Exciting! We have five delightful grandchildren and trust us—your grandchildren are your reward for never killing your kids.

In your fifties, your world will expand and you'll find new opportunities to reach out to others. And your relationship with your parents will change. You'll see your roles reverse. You'll watch with wonder how the cycle of life continues. You'll grow older, but life gets better. The poet Robert Browning summed up the challenges of the fifties when he penned, "Grow old along with me; the best is yet to be."

Fabulous Fifties? Absolutely! Especially if you take the following pages to heart. You can make the rest the best. We wouldn't be any other age, and after you read this book, you wouldn't either.

Blessings from your fellow travelers,

David & Claudia Arp
Authors of *The Second Half of Marriage*

INTRODUCTION

I'm part of the Baby Boomer class of 1946–1964, the huge generation passing through American society like a tennis ball through a snake. I know that most of my Boomer compatriots have crossed the fifty-years-and-older divide, and they are doing just fine, thank you.

I'm looking forward to what lies ahead. Not that I want to race through my final third of life (if God grants me the days), but I'm hearing more and more that the years between fifty and seventy can be richest of all. Experience has replaced youth, wisdom has replaced impetuousness. People in this age-group are healthier, more active, and more financially secure than ever before.

It's also a wide-ranging group. Some of you in your early fifties are empty-nesters, while others still have a handful of teenagers in the house. Some of you in your late fifties or early sixties have grandchildren living far away from home, while some of you are *raising* grandchildren. In the work arena, some of you see yourselves staying gainfully employed for a long time, while others of you have retired to work full time on your golf handicaps.

I imagine that many of you are like my parents, safely into their sixties, where no traditional "Grandpa" and "Grandma" roles and rocking chairs wait for them. When my eldest daughter, Andrea, was born, my mother informed me that she wanted Andrea and all successive grandchildren to call her "Mimi." The name has no special meaning in our family, but it's become a term of endearment that sounds right.

As for my dad, he's called "GD" by Andrea and Patrick, not Grandpa. GD stands for "Grand Dad," of course, but again, that moniker sounds better for an active grandfather who likes to putter around the house or the golf course.

I was asked to be the general editor for this book because it is the fourth in a series for Cook Communications/Chariot Victor Publishing. Thank you, Chariot Victor, for the vote of confidence.

So to all you "Mimis" and "GDs" out there—and those still waiting for grandkids or your kids to leave the nest, *Your Fabulous Fifties* book is for you. And thanks for letting me work on it in advance of my fiftieth birthday!

Mike Yorkey

1

You and Your Spouse

How's Your Marriage Doing?

. . . .

You'd think that after spending twenty, thirty, or forty years as husband and wife, your marriage would be trouble-free, right? Wrong! Statistics shows while the first seven years of matrimony is the most difficult for couples, too many couples decide to split the sheets after their silver anniversary.

So, how strong is your marriage? It's time to find out. This short quiz is designed to help you spot any trouble areas that may be cropping up in your relationship.

Answer the following:

1. Which year of marriage is the hardest?

(a) any year (b) the seventh (c) the first

2. I tell my spouse I love him (or her):

(a) all the time (b) once in a while (c) enough

3. When I look at my spouse, I:

(a) still get butterflies (b) try to recapture those old feelings
(c) wonder who this stranger is

4. The three C's of marriage are commitment, communication, and:

(a) change (b) control (c) cash

5. It's all right to be angry with one another if:
(a) you talk your problems out (b) scream your frustrations away
(c) walk away from the disagreement

Give yourself three points for every A answer, two for every B, and one point answer with C. Add up your score. If you score between nine and fifteen points, you have nothing to worry about. Your marriage is steadily paddling down Old Man River.

If you scored between six and nine points, your marriage has run aground a couple of times. You'll need to shore up your marriage's weak points.

A score of zero to eight could mean that your marriage is heading for level five rapids or even a waterfall. Have you thought about talking to your pastor or a counselor?

To help you better understand your score, writer Maurcia DeLean met with eleven couples who brought 534 years of combined marriage experience to the table. Here are some of their observations, which may help you:

1. Which year of marriage is the hardest?

Contrary to what most people believe, the first year is not the hardest. That's the time when the bloom is still on the proverbial rose. Most marriages begin with lofty goals when couples have the time and energy to build their relationship brick by brick.

The onset of the parenting years, however, causes many couples to shift their focus and energy onto the kids. During this season of life, often lasting twenty or thirty years, the romantic side of marriage is often put on hold. Couples are working hard just to get through the day, and life's everyday irritations can pile up, causing tempers to flare.

No matter what threatens your marriage—anger, frustration, boredom, even a lost trust—now is not the time to walk away. You've made it this far by surviving more than a few trials, and you can survive this one as well. Stick by one another. Renew a date night. Keep talking. If need be, ask for some "casual" counseling with one of your church pastors.

Most of the expert couples agree that, although couples in long-term relationships often know each other better than they know themselves, they often resort to this comfortable oneness to solve problems instead of hashing them out. After you've talked it through and aired both sides, don't forget to say "I love you."

2. Does saying, "I love you" really make a difference?

The obvious answer is yes. "Never hesitate to offer that verbal reinforcement to your mate," stressed Ruth. "Every night for the past fifty-five years, my husband has made it a point to tell me that he loves me, so I've never doubted it."

When questioning the importance of saying "I love you," remember Solomon's reply in Song of Songs 2:1, when the woman tells him that she's not special, just an ordinary flower. Does Solomon say, "Oh, yes, you're right"? Of course not! He expresses his feelings using the language of love. Even the Bible tells us that there is nothing more important than encouraging and appreciating our spouses. Remember that the next time you wonder whether saying "I love you" makes a difference.

3. What do you see when you look at your spouse?

"Romance," answered Joe, who's been married sixty years. Just because you've been married for oh, six decades, doesn't mean the romance must grow old too. The flame can continue to burn and burn strongly over the years.

4. Change is the last C in marriage.

Yes, folks, change is inevitable, just as the sun will set at the appointed time. Two individuals can't share a life together without changing, at least a little bit. Think about all the changes that have occurred in the world since you first said, "I do." Embrace change. Revel in new hobbies, new friends, new surroundings. Yes, there is much to be said for stability and routine, but even if we live in the same house and attend the same church, the world will change around us. That's a guarantee.

5. Anger is natural in any relationship.

That's a consensus opinion among long-term couples. They agree that the important thing is to talk things out and listen to what their spouse is saying. No marriage is trouble-free, even the ones that have lasted into the golden anniversary years. First Corinthians 7:28 says it best: "But those who marry will face many troubles in this life."

The key to overcoming these problems is to not hide or shy away from them. Deal with them head-on, let yourself be angry, then move on.

Finally, all of the interviewed couples agreed on this: Remain friends no matter what. In a healthy marriage, lovers are also friends who enjoy being with one another and who take the time to listen to one another, share their dreams, and care what the other is thinking.

But hey, you already know that. You're a married veteran, right? How else could you have made it this far? What you've just read is a just a little reminder, if you needed any reminding at all.

This chapter is adapted from writings by Maurcia DeLean of Abington, Pennsylvania.

LOVE IS A LONG-TERM DECISION

Clebe and Deanna McClary, authors and speakers from Pawleys Island, South Carolina, say that love is a decision, not based on feelings but on commitment. They say they've gone through some incredibly difficult times over their thirty-two years of marriage (Clebe was nearly killed in Vietnam, losing his left arm and left eye), but they made the decision that surrender was not an option. They would not—and did not—quit.

Clebe's truck has a license plate bearing these four letters: FIDO. It stands for "Forget it, drive on."

"If something goes wrong in our marriage, or we have an argument, we deal with it and then we drive on," said Clebe. "We don't keep digging up the past. We learn from it, but we don't dwell on it."

Deanna says she had to learn a lot in this area because in their first decade of marriage, she wanted to keep talking about all the "what-ifs" and "if-onlys." Clebe would listen to her and then he would say, "That's over with, and we can't change a thing. Let's learn from it and move forward."

Deanna says she is more in love with Clebe today than she has ever been. "Our relationship has matured and strengthened over the years, and I am very secure in his love after more than three decades of marriage. It's a great feeling, a priceless treasure," Deanna says.

2

The Lifeblood of a Good Marriage

. . . .

■ I joke with my husband that we've been married so long that we can finish each other's sentences. Still, like many married couples, we've experienced our share of communication miscues. Nothing major, but when it happens, things get frosty around here. How can we stay in good communication?

Whether you call it talking, sharing, staying in touch, or just being a sounding board, communication is the lifeblood of marriage, no matter how many decades it's been since you tied the knot.

As much as us old guys don't want to admit it, the ball is in our court much of the time. We're the ones who feel like our allotment of spoken words is used up by 6 P.M. We're the ones who barely ruffle the pages of the newspaper when our wives describe the bargains they found at the farmer's market. We're the ones who emit grunts when our wives ask us how our day went.

A typical one occurred a few years ago on the eve of Focus on the Family's building dedication in Colorado Springs. As editor of *Focus on the Family* magazine at the time, I (Mike Yorkey) thought I had told my wife, Nicole, months before that I would be gone all day covering the event. That seemed only natural, since the dedication ceremony was on a Saturday.

The night before the event, however, Nicole heard me making arrangements to meet photographer John Russell at 6:30 A.M.

"What are you doing tomorrow?" Nicole asked as soon as I hung up the phone. *(You better not be working on a Saturday.)*

"I'll be at the Focus dedication, probably most of the day," I replied evenly. *(Surely, she remembers.)*

"Don't you think you should have let me know that you were going to be gone for a whole Saturday?" *(Turkey. You forgot to tell me again.)*

"Didn't I tell you I have to write a story on the building dedication for the magazine?" *(I sure hope she remembers.)*

"No, you didn't. That's so typical of you, to forget to tell your wife." *(You're going to pay for this.)*

"OK, OK, OK." *(I'm in trouble now.)*

Yes, we've all had rough patches like that, but if we can remember to tell our spouses about our plans *before* the event, conference, golf tee time, or meeting, life will go much smoother.

■ **In our family, I can barely find a few minutes to take a shower before bed, let alone have a meaningful conversation! Meanwhile, I'm dying on the vine. When my husband comes home from work, he's got nothing left in his tank, and it takes everything I've got to muster more than four sentences out of him. I need some two-way conversation. How can I make this happen?**

Short of your husband having to find a second wind, he's going to have to work to get those communication muscles in tone. Here are a few ideas:

1. Be willing to open up, and be willing to listen. Back in their early days of marriage, Todd and Tracey Thomas were sitting on swings at a nearby park, making small talk. Todd had a penetrating question: "Can you tell me something about yourself that you don't want me to know?"

Tracey considered the inquiry for a moment. Should she tell him? They had been married for only a couple of years, but not all the cards had been played. *OK,* she thought, *I'll take a chance.* "You're probably going to laugh at me, but I don't like my feet. You see, I have a toe on my right foot that is not the right size. See?" she asked, taking off her shoes and socks.

Todd peered closely at the offending toe and then at the others. He took a second look. "No, I don't see any difference between your toes," he said.

"Oh, honey, I knew you'd understand!" Tracey said as she hugged him.

All the while Todd thought, *Women are strange!* Fortunately, he didn't voice that thought, but that afternoon in the park helped him understand two things: One, Tracey's self-image was tied up in how she thought she looked to him; and two, she wanted to know if it was "safe" to confide in him.

Have you informed your spouse that it's "safe" to bring up sensitive subjects? Can your spouse *really* tell you what's on his or her mind? If you're afraid of your parents dying, have you confided that to your spouse? If you're mortified about your own mortality, have you had a heart-to-heart with your loved one?

You can do it. It just takes some effort and resolve.

2. If you can tell something is bugging your spouse, ask him or her about it. Many times a husband wants to air his frustrations about work, but he doesn't want to come across as a griper. Or a wife's frustration index just skipped off the chart because a friend stood her up for lunch. Slowly draw out your spouse. Ask gently but directly, "Is anything bothering you, honey? I'd like to hear about it."

Not only will you both feel better, but the conversations may turn to deeper subjects, which will increase your feelings of intimacy for each other.

3. Relearn walking. People who want their marriage to be the best sometimes think they have to do something huge like take a two-week romantic cruise or a ten-week "marriage builders" course. It's much smaller than that: Take walks together. Walking may sound pretty basic, but it will rejuvenate your relationship. You can focus on each other and just talk as the houses go by. No TV blaring, no phone ringing.

What if you're watching the grandchildren? Take them along! Kids love the fresh air and the world's-eye view from the stroller.

4. Have one TV-free night a week. Who knows? The deafening silence in the living room, with the two of you just sitting there leafing through the magazine pile, may cause a conversation to break out. Another approach is to turn the TV off after the show ends, instead of flicking through the channels to "see what's on." Either way, turn that communication-buster off!

5. Don't discuss the real important stuff after you go to bed. When you're tired, you're more apt to say something you'll regret in the morning. At the same time, sometimes a spouse just *has* to get something off his or her chest before it's lights out, heeding the biblical advice to not "let the sun go down on your anger."

A balance has to be sought here. Yes, meaningful conversation can happen late at night, but keep the volume down. If you can, save the important topics for the light of day.

6. Check with your spouse before agreeing to something. If I don't say, "Let me check with Nicole," before saying yes to a friend, I always get burned. Your spouse will appreciate the marital courtesy.

7. Join a couples Bible study. Usually, great discussions ensue among couples whose common bond is Christ. Those discussions can serve as a springboard to later talks between you and your spouse.

8. Finally, don't forget the "three C's": communication, compromise, and consideration. Compromise is the cornerstone of marriage, but it works best when both sides have aired what's bothering them. In order for give-and-take to work, offer to hear what your spouse has to say first.

If you take these ideas to heart, you'll be finishing your spouse's sentences in no time.

■ **What should we do when the hurricanes of life hit? My wife is not above raising her voice and slamming a few doors. She said she once read in a women's magazine that it's a good idea to verbalize anger, to scream, let it out, and vent your spleen. The article said you'll feel better afterward because "meaningful" communication has occurred. I'm not so sure. What gives on this subject?**

Slamming doors and screaming is not good communication. Although you can "get if off your chest," everyone is left with a hangdog feeling. The yeller may win the battle, but that is no way to win the war.

Of course, screaming bouts are inevitable over the life of a marriage, but we should view them as weather forecasters view tropical cyclones. Here's how the comparison goes: The U.S. Weather Service divides tropical cyclones into four classifications:

- ► Level 1—Tropical Disturbances: a low pressure area with beginning surface circulation.
- ► Level 2—Tropical Depression: a low pressure area with close circulation and winds up to 31 m.p.h.
- ► Level 3—Tropical Storm: winds now between 32–72 m.p.h.
- ► Level 4—Hurricanes: winds more than 72 m.p.h.

■ So what does this all have to do with marriage communication?

You should realize that tropical storms will build up and occasionally burst into full-blown hurricanes. What that means for married couples is that if a "discussion" starts at Level 2 (fairly heated), don't escalate matters and turn the argument into a Level 3 tropical storm; your spouse may use that as an opening to go on a dish-tossing, lamp-throwing Level 4 hurricane.

Instead, let your spouse vent at Level 2, and then try to calm the

---

**THE TOP TEN LEAST POPULAR
HUSBAND–WIFE DATES**

10. A romantic evening listening to her Don Ho CDs.
9. Watching hubby go for a new personal best at the all-you-can-eat joint.
8. A greasy, gut-bomb burger at Joe Bob's Barbecue, followed by pool at Mr. T's Highland Park Bowl.
7. A heart-to-heart conversation with your urologist.
6. A retro look at Arnold's *Terminator* flick.
5. A living will seminar.
4. The motorcycle parts swap meet.
3. A multilevel marketing presentation.
2. Your best friend's Super Bowl party.
1. A time-share presentation in the middle of the desert.

waters. Repeat what he or she said. Validate her feelings. Doing so may get the discussion down to Level 1, where a more fruitful conversation can ensue.

This chapter is adapted from writings by Mike Yorkey and Greg Johnson.

3

Living with a Messie for All These Years

. . . .

■ When I married Ken twenty-five years ago, I knew he was disorganized, but I thought I could change him. Here we are celebrating our silver anniversary, and Ken has never cleaned up his act, and my house has become a messy nightmare. He's incapable of throwing anything away!

Sometimes when Ken travels on business, I carefully thin out his clothes or papers, and he's never the wiser. One time, though, I went a step further and pitched out an old rocking chair. Ken was infuriated when he returned. "Don't you know that chair was a valuable antique?" he bellowed.

With all the stuff Ken brings into our home, my efforts to keep things organized are futile. Although he is a wonderful husband, I can't have friends over because of the messy surroundings.

Short of giving him his walking papers, is there any way I can live with this messy guy?

Yes, you can, says author Sandra Felton, who's written the book on living with "Messies" (actually, several of them). Sandra, a former Messie, was so disorganized that she never threw out expired sale flyers that came with her junk mail. Why? Because when the next sale flyer arrived, she could tell if it was going to be better sale.

At least, that was her thinking. Meanwhile, she could never dig up those sales flyers from underneath the mounds of stacked papers, magazines, and newspapers lying around her house. Nor could she find a simple Band-Aid when one of the kids scraped a knee.

Sandra managed to turn her topsy-turvy life around, however, and keep a presentable home. You can too, although living with a Messie presents its challenges.

If you're wondering what makes a Messie tick, or hoping someday he'll change—forget it! Instead, you should confront the real issue: What are you going to do to make your life satisfactory, even enjoyable?

■ **That's a tall order. So what can I do to make the most of living with a Messie?**

First, give your Messie his freedom—freedom to change or not to change as he sees fit. You can only entrust him to the care of God, who has the power to change people. Though you would like for the Messie to change, that is not your area of responsibility. Your responsibility is for your own life.

Without trying to change the nature of the Messie, first decide what you most want changed about the house. Choose a specific

---

HOW TO TELL IF YOU'RE REALLY A MESSIE

Do you:
- ► have medicine over five years old in your medicine cabinet?
- ► clip newspaper articles, but don't have any special plan for keeping and finding them?
- ► lose things in your house?
- ► keep the bedroom door closed when you have guests?
- ► have to work all day on the house to have dinner guests that night?
- ► buy things you don't need just in case you might need them someday?
- ► hope unexpected visitors will not drop in?
- ► still have your high school dance program somewhere in the house?
- ► find it hard to throw away newspapers because they might have something good in them?

short-term goal—one thing about the house that is bothersome to you. Here are some suggestions to get you started:

- ▶ I will not allow the table by the door to be used as a dumping ground. I will not have a cluttered dining room table.
- ▶ I will not allow stacks of books to be left in the living room.
- ▶ I will not allow the beds to be left unmade all day.

■ In order for me to be successful with this strategy, what are the pitfalls?

Problems with keeping the home in order seem to fall into five main categories:

1. Storage or Organization

This includes maintaining orderly drawers and closets and the storage of seldom-used items like Christmas things and light bulbs. How you handle storage is basic to other cleaning. If you don't have a place for everything, how can you put it away?

2. Neatness

A neatness problem is best identified by how you feel when people drop in on you. Messies are frequently warm, sociable people who would enjoy sharing their homes with others, but the house won't allow it.

3. Paper

Messies love paper. They don't throw away anything that might be important. And everything could be important . . . someday!

4. Bills and Banking

This is an area that requires organization or it falls apart. When bills and statements come in, it's easy to let them sit in a pile, knowing "they are there somewhere."

5. Collecting

Either for the past or for the future, Messies collect lots of things because they "might come in handy someday." Or they keep them for the sake of the past or a deceased loved one.

Choose one. Start wherever you want, then move slowly into other areas as you discover what works for you. Before you begin implementing any plan, however, have Plan B ready. For instance, what will you do if the Messie continues to thwart your will? Will you begin to engage in life away from the house—taking classes or meeting friends in restaurants? Will you find a spot in the house where you can carve out an island of beauty and order? Will you take up gardening and other outside pursuits? Will you hire a cleaning woman? If the Messie is an adult child, will you ask him or her to move out?

The Messie may threaten your relationship in a way that makes you more uncomfortable than you are willing to be. Or, though he tries to change, he may continue to maintain messiness at a level higher than you can handle. What will you do then?

Having an alternative plan will help you keep your head when things do not go right.

■ **I don't think I'm going to get Ken to change at all. Are there any in-between steps I can take?**

Yes, you can start teaching him the "Mount Vernon Method," as Sandra Felton calls it.

One of the "Cleanies" that Sandra talked to years ago told her how impressed she was with the maintenance of Mount Vernon, George Washington's home. It seemed the housekeepers arrived each day and started at the front door and worked to the next, cleaning each room one room at a time.

That's what you're going to have to do with Ken. Begin by getting three boxes and label them "Throw Away," "Give Away," and "Store Elsewhere." Then the two of you should begin at the front door and gravitate to the first piece of furniture with a nook, cranny, or drawer.

Begin by throwing away all the true junk that has accumulated in the drawer. Put it in the "Throw Away" box. Be serious about it. Don't keep the pen that works only half the time and the year-old calendar even if it has nice pictures on it. Your freedom from clutter is more important than they are.

Be kind, but tell Ken that it may cause temporary pain to throw something out, but it also causes definite pain to keep it. Put items you want to keep back in the drawer or in one of the other boxes.

Do not worry about cleaning walls, drapes, upholstery, and furniture as you go. Basically, you organize each spot around the inside periphery of the house. When you have done enough for one day (about an hour), stop, put the boxes away, and wait until tomorrow.

Don't overdo it. This is a marathon, not a sprint.

■ What should I do if my hubby loses, ah, his enthusiasm for this cleaning project?

Start by stating to your Messie (or Messies, if you're including the whole family) your I-will-not statement.

It might go like this: "Ken, kids, I want to keep this table by the front door clear. When you come in, take your things to where they belong." Then, before anyone has a chance to place something on the table, polish it nice and bright, and put a potted plant on it. Perhaps the family will immediately comply. If so, you have accomplished your goal. Now choose another and go from there.

Realistically, it is unlikely that things will go this smoothly. Old habits die hard. So let's suppose that the next day someone comes home, moves the plant a little bit, squeezes school books onto a corner of the table, and goes into the kitchen for a snack. Having already anticipated this breach in your brief agreement with the Messie, now implement your next move.

"Karen, I want to keep that table clean and clear. Will you take your books to your room?" you state calmly.

"Just a minute! I'll get to it!" she calls, cookie in mouth.

You may choose to reply, "I don't want to wait a minute. Please remove them now."

If she moves the books, great. If not, wait a minute or two, then take the books to Karen's room yourself. It's not fair for you to do the work, but remember that your goal is to have a nice-looking table.

Perhaps Karen will say, "Mom, I told you I would do that!" or "Mom why did you do that? I would have gotten them in a minute."

Your reply could be, "I want the table clear of books all the time." No fuss, no blame, just facts. Keep your goal in mind.

The next time—and there will be a next time—put them under her bed or in the basement. When she complains that she can't find them, tell her where they are and suggest she put them in her room next time. Never act fussy or annoyed.

If she says, "Mom, you're getting kooky about that table!"—do not defend yourself.

Agree with her and say without rancor, "Yes, indeed I am. Remember that the next time you want to put your books on the table."

■ But what about my husband's dirty clothes on the floor?

If you have said you want to keep the bedroom clean and he continues to leave dirty clothes lying around, put them in the back of the closet or under the bed so they are not cluttering the floor. Don't wash them. When he complains about having no clean underwear, explain that you did all the laundry in the hamper. His underwear was not there. If he would like to put his underwear in the hamper, you will be happy to wash it with the rest of the laundry.

■ Can you explain to me why it is so hard for a Messie to throw something away?

Messies have the feeling that some part of the former owner is mixed with a particular belonging. In other words, if the old plate belonged to Aunt Nan and she is dead, a little of Aunt Nan lives on in that plate. If the old plate is discarded, some part of the Messie is lost. We are talking deep emotions here. Messies live with the fear of being without what they need. If they have a lot of stuff, they feel safe—cared for. To get rid of anything is to risk kicking up that old fear of being in need.

That's why you should care for the Messie. He is not your enemy. You will not escalate the problem by taking a tough stand when patience, understanding, and responsible actions will accomplish your goals and work for the Messie's benefit. In the end, however, the choice of what he does with his private stuff is his problem.

Resolve to improve the degrading living conditions that have been forced upon you.

▶ Let the Messie know of your plans to throw something out ahead of time.

▶ Speak reasonably and calmly.

▶ Don't go into details.

▶ Give him a chance to retrieve his things.

If you do each of these things, the best-case scenario is that the Messie will be relieved that a job was done that had weighed heavily on him. At the very least, your life will be better.

This chapter is adapted from writings by Sandra Felton, author and president of Messies Anonymous, 5025 S.W. 114th Ave., Miami, FL 33165. Or you can call (800) 637-7292. Her Web site is www.messies.com.

4

Seven Secrets of Marriage Success from Golden Anniversary Couples

. . . .

■ Denine and I were in our mid-thirties when we tied the knot. We'll celebrate our twentieth anniversary soon, but our two children are still in high school.

Although Denine and I are in our mid-fifties and have settled into a lifelong marriage, we want to see our union go the distance—fifty years together, if the Lord allows us that much time. What can couples who've celebrated their golden anniversary—who must have been married as baby-faced kids—tell Denine and me about marriage?

Barbara Curtis, a writer living in northern California, recently received an article assignment from a magazine: "Find the secrets of successful marriages to share with our readers. Ask couples married fifty years or more."

She asked around and heard about several couples, including one named Stan and Helen Warner. After a long interview, she fell in love with their story. See if you don't agree:

Stan and Helen Warner
He noticed her right away. Dainty and demure, she was fine as the filigree she fashioned each day for a large jewelry maker in San

Francisco. He was just an apprentice, hired on for sixty-nine cents per hour to learn the art of engraving. World War II was over, and twenty-two-year-old Stan Warner was ready and eager to make a living.

But no matter how serious he was about his work, he couldn't help but be distracted—even though "she" worked all the way across the building.

He finally wrangled an introduction from a coworker, then asked Helen if she planned to go to the company Christmas party. She did. "Good. We'll dance together," Stan promised.

Dancing at the Christmas party, he asked her out for New Year's Eve. She didn't hesitate.

They feasted on seafood at Bernstein's, then strolled down Market Street, tossing confetti with the crowd. On impulse, they caught a streetcar to the beach and found an abandoned, still crackling bonfire made from railroad ties. In the rosy glow, Stan and Helen warmed their hands and made small talk. Finally, in the earliest hours of '46, he took her home—again by streetcar—to her parents' flat across from Golden Gate Park.

The following week, he did a little work behind the scenes. He persuaded her supervisor to move Helen's desk from one end of the building to his own, even placing her workbench next to his. A week after that, he bought her a ring and worked up his nerve to pop the question.

They were standing in the pouring rain at the corner of Fillmore and Polk, waiting for their respective streetcars, when he asked, "Will you marry me?" She gave a little scream and put her hands over her face.

They had known each other all of ten days.

"She didn't say yes, and she didn't say no, but she did accept the ring," Stan remembers now. "She put it on her right hand though."

Eleven days later as they shared their brown bag lunches at a nearby park, Stan noticed Helen had switched the ring to her left hand.

"Does that mean what I think it means?" he asked.

The answer was yes; the question was when.

"When's your birthday?" Helen asked.

"April 18th."

"Let's do it then."

That year April 18 fell on Maundy Thursday. It took some searching, but they found a Lutheran minister who agreed to perform the ceremony.

The major difficulty was Helen's mother, who balked at her daughter's marriage. On April 17, she invited Stan to dinner. He found Helen with red and swollen eyes, dutifully sewing the last stitches of their wedding quilt. Helen's mother's arms were crossed stubbornly. The tension within was thick as the fog outside.

"What's wrong?" Stan asked.

Helen's mother shoved a box of papers toward Stan.

They were adoption papers for a child with no legitimate heritage—his future bride.

"Now what do you think?" Helen's mother said triumphantly. Surely no one would want to marry her daughter now.

"To tell you the truth, Ma'am, I'm relieved. Relieved she's not really related to you!"

Even now, Stan's eyes twinkle when he pulls the punch line. But Helen's eyes could light up the room. According to her, until that point her agreement to marry Stan had been an act of faith. Stan had yet to prove himself. But in that moment he became her Knight in Shining Armor.

You see, until that day, Helen had never known she was adopted. The cultural milieu, along with the punishing manner in which her mother told her, made Helen feel unworthy of any love at all. Stan's unconditional acceptance, at a moment when Helen could barely accept herself, would become the cornerstone of a marriage built to last.

It was a small wedding with big results. Not only did it mark the beginning of a new marriage, it also revived a marriage that had died ten years before. Stan's parents, divorced for a decade, renewed their relationship at their son's wedding, remarried, and spent their remaining twenty years together. Surely God was smiling on a very special event when Helen and Stan took their vows.

After a ten-day honeymoon a couple hours down the coast in Monterey, Stan and Helen returned to find a place of their own. Their first "home" was a furnished third-story room with kitchen and bathroom privileges. Their rent was $5 per week. They didn't own a car, a television, a typewriter, nor a stick of furniture. But they felt rich having found each other.

"I wasn't worried," Helen said. "We just took it one step at a time."

One step at a time they've walked through life together—for more than fifty years.

■ **That's a touching story of real love. Suddenly all those marriage manuals written by my fellow Baby Boomers seem to come up short. Why had we never asked the real experts like the Warners?**

The experts aren't too hard to find, if you know where to look. Nowadays in local papers, fifty-year anniversary announcements are a regular feature—some weeks outnumbering weddings. This shouldn't come as a surprise. Before the Baby Boom, there must have been a marriage boom. The only reason we haven't noticed is because—as usual—the spotlight is on us Boomers—now beginning our round of fiftieth birthdays—rather than on the generation that thrust us on the stage.

That's really been our loss. Somehow always relegated to the background, these were couples whose marriages survived the turmoil of the '60s (when "experts" were saying that marriage was a dying institution), and the resulting fallout of their children "doing their own thing" through sex, drugs, and rock 'n' roll.

During her interviews with several couples married fifty or more years, Barbara Curtis came across seven secrets of long marriages. Here they are:

Acceptance

People once referred to a future spouse as the recipient's "intended." In other words, this mate was uniquely planned, a special gift for one another. Because Stan had already chosen to receive his own gift—Helen—it didn't matter when her mother pressed on him the unfortunate circumstances of her birth. Stan's acceptance of Helen broke all the barriers she might have faced, but more importantly, it demonstrated that she was worthy—just the way she was.

Commitment

The bottom line of any marriage is the wedding vows. No way around it: some couples will go through periods of wondering why in the world they ever got married. From the point of view of the

Survivors, *why* doesn't matter. What matters is the *promise*. Dr. James Dobson puts it this way, "Love is not a feeling. Love is a commitment." This commitment is often strengthened through the birth of children. David and Susan Younan withstood tremendous trials over five decades of marriage. Raising children kept their feet on the ground, said David. "It is amazing how that first baby changed my life from top to bottom, made me a more responsible person, and brought joy and happiness and unity to my life."

Leaving and Cleaving

Let's face it, some parents have a hard time letting go. In these cases, grownup children must assert their independence as a couple. U.S. Coast Guard commander Lynn Parker was so convinced of the importance of this principle that when one of his men got married, he had him transferred immediately as far from home as possible.

On the other hand, parents who share a deep commitment to the Lord can be an invaluable source of support. The Younans remember that every time they had a problem or disagreement, they were surrounded by people who could share their experience or wisdom. "Our marriage was never empty," said Susan.

Realistic Expectations

Survivors are emphatic that they never expected to change their mates, nor certain circumstances of their marriage. Betty Parker knew she was marrying a career Coast Guard officer. Melba Meakin knew she was marrying a minister. Each knew her husband's work would entail relocating, and neither quarreled with this later on. Within each marriage gender roles were respected: while there was a sense of mutual submission, the husband was responsible for his house.

Careful Finances

"Don't spend what you don't have." Every couple uttered words to this affect. They described making do with less in the beginning years of their marriages—with no hard feelings. The long-married couples expressed concern for today's newlyweds, many who expect to begin marriage at the same standard of living as their parents. So often they end up disappointed or in debt. During the 1940s, everyone knew that they would start with little more than each other. "We never felt deprived," Betty Parker says. "It was just the way life was."

Mutual Respect

Self-control and respect for each other were hallmarks of the successful, long-term marriages. Helen and Stan Warner made it a rule never to fight in front of their children—specifically because Stan's parents' fighting had driven him from home at an early age. Waiting to discuss something later often cooled off hot topics, averting major disasters.

"From the time I married Susan," David Younan said, "I realized she was a gift of God. God was telling me, 'Here, David, this is My daughter. Take care of her.' " Thinking of your spouse in this way brings forth an uncommon tenderness and respect.

Generosity

"Don't be selfish," Betty Parker urged. "Put the other person first." Stan and Helen Warner carry this spirit of generosity even further. Though their two sons grew up and left home long ago, the Warners have never suffered the empty nest syndrome. That extra bedroom is usually put to good use. When Barbara Curtis went to interview Stan and Helen, they introduced her to a man newly released from the county jail whom they were helping get back on his feet. Hospitality like this has been a way of life for them.

■ **Looking back over those seven secrets, I wonder if we modern types can handle such an old-fashioned no-frills approach.**

If you think about it, the long-time couples take us back to the basics, reminding us that marriage was made not to fulfill us, but to fulfill God's purpose.

Think about it. Without couples' conferences or marriage manuals, these Survivors muddled through—while their Boomer children fell apart, in many cases. Maybe they knew more than we ever gave them credit for.

After all, it's hard to argue with success.

This chapter is adapted from writings by Barbara Curtis of Petaluma, California.

5

The Second Half of Marriage

. . . .

Your eyes blink open in the dark room.

As you roll over, you check the red numbers illuminating the night-stand. It's 7:17 A.M. Another Saturday morning.

But this one is different. You're waking up with no children in the house. Besides a few days here and a few days there, it's the first time this has happened in twenty-five years.

What makes this day even more unique is . . . they won't be back.

The nest is empty.

It's just you and your spouse.

Together.

Alone.

As you turn back over, you catch the sleeping silhouette of the person you said "I do" with so many years before. Time has passed quickly. Though some body parts have sagged and the hair has a slight silvery glint, it's the same person you used to dream about waking up with in those crazy courting days.

Your mind fast-forwards through footage of dozens of memories.

The kids were your life. Did you even have a life before kids?

Now they're gone, and it's just the two of you.

What are you thinking right now?

Does your marriage have you exchanging high fives . . . or is it a ho-hum affair?

Are you wondering if your relationship will be a rerun of the last five or ten years, or are you excited to see how your marriage will change now that the kids are gone?

Are you hopeful about the future, or do you dread having to spend the "rest of your days" with your spouse?

In the first years of marriage, it was just the two of you. Waking up with bad hair days and asking your spouse not to kiss you until you swished Listerine was fun.

Then you entered the enthralling season of child-rearing, that difficult yet satisfying period of life filled with purpose and Kodak moments. You finally understood what your parents did for you—and how God's plan for replenishing the next generation makes sense.

Now you're entering the second half of marriage, full of wisdom and experience. These golden years can be rich and meaningful, and you are excited to make the most of the days God has given you. The start of the "empty nest" years is a great time to renew those vows "to love and to cherish," because it's just the two of you.

David and Claudia Arp, authors of *The Second Half of Marriage*, say it didn't take them long to realize their marriage was changing once the last Arp left for college. Their roles and responsibilities were turned upside down. Their family's hectic and crisis-filled rhythm was disrupted. With no children at home, their schedules filled up, and overcommitment became their constant companion as they moved from a child-focused marriage to an activity-focused one.

Were the Arps alone? They didn't think so. The Arps, who had written several parenting books, began surveying hundreds of "empty nest" couples around the country. They discovered that many couples stay together when children are the focus on the relationship, but when the children left home, so did the reason for staying in the relationship. Couples told them that they needed to be reminded that life is a series of adjustments, that changes are as certain as the seasons. As you face the second half of your marriage, embrace change—but embrace it together.

From their national survey, the Arps learned that the greatest indicator of a long-term successful marriage is the friendship of the couple. In other words, you need to become best friends!

■ **Ever since the kids went off to college, we became heavily involved with activities outside the home. One of our areas of service is church. Rick is on the elder board, and I sing in the choir. We also lead a couples' Bible study one night a week. One evening when we were finished, we sat in our car, exhausted, glaring at each other.**

"Why do we do this to ourselves?" I asked.

"I don't know," Rick answered, "but something has got to change!"

Over the past several months, we've had no dating life of our own. That evening was no different. We didn't have time even to stop for coffee on the way home because we had to get to bed.

We both saw the irony: While we were helping husbands and wives grow stronger, we were violating the very principles we taught. We easily rationalized our behavior, telling ourselves that working with other couples kept us on our toes, but we were kidding ourselves. Is that a fair assessment?

You're not alone: Couples who risk giving too much of themselves can endanger their own relationships. But it doesn't have to be this way. How can you begin to turn things around? By becoming intimate again.

■ **What kind of intimacy are you talking about?**

Intimacy means different things to different people. While most men tend to equate intimacy with sex, women tend to think of emotional closeness. Both are components of a healthy love life, but true intimacy includes other ingredients:

▶ Trust: the ability to feel safe with each other.
▶ Mutuality: the freedom to choose to love each other.
▶ Honesty: open communication of your true feelings.

▶ Pleasure: giving joy to each other.

A beautiful picture, isn't it? All work together to create an atmosphere of romance and intimacy. But while just the word intimacy rings of romance and closeness, it's a word that is easily misunderstood and difficult to achieve.

■ What can we do to improve intimacy at this late date in our marriage?

Many marriages lack intimacy because the partners hold different expectations about their relationship and don't discuss them. For instance, if your idea of a romantic evening is lovemaking ten minutes after the late news, while your wife envisions an intimate dinner and an evening at a cozy bed and breakfast, you can see the potential for trouble.

It's hard enough to satisfy your mate's expectations when you know what they are; it's impossible when you don't. Talk about them. Once you understand each other's expectations, the next step is to establish some boundaries, which the Arps found difficult to do. Once when their twenty-eight-year-old middle son, Joel, was visiting, he asked a pointed question: "Mom, when are you and Dad going to get a life?"

"We have a life," Claudia replied.

"I'm talking about a life apart from all your writing and speaking," he said.

The Arps' discomfort suggested that Joel's observation may have been valid. David and Claudia knew it was up to them to claim time for deepening their own intimacy, which is not always an easy job.

They thought about some encouraging stories they had heard. The remembered hearing how friends of theirs, Frank and Kim, checked into a downtown hotel. Kim brought a picnic basket, a CD player, and a stack of their favorite CDs. They signed for a room and enjoyed swimming with each other in the indoor pool—in the middle of winter.

Jack and Norma, who are in their late sixties, told the Arps they had developed a habit of showering together in the mornings. "It's also a time-saver," Norma told Claudia. "Besides, now that we're older, we can steady each other and prevent falls in the shower!"

■ **Besides showering together, how can we revive a tired love life?**

Here are some ideas:

► Refuse to be the slave of technology. You don't have to check your e-mail "just once more" before you go to bed.

► Delegate. If you're involved with school boards and church leadership, find others who can help carry the load. Enlist the help of a good friend or member of your congregation.

► Pray together just after the lights go out. Prayer will bond you even more together.

► Get back on a regular date schedule. It doesn't have to be for dinner. How about lunchtimes together? Starbucks coffee dates?

This chapter is adapted from writings by David and Claudia Arp. For more resources and tips for building better relationships, visit their Web site at www.marriagealive.com.

6

When Hubby Is
Around the House

. . . .

■ **My husband and I have different tastes in things. He doesn't like the same kind of food I like, the same kind of movies, or the same activities. He loves action films, TV sports, and his steak and baked potatoes. At this late date, will he ever change?**

Nope. Next question?

No, seriously, you shouldn't try to get him to change. These things are relatively harmless. He's a man. Men like their steaks, their sports, and their physical activities. Play along with him on this stuff. If possible, get into his sports with him, or start new ones with him.

Can you bowl together? Can you take up golf? Have you ever fished? If so, he'll love you for it. Men like to have a "buddy" in what they do, and in what they like. Learn to accommodate these things. Be grateful that what he likes falls within the "normal" range of men's behavior. If he wants you to go out in the desert in a four-wheeler with him, try it!

When you go to a restaurant, let him order his steak and don't criticize him for it. Besides, at home you have more control of what gets put on the dinner table. If he's enjoying his top sirloin in a restaurant but you're on his case, he'll resent you. Eat your rabbit food, or whatever you prefer, in peace and let him be.

One of Solomon's proverbs provides us with some wisdom: "Better a dinner of herbs where love is, than a fatted calf with hatred" (Prov. 15:17). The stress of fighting over a meal could do more harm than the food itself. A meal should always be a joyous occasion, never a time for bickering, criticizing, and arguing. If your husband is going to come in for criticism every time he orders something from the menu that he likes, he's not going to want to go out to dinner with you anymore.

Besides, we Christians can learn some lessons from Judaism about the importance of the dinner table peace. Marvin Wilson writes, "The dinner table of the home became, as it were, the altar of the Temple. Seen as an altar, the table was to be consecrated. It was a place for more than food was to be passed; it was also to be set apart, that words of Torah might be exchanged. For one 'does not live by bread alone' (Deuteronomy 8:3; cf. Matthew 4:4; Luke 4:4)."

In traditional Jewish homes, the family actually sings songs (*zimrot*) in praise of the Holy One. The father often instructs his family in the Torah at mealtimes. Clearly this is not an occasion for arguing and bickering.

Everyone has differences of opinion. Husbands don't always say or do exactly the right thing. They don't always make the wisest choices in food selection, but marriage is about accommodation. We learn to bend to each other, adapt, and accommodate, especially when we're talking about mere preferences or natural differences.

If you think your husband's preferred diet is bad for him, let him learn it from an authority he respects on the subject, such as a doctor or book author. Chances are you won't be able to nag him into changing it.

■ **My husband just won't fix anything. The house is falling apart, and all he does is sit in that oversized chair and loaf. Worse, he won't let me ask George, a friendly neighbor with time on his hands, to help us out. What can I do?**

Not all husbands are "Mr. Fixits." Some men simply don't have the ability or capacity to fix things. At the same time, it hurts their male pride when you hold up someone else's husband who is handy around the house. If your husband finds himself in this predicament, he may think you won't love or respect him unless he's like George next door who sleeps in a nail apron and fixes everything.

The idea that he either has to be like George, or get George to fix things he should be fixing, can immobilize your husband. He knows that if he tries to fix something, chances are he'll blow it. If he fails, that's worse than not trying. Then you'll really come down on him. If he invites George to fix it, and he does, then George will become your hero who saved the day. So he does nothing.

The key to this dilemma is providing your husband with a face-saving device. Let him know that the sink, for example, has a leak that needs fixing, but that you realize that he probably doesn't have the skills or the tools to fix it. Just say to him something like, "Honey, I wonder if you'd mind getting someone to fix that sink. I know you're busy. Just get anyone you wish. I trust your judgment."

Now the ball's in his court. He's in the driver's seat. He'll find a way to get it done without having to struggle with it himself. He may even invite George to do it, since George is now in a noncompetitive position to help him.

■ **My husband was caught in one of those corporate downsizings, even after serving his company for fifteen years. He has been out of work for some time. Fortunately, I have a good job that helps us keep the wolves away from the door. But, I wish he'd get off his duff and start working again. Can that happen?**

If your husband has lost his job, he's experiencing a painful time. Again, much of a man's identify and self-esteem comes from the work he does. When a company lets a man go, his self-esteem is devastated. He feels like a failure and someone who isn't wanted anymore.

He needs time and space to work that through. Give it to him. It's going to take awhile. In addition, the older he is, the more difficult it may be for him to find work. The higher his pay, the longer it can take. (A rule of thumb is one month for each $10,000 per year he earned, so if he was in the $50,000 range, he could be waiting five months.)

What he needs during this difficult time is for you to believe in him. This is more important than anything. When he's feeling that he's been rejected by his professional peers, he needs to know that you are behind him.

Don't lord it over him because you're making an income and he isn't. Nothing crushes a man's self-confidence more than to believe that he is no longer capable of bringing home a paycheck. His whole manhood is tied up with the idea of earning a living.

If you carp and criticize, it will only drive him deeper into a pit of despair. In such a state, men often do crazy, irrational things. Try to help him keep his spirits up. Exude a sense of optimism and confidence. The feeling could be contagious.

Perhaps the most important thing you can do for him at this time is devote yourself to consistent, intercessory prayer for him.

■ **My husband just doesn't seem to care about spiritual things—going to church, praying, or studying the Bible. If the grandchildren spend the night, I have to be the one to read them a Bible story. How can I get him to be more spiritual?**

Statistically, women have been shown to be more religious than men. Many churches report a higher female-to-male attendance ratio. There are many reasons for this.

Men are conditioned, especially in our culture, to do everything themselves. They have to be problem-solvers. They get things done by hard work. The bigger the problem, the bigger the challenge.

Women are conditioned to be more dependent, less inclined to take the initiative. This is a generalization, of course, but it is naturally easier for women to pray and depend on God. (We are not including radical feminists, who feel they have to take on the role traditionally reserved for men.)

For many men, Bible study is drudgery. They see themselves "wading through" King James English and trying to understand obscure words from a distant time. Have you looked for an exciting Bible study that uses a modern translation of the Bible?

Don't forget that most men don't like sitting in church, doing Bible study, meditating on the Word, etc., which are viewed as boring and passive. Realizing this, more and more pastors are generating more appealing church programs, and this type of church may appeal more to your husband than a teaching-type of pastorate. Chances are he'll identify with a more masculine, sports-oriented pastor rather than a traditional platitude-passer.

Look for a church where the pastor gives the men things to do. This will get him involved in a youth program, sports team coaching, painting widow's homes, or some other physical type of service.

Another important point to realize is this: as with their sexuality, men express their relationship with God somewhat differently than do women. Men are no less spiritual, no less sensitive, but they do manifest their spirituality in uniquely male ways.

Don't try to get your husband to be like you in this regard. Let him be who he is. If he's not "into emotion," don't force him into it. Ask the Lord to work with him.

■ **My husband just won't read the directions for anything. He won't read maps when we're driving either. Some things don't work after he finishes assembling them, and we always get lost when we're driving. This frustrates me. What can I do about it?**

Men often like to figure things out for themselves. Some are better at it than others. Back in 1947, Art Knowles of Los Angeles bought his first car—an Austin. Instead of studying the user's manual, he took the whole car apart in the driveway. He examined everything, figured out how it worked, put it back together again, and listened to the engine purr the first time he turned the key.

It helped that Art Knowles was a marine engineer, which gave him a leg up on those of us who have no mechanical aptitude. Most of us need to read directions and look at maps.

Then there is the story of the minister who once took a ministerial trainee on a ministry tour in the Midwest. The elder man refused to read the map. In fact, he insisted that the map was printed wrong. Consequently, the two men drove around for hours before they found the house they were looking for. The senior man had too much pride to admit he didn't know where he was going.

If your husband is lost, don't ask him to read a map. Instead, pick up the map yourself and offer to help. Face-saving is important here. If you make fun of your husband because he can't find his way, you may find yourself walking to your next engagement (just joking!).

This chapter is adapted from writings by Brian Knowles of Pasadena, California.

7

Do I Still Have to Cook?

. . . .

■ **Fresh-baked bread. Barbecued chicken sizzling on the grill. Homemade apple pies.**

I love to cook as much as anyone, but after thirty years of slaving away in the kitchen for my husband and family, I deserve a break today. In fact, since the children left the nest, my husband and I have been eating out more, but we're noticing that that practice has put a dent in our pocketbook. What is it costing us to eat out?

A lot, and in many two-person households, too much for what you get. If we're a nation that has forgotten to cook, then we've become a nation that loves to be served in restaurants. We eat in restaurants an average of 4.1 times per week, according to the National Restaurant Association, or 213 restaurant meals a year. If you attach a dollar figure—let's call it $8 a meal—then you're spending $1,704 a year *per person!* Multiply that by two for you and your husband, and the figure approaches $3,400 annually or nearly $300 a month.

■ **It's nice to be served, enjoy some tasty food, and have someone else do the clean-up. Besides, I went back to work to help pay for the kids' college tuition, so I'm too pooped to cook.**

Yes, but no matter where you eat, it's going to cost more than you think. Most of the time, you'll be paying $15, $20 a head for dinner, which probably costs you three hours of take-home pay (figuring you make $10 an hour). Looked at another way, three hours is 37 percent of your work day—all to pay for a green salad, chicken marsala, and a beverage?

The problem is that we've forgotten to make eating out an *occasion*. Sitting down in a restaurant should be a time of unhurried conversation, a period of spousal interaction, a respite from the daily routine. Instead it's a quickly served mesquite chicken breast, soggy fries, and a flat Coke amidst a raucous atmosphere in which you are expected to "turn over" your table in one hour.

■ **We will probably eat out less, based on this information. But given the fact that we will be eating out on occasion, what are some effective strategies?**

Here are some ideas:

▶ **Eat out less often—it's as simple as that.** If you're looking for another rationale for staying home, remind yourself that you can eat better at home. You can purchase a nice piece of pork tenderloin or even Alaskan king crab for the price of a simple meal at Applebee's Neighborhood Grill & Bar.

▶ **Know that it's going to cost you more than you think.** Let's say you and your spouse have a date night at T.G.I.Fridays. You go easy, passing on appetizers and ordering two Blackened Cajun chicken meals, priced at $7.59. Mentally, you're figuring a total $16, maybe a couple of dollars more with tip.

Actually, your two meals will set you back more than $30! Beneath the description for the Cajun chicken, the fine print said you could order a house salad for an extra $1.89. *That doesn't seem like much to get some greens.* Then you ordered two ice teas at $1.49 each. Although your waitress did her best to entice you with the dessert tray, you stood firm, but you ordered coffee to round out the meal ($1.49 each). The cost of the two meals, when you add 6 percent sales tax and a 15 percent tip, comes to $30.42.

▶ **Brown-bag your lunch at work.** You'll feel a twinge of jealousy when you watch coworkers eat out every single weekday, but bringing your own lunch to work saves you $6 a day or $120 a month.

▶ **Sign up for dining clubs.** Every major city has them—entertainment books or dining clubs that cost $20 to $45 for a one-year membership. What you get is a card that allows you two-for-one dining at participating restaurants. There's a caveat, however: it's buy one entree and get one free, not 50 percent off the entire meal. You add appetizers, salad, dessert, and drinks at full price.

▶ **Speaking of add-ons, watch the add-ons.** You should eat at restaurants that serve complete meals—entrées served with bread and salad or soup. Appetizers and desserts can turn a $25 check for two into a $50 check quicker than you can say shrimp cocktail and tiramisu. Besides, you can eat dessert at home.

▶ **Drink water.** Most restaurants charge at least a buck for a soft drink or lemonade. Drinking water may take some getting used to, but water is much healthier than high-calorie soft drinks. Also, can you do without the dessert coffee? That can add another 10 percent to the bill.

▶ **Go out for lunch instead of dinner.** Many restaurants serve the same menu for lunch and dinner. You just have to pay 25 percent more for the privilege of eating after 4 P.M.

▶ **Look for coupon and "early-bird" specials.** Saturday is the most popular day to eat out, followed by Friday and Sunday. Restaurants are not willing to discount these high-peak times. But newspaper or junk-mail coupons can be found for other weekdays or early-bird specials before 6 P.M.

▶ **If you still have teenage boys in the house, get to know your country buffets and smorgasbords.** If your teen boy asks what's for dinner after three pork chops and mounds of mashed potatoes, country buffets are the place to go.

continued next page

THE FOOD SPOILAGE TEST

When it's just the two of you in the home, you're probably used to cooking and serving simple meals. But what if your children and grandkids come over and before you know it, the fridge is filled with leftovers? If that happens, then you want to know what to pitch and what to save. Here's a humorous look at leftovers:

Eggs

When something starts pecking its way out of the shell, the egg is probably past its prime.

Dairy Products

Milk is spoiled when it starts to look like yogurt. Yogurt is spoiled when it starts to look like cottage cheese. Cottage cheese is spoiled when it starts to look like regular cheese. Regular cheese is nothing but spoiled milk anyway and can't get more spoiled than it is already.

Mayonnaise

If the mayo makes you violently ill after eating it, it is spoiled.

Meat

If opening the refrigerator door causes stray animals within a three-block radius to congregate outside your house, the meat is spoiled.

■ **To help pay for the kids' college tuition, we are not eating out very much, which means I'm relegated to more kitchen duty. How can I get out of my thirty-year cooking rut?**

Besides buying a new cookbook, the simplest is to cut your food preparation time by doubling or tripling your recipes, then serving the leftovers two or three days later.

Of course, you'll have to manage your leftovers because you don't want your refrigerator filled with Tupperware containers with gross fur balls growing inside them. Some women stick a little notepad on the refrigerator and keep an "active list" of stored leftovers, complete with the date it first went into the fridge.

Don't turn your nose up at leftovers: Lasagna, chicken, pasta, and just about any casserole often tastes better the second time around, especially if you warm it up in a butter-filled pan.

If you're not a leftovers fan, then consider the 15-Minute Cooking plan, devised by Rhonda Barfield. If you're looking for a way to prepare food in very short segments, 15-Minute Cooking is a good idea, and it works well if you want to prepare something quick and nutritious after you get home from work.

Rhonda invented this system and then wrote a step-by-step plan called *15-Minute Cooking*. (The spiral-bound book is 168 pages and costs $12.95, which includes shipping and handling. Write: Lilac Publishing, P.O. Box 665, St. Charles, MO 63302-0665.) The advantages are home-cooked meals, having leftovers that can make a good breakfast and lunch, and better managing your time.

The 15-Minute Cooking system includes food preparation time only, so this doesn't mean you'll be able to set the table, put the food away, and wash the dishes in fifteen minutes. Besides, some of Rhonda's recipes have baking and cooking times beyond fifteen minutes. But if you'll devote one-quarter of an hour to this, you and your hubby will enjoy some tasty fare.

■ **What if I'm not a good cook?**

We've got news for you: Most women today cook very little, if at all, so if you think you are an average cook, you're probably excellent by today's standards. Remember this: If you can read, you can cook.

Bread

Fuzzy and hairy-looking white or green growth areas are a good indication that your bread has turned into a pharmaceutical laboratory experiment.

Lettuce

Bibb lettuce is spoiled when you can't get it off the bottom of the vegetable crisper without Comet.

Canned Goods

Any canned goods that have become the size or shape of a football should be disposed of. Carefully.

Raisins

Raisins should not be harder than your dentures.

Potatoes

Fresh potatoes do not have roots, branches, or dense, leafy undergrowth.

Chip Dip

If you can spoon the dip out of its container and bounce it off the floor, it has gone bad.

General Rule of Thumb

Tupperware containers should not burp when you open them.

But it really doesn't matter *how* you cook. Just do it! And go with what works for you and your family.

■ **I'm on a tight budget. Can I save money using the 15-Minute Cooking principles?**

Most couples and families will save a huge amount of money with 15-Minute Cooking because the system avoids high-priced supermarket convenience foods. Many of the 15-Minute Cooking recipes use "from scratch" principles. In fact, that's the key to all this—staying away from the Lean Cuisines and Stouffer's frozen entrees, which can cost upwards of $3 to $5 for a ten-ounce serving. Ouch!

■ **We can't save money on groceries because my husband is a big meat-and-potatoes man. How can I still keep beef on the table without busting our budget?**

Make it a point to buy meat that's on sale. Supermarkets generally discount certain cuts each week to draw shoppers into the store. If your husband is looking forward to top sirloin on Friday night (at $5.29 a pound) but beef brisket is specially priced at $1.99 a pound, go with the latter meat. In addition chicken is cheap and works wonderfully in dozens of recipes, from chicken parmesan to Crock-Pot soup.

■ **Can I save money by cutting up meat myself?**

For chicken, the answer is yes, which is why you should purchase whole fryers that can be cut up and baked. Chickens are not too difficult to cut up. You can find whole fryers at 79 cents a pound, but if they are cut up by the butcher, the price jumps to $1.29 a pound. That's a 63 percent increase.

As for beef, it's not worth it. For instance, let's say a rib-eye roast costs $4.69 a pound. When the roast is cut into slices, it's called rib-eye steak and sold for $4.99 a pound. You'd need a strong hacksaw to saw through the bones to make the roast into a steak. Is it worth thirty cents a pound? No.

■ **Any other things we should be doing to get out of the cooking rut?**

Don't feel guilty if you fail to put a gourmet dinner on the table every night. We sometimes have better things to do with our time than cook. Plan variety, but also keep in mind what your husband likes. There's really no excuse for cooking the same meal more than once every two months.

This chapter is adapted from 21 Days to a Thrifty Lifestyle *(Zondervan) by Mike Yorkey, and writings by Rhonda Barfield, author of* Eat Healthy for $50 a Week *(Kensington). She lives with her family in St. Charles, Missouri.*

8

When You Lose a Spouse: Finding Hope Again

. . . .

■ **The funeral is over. The flowers are wilted. My friends are telling me it's time for life to get back to normal. But how can it? I just lost a husband that I shared my days, my nights, my children, my dreams, and my life with for four decades. And now it is all over. There are days that I cannot find the strength to get out of bed until noon. How can I find hope again?**

The death of a spouse—and learning to live as one instead of two—is one of the most difficult passages of life. You will suffer in the next few weeks, few months, and few years. Time is a great healer, but you will probably never completely get over the loss of your beloved. Your whole life will be different, and special occasions and holidays times (birthdays, Christmas) will cause another cycle of grief as you look at the "empty chair."

Dealing with grief may remind you of the childhood game hide-and-seek—ready or not, here you come. But as you deal with the whirlwind of emotions, the deep hurt in the pit of your stomach, the aching heart, "Trust in the Lord with all your heart and lean not on your own understanding" (Prov. 3:5).

■ What can I do to make the pain go away?

The pain won't go away, and understanding that is the first step to dealing with your new life without your spouse. Grief is also a unique experience; no two persons handle a spouse's death in the same manner. Sometimes death is sudden: a heart attack or being hit by a drunk driver, and sometimes death is something to be anticipated, the result of a lingering illness or a long, debilitating condition.

Obviously, the spouse who loses his or her loved one overnight is going to be dealing with sudden shock and a whirling maelstrom of funeral preparations, cleaning out closets, dealing with insurance companies, and the wearying task of trying to make it through another day. The spouse who loses a husband or wife to a long bout with cancer, for example, has more time to get *used* to the idea of being a surviving spouse. Sometimes that helps; sometimes it doesn't.

Grief is a very unique experience. You can't judge youself or your grief by the way others around you have grieved. Some actually feel as if they are going crazy, finding it difficult to function after the death of a loved one. That can be pretty normal—even healthy.

■ I dreaded getting out bed in the morning after my husband died. Not because I couldn't face a life without Jake, but I just couldn't face walking into the bathroom and not finding his shaving stuff and toiletries scattered all over the counter.

It's the little things that make us miss the ones we love, and again, time is the best healer. But don't try to black out memories. Let them warm your soul.

■ One of our family traditions was to host a family dinner every Sunday for one of the kids and their families. Is it okay if I stop hosting that dinner?

Okay? Of course it's fine. If you're having a problem getting "up" for a Sunday family dinner, let it go on hiatus until you're feeling better about it. When you are ready to resume the family tradition, invite family members to bring a favorite dish to lighten the load. A simple alteration like this will help you enjoy the time with your family without the stress of planning, shopping, cooking, and cleaning up the kitchen.

The nice thing about family traditions is that they are easily bent and changed, but don't try to pretend that no one is missing. Some widows and widowers have been known to set a place at the table and place a flower on the plate in his or her memory. If that is too difficult, take the chair completely away from the table so it doesn't sit empty during the meal.

This chapter is adapted from writings by Maurcia DeLean Houck of Abington, Pennslyvania.

9

Sex and Singlehood

. . . .

■ I was going on my first blind date since my husband's death a few years before. My friends Mike and Leslie had run into a friend named Ed after having lost contact with him for several years. He was a widower, and they asked if he would like to meet a widowed friend of theirs—me. And so my eye-opening adventure began.

Ed came to take me to the restaurant where we would meet Mike and Leslie. Before they arrived, Ed leaned over the table and said, "You know, I think it is unrealistic for people our age [mid-fifties] to date and not sleep together." He went on to explain that if two people were single, adultery was not involved, and that the struggle with sexual temptation was too great to manage.

I was speechless at first, but what he said struck a chord. By the time Mike and Leslie walked into the restaurant, we were engaged in a heated discussion. Mike and Leslie were dumbstruck as we continued to debate the biblical acceptability of Christian singles engaging in sex.

Neither Ed nor I changed each other's mind that night. He was convinced that sex for singles was fine if both partners were honest about their feelings. I maintained that sex between singles is prohibited by God, along with adultery. Though I never saw Ed again, the issue remained close to my heart in the days that followed.

Why is there so much sexual confusion out there, even among Christians?

Widows and widowers, especially those under sixty, say that the struggle with sexual temptation continues to be a major issue for dating adults.

■ Is it confusion about what God says?

Many single people admit that premarital sex is wrong. But others, like Ed, believe that the admonition against sex outside of marriage only applies to married people. For instance, Bob, a divorced father of two young adults, also isn't sure about the biblical standard regarding sexual activity. He says he doesn't find evidence in the Bible that he should live a celibate life, but he struggles with his own sense of right and wrong.

"My logical self says, 'Don't engage in sexual intercourse, and keep it for marriage.' But when I trust the other person, know her intentions are good, feel physical chemistry between us, and believe there is a future in the relationship, then I let my guard down."

■ Well, in times like this, it's always good to go back to the Bible. What is God's standard?

Perhaps the most familiar verse that prohibits adultery is Exodus 20:14: "You shall not commit adultery."

According to *Webster's New Collegiate Dictionary*, adultery means "voluntary sexual intercourse between a married man and someone other than his wife or between a married woman and someone other than her husband."

Another word, "fornicators," applies to unmarried people. *The Evangelical Dictionary of Theology* says that in its widest sense, the Greek word *porneia* [fornication] "denotes immorality in general, or every kind of sexual transgression." This is the word used, for example, in 1 Corinthians 6:18: "Flee from sexual immorality. All other sins a man commits are outside his body, but he who sins sexually sins against his own body." Even if two people are single consenting adults, the Bible says that God considers sexual communion between them sin. God's standard is purity. We hinder our relationship with Him and miss His best when we ignore or misunderstand His teaching on sexual thoughts and behaviors.

■ **The Bible does not spell out what acceptable behavior** *should* **be when adults are dating. So if sexual intercourse is not allowed, what is?**

Ah, the question everyone wants answered. Does the Bible mean no physical contact at all? Is hugging, kissing, holding, or touching each other permitted? If the two adults are committed to God and to each other, does that allow for more intimate sexual expression?

Elaine admitted that she and a longtime dating partner had participated in mutual masturbation, and she felt enormous guilt over it. The man she was dating seemed apologetic for moving beyond her comfort level, but he wasn't convicted that the behavior was ungodly. The relationship didn't last, and Elaine decided she would not go that far sexually again.

Tammy dated a single pastor for six months and described their relationship as "as a Christian version of going all the way." She went on to describe that while this man felt that abstaining from sexual intercourse was the standard for godly behavior, any other sexual expression was acceptable.

The reality of dating for Christian singles is that sexual relationships are a constant struggle. Natural, God-given desires reside in most healthy adults and scream for expression and fulfillment. All widows and widowers have been sexually active, and they face the challenge of relating to members of the opposite sex and limiting the behavior that used to be a regular part of their lives.

PRACTICAL HELP

Here are suggestions that can help if you have made a commitment to the Lord. Allow the guidelines on this list to help you move into a deeper relationship with Christ.

▶ **Take a break.** If you are in a relationship that is not sexually pure, take a break from it and reevaluate your thinking and behavior. This will be difficult to do, but it may result in an enhanced relationship later.

If you are in a relationship that is sexually pure, talk about spiritual issues with your partner. Discover your similarities and differences and how they may affect your future.

If you are not in a relationship, take this opportunity to grow spiritually.

▶ **Make a decision.** After evaluating where you are spiritually, decide why you are dating, how you want to date, and what you are hoping for in the future. Decide what behavior is godly and what you will avoid.

▶ **Take an escape route before it's too late.** Don't wait until you are in someone's bedroom to flee temptation. Decide what precautions you will take to prevent getting into compromising situations.

Jane has a warm and growing relationship with David. They both are committed Christians who have faced the issue of sexual expression openly. They want their relationship to honor God and each other, so they have limited the time they spend alone.

Recently they went to see a popular film that left audiences sighing with romantic emotion. Jane said that after the movie, she and David had planned to go back to her house for dinner, but they decided it would be better not to be alone. Instead they went out to dinner and talked. By the end of dinner, their emotions were back on an even keel, and their overpowering temptation to compromise sexually had passed.

▶ **Maintain involvement with other couples.** Other couples can help you establish accountability and ease the sexual intensity that grows when you're alone together. If you are not in a dating relationship, you still need involvement with people who care about you and will hold you accountable for your behavior.

▶ **Relate to God on a meaningful level.** Your relationship with Him is the key to every aspect of peace, happiness, and fulfillment in your life. If you don't nurture that relationship, you will slip back into old ways of feeling, thinking, and acting.

The pressures of our culture and your own nature will draw you back into

continued next page

compromising situations. You will miss God's best. God wants to bless you. He wants you to experience His love with power.

At all costs, stay involved with Him. Read, pray, and sit in His presence. Wrap yourself in His love and enjoy the rich, godly relationships He has for you with Him and with others.

■ Knowing this, how can I experience God's best?

A wide chasm exists between no sexual contact and sexual intercourse. Somewhere between these two extremes lies God's best for us. While God does not want us to be relational islands who communicate with each other from behind a sea of prohibitions, God also doesn't want us to compromise on living godly lives.

Some recommend making a list of behaviors and committing to stick to the list. But the reality is lists don't work unless a deep conviction about our intimate involvement with God grips our very souls.

The answer to sexual purity lies in our love relationship with Christ. If Christ isn't first in our lives, we will have little motivation to limit sexual expression. From the moment we accept Christ as Savior and Lord, we are encouraged to give up control of our lives and give it back to Him.

Paul's prayer to the Ephesians says, "And I pray that you, being rooted and established in love, may have power, together with all the saints, to grasp how wide and long, and high and deep is the love of Christ, and to know this love that surpasses knowledge— that you may be filled to the measure of all the fullness of God" (Eph. 3:17-19).

This side of heaven, we will not arrive at godly living without struggle. But we can experience God's love in ways that lift us above our circumstances. We can find fulfillment by choosing to listen to our consciences and to live with discipline for the sake of our relationship with Christ.

This means that we continually run back to Jesus, sit in His presence, pour out our hearts, then hear His voice and feel His love. Those who focus on Him grow in strength and discernment and can make wise choices about all aspects of life, including sexual behavior.

Jim is a divorced father of two teenagers who summed up his standard for dating in one sentence: "I'm a Christian, and I don't mess around." Jim talked about the struggle that surrounds his position. He found that many Christian women were more willing to engage in sexual intercourse than he had anticipated. Jim set a personal standard by asking himself who he was and what he stood for. He said, "It's a matter of discipline and drawing the line."

Jim limits sexual activity to putting his arm around a woman and maybe kissing her good night. He feels that anything beyond that is unsafe. The issue for him is based on his relationship with God and his desire for God's best for him.

Lists won't work without conviction and a deep relationship with the Lord. But even with that level of commitment to God, guidelines are needed.

■ **What about if we are moving toward marriage? That's what happening for me after I lost my wife ten years ago to breast cancer.**

In his book *Life on the Edge*, Dr. James Dobson quotes from Desmond Morris in *Intimate Behavior*. Dr. Dobson says that the quality of the bond made during courtship is one of the keys to a successful marriage. He supports Morris' assertion that couples are more likely to bond securely if they have not rushed the dating experience. Morris advocates twelve stages of intimacy through which couples should progress if they want to develop a firm commitment to each other. They are:

- ▶ **Eye to body.** One person sees another.
- ▶ **Eye to eye.** They exchange glances.
- ▶ **Voice to voice.** They talk.
- ▶ **Hand to hand.** They hold hands.
- ▶ **Hand to shoulder.** They develop a "buddy" type of relationship in which they are still side-by-side instead of facing each other.
- ▶ **Hand to waist.** They begin a romance by embracing.
- ▶ **Face to face.** They kiss, hug, and gaze into one another's eyes.
- ▶ **Hand to head.** They stroke each other's hair.

The final stages are distinctly sexual and private and are to be reserved exclusively for the marriage bed:

- ▶ **Hand to rest of body.**
- ▶ **Mouth to breast.**
- ▶ **Touching below the waist.**
- ▶ **Sexual intercourse.**

Purity in thinking keeps bringing us back to what God wants for us. It flies in the face of everything our culture and our unleashed desires tell us. Somehow, we have come to believe that it is not humanly possible, or even healthy, to have desires and needs that go unmet.

While our hearts move toward purity, our emotions may continue to rage toward the temptation to satisfy sexual desires. Godly behavior is based on what we know, not what we feel. Despite tumultuous feelings and longings, we can choose behavior that honors God, ourselves, and each other.

This chapter is adapted from writings by Lois Rabey of Colorado Springs, Colorado.

10

For Your Eyes Only

■ After all these years, you'd think I'd be used to it, but a nice-looking female body still has a mighty hold on me.

Everywhere I look, there they are—joggers in sports bras and pink biker shorts, bikini-clad babes in beer commercials, half-clad models in unsolicited Victoria's Secret lingerie catalogs, secretaries wearing tight, low-cut dresses to work. The Old Testament Job didn't have to deal with half of these!

My eyes always seem to bounce right to the sexual, as my wife is fond of pointing out. Once we were casually flipping through a magazine together, and we stopped at a very "busy" picture of a room set up for a celebration. There were tons of things to look at, but she was stunned when I said, "Now, why did they have to put those legs sticking out of the top of the cake?"

Yup, two attractive female legs with black fishnet stockings were sticking up out of the top of the cake, as part of the decorations. My eyes had rocketed to the sexual, but Linda had never even noticed them.

So what do I do? With sexual images everywhere and a pair of "heat-seeking" eyes, what are my options? Do I have to pluck them out?

No, you don't have to go that far, but you will need to train your eyes to "bounce" away from sexual images. It will have to become almost as a reflex action, something as quick as pulling your hand from a hot stove.

This whole idea of "starving the eyes" and "training the eyes to bounce" is based on Job 31:1: "I made a covenant with my eyes, not to look lustfully at a girl." There were a few babes in Job's neighborhood, but the key is that he determined not to "look lustfully."

This is all part of a "look-lust-sin" pattern for males. The "look" is not dangerous in itself, except that it leads to the "lust" part. The "lust" part is the quicksand. Once there, sin usually abounds.

Fred Stoeker, who has written about this issue, says he has a friend who goes into a video rental store, eyes a couple of sexually explicit video covers, and he becomes helpless. The man is then stuck in the store for sometimes up to two hours, as the lust grips him and he walks from video to video, gazing at images. To a woman, this sounds sick. To men, we understand.

■ When does "looking" become "lusting"?

Because the human heart is desperately wicked, we always will define sin loosely. Take drinking, as an example. The Bible clearly states that you should not get drunk: "Do not get drunk with wine, which leads to debauchery. Instead, be filled with the Spirit" (Eph. 5:18).

The Bible does not specifically say that you can't drink alcohol at all. So when do you pass from "drinking" to being "drunk"? It's a blurry line, literally, which is why drinking should be very limited. It's the same way with seeing sexual images.

Given that the human heart is rebellious, and given that "lust" is a dangerous slippery slope, it is prudent and proper that to keep from sinning, you will need to train your eyes to bounce away immediately.

■ What are some good ways to train my eyes to bounce away? This is easier said than done, you know.

In one sense, it is no different from any other habit. They say that if you do anything for twenty-one days, it becomes a habit.

You have to do it consistently and in an orderly way. You must consciously practice to imprint a new habit. Your body will be fighting against you in a special way, however, since there is an addictive nature to this problem.

Then you must make a list of your "greatest enemies." Fred Stoeker made such a list, which might look something like yours:

1. Female joggers in tight nylon shorts
2. Lingerie advertisements
3. Billboards
4. Beer commercials
5. Movies rated PG-13 and up
6. Pretty receptionists

Here's how Fred handled each category. See if you can adapt any ideas to your situation.

1. Female joggers

Whenever Fred approached a jogger on the road, his eyes would fix on her, appreciating her beauty. He had to create a new habit. Whenever he approached a jogger, he would look to the opposite side of the road, keeping the jogger in his peripheral vision so he wouldn't run over her. He found that it was impossible to "lust" using peripheral vision.

Fred began practicing this defense with fervor—bouncing his eyes away. It became immediate habit, and he never got in a car wreck! (Besides, more accidents are caused by looky-loos than those trying to point their eyes elsewhere.)

2. Lingerie Advertisements

This will be difficult because full-color photos of women in their underwear and bras is among the most sexually satisfying of all of them. And they are there every Sunday in the newspaper!

But wait, it gets worse. Nearly ever sports magazine has its own "swimsuit edition," patterned after the famous *Sports Illustrated* special issue each February. Believe us, you don't want to go *there*.

Your defense is to stay a step ahead of the curve by cutting off the problem before the "look" stage and well before the "lust" stage.

To accomplish this, Fred formulated two hard-and-fast rules:

Rule #1: Whenever his hand reached for a magazine or newspaper insert and he sensed in even the slightest way that his underlying motive was to see something sensual, he forfeited the right to pick up that newspaper or magazine.

This didn't work well at first, because even though sensing the motive was easy, forfeiting his right to pick it up was not. Fred's flesh simply ignored his spirit, telling him to "shut up!" But as Fred began to succeed in other areas, his hatred for the sin grew and his will and discipline got stronger.

Rule #2: If you are genuinely looking for sales on camping equipment or tools in those department store inserts, you are allowed to pick them up. However, you must only open them from the back. The lingerie ads are always on pages 2 and 3. The camping, automotive, and tool ads are on the last pages.

3. Billboards

Billboards are notorious for having long, tall, slinky, big-busted women silently catching your eyes and whispering, "C'mon, big boy, buy this stuff and you'll get me too!" These billboards are getting racier all the time.

Fred's defense, of course, was to bounce his eyes away. But he also made it a habit to memorize where the racy billboards were on his daily commute to he could be sure he could avoid them each day before they came into view.

4. Beer Commercials

It's difficult to say which came first, "Baywatch" or sexy beer commercials, but you catch the drift. This one should be the easiest to overcome because of the remote control. Just zap it away. Who wants to watch commercials anyway? Go to "ESPN SportsCenter" during commercial breaks.

5. PG-13 Movies and Above

What is PG-13 today used to R-rated fifteen or twenty years ago. That's how far this culture has slid down the slippery slope. You will have to very careful what you rent (or watch at first-run theaters). Try to rely on the advice of friends who have the same worldview as you. You can also subscribe to *Preview*, a Christian-based movie review newsletter. A one-year subscription with twenty-four issues is available for a suggested donation of $34. Call Preview at (972) 231-9910, or write Preview, 1309 Seminole Dr., Richardson, TX 75080.

A bigger problem is the sexy "Debbie Does Dallas" videos that are piped into the pay-per-view services of hotel TVs. When you check into a hotel during a business trip, ask the front desk to block those racy channels.

6. Pretty Receptionists

All too often when Fred entered an office building, he would enter the business and encounter a receptionist who was standing up to do some work. Inevitably, the phone would ring, and rather than sitting down, the receptionist would bend over, giving Fred an eyeful down her blouse. It never occurred to Fred to turn away from something like that; the view was rather nice.

The practical defense is easy. If a receptionist is standing and you know she is going to bend over, turn away before she even bends.

■ **I'm going to try to make a covenant with my eyes to train them to bounce. When can I expect to see progress?**

You will probably experience failure after failure for the first couple of weeks. Your eyes will simply not fall in line and bounce away from the sexual. If that happens, remember the example of Job and how he was just a man like you, and that there must be a way. Keep praying for more insight and understanding, that God will make the path clear.

Fred Stoeker reports that during the third and fourth weeks he began seeing changes; he began winning about as often as he failed. It was during this time that there was a noticeable impact in his life. His sex life improved. He thought his wife, Brenda, looked very different, very ravishing, yet she hadn't done a thing.

Once Fred's eyes were starved from any other source and his eyes were focused on her and her alone, her perceived beauty rocketed out of sight. "I cannot overemphasize how impressive this change can be," says Fred.

It was also during this time that his marital sexual satisfaction flew off any known scale. They had always had a satisfying sex life, but he found that even their good sex life had been hurt by his impurity. How? Because when the sin was removed, it became far better.

During the fifth and sixth weeks, when his eyes began to learn to consistently bounce away from the sensual, Fred had more victories than failures. If he saw a jogger in the distance, an automatic turn of the eye would occur without conscious thought. His eyes began to bounce from billboards and TV ads and sexual scenes on TV. He began to get stronger in regards to magazines and ad inserts.

As you live purely, the "hedge of protection" from temptation will grow thicker and thicker around you. Over time, if you are diligent, it will become more difficult for Satan to lob a "temptation grenade" over the hedge. Keep your eyes on the Lord, and you'll be less likely to fall in the area of sexual impurity.

This chapter is adapted from writings by Fred Stoeker of Johnson City, Iowa.

2

You and
Your Family

1

Family Reunions: Celebrating the Ties That Bind

. . . .

■ My image of family reunions is a bunch of hayseed relatives who don't know each other from Adam's housecat meeting in some dilapidated church fellowship hall in a dusty town forgotten long ago by the rest of the world. Then we recently received an invitation to our first big family shindig next summer in Nebraska. That's a plane trip for us, plus nearly a week away from the house. Is it really worth it?

Well, if you pack that attitude with you, then yes, you're better off staying at home.

But if you go, the odds are high that you'll be glad you did. Let me make a bold statement: Family reunions are well worth the effort of getting there and staying there.

Kerry Klaassen Veale is a mom who just turned forty and who had never attended a family reunion until a decade ago, and now she attends every few years, even though it's a trek from her Southern California home. What hooked her was hearing this story at her first reunion:

> *It was the summer of 1945. As the yellow Oklahoma*
> *wheat fields rippled in the warm breeze, thousands of locusts*

whispered their monotonous chant. A thirteen-year-old girl walked briskly along the country road, kicking up little clouds of red dirt with each step. Sweat trickled down her face to her faded cotton dress. The young girl was returning from a revival in town, where she'd accepted Jesus Christ as her Savior. Knowing instinctively that life was somehow going to be different, she burst through the back door and told her mom the exciting news.

"You don't know what you're talking about," was her mother's angry response.

The young girl stumbled outside, crying. She ran to her chicken coop—at least the nesting hens would listen. She didn't know it yet, but for many years her parents, still rebellious from their own upbringing, would forbid her to visit her relatives—the ones who already shared her new faith.

■ **That's quite a story. What else did Kerry learn at her family reunion?**

The Karber family reunions happen every couple of years in Oklahoma prairie towns, where several hundred descendants explore their common heritage. Kerry learned that she is part of the fifth generation, living halfway across the country from most of her relatives (Kerry grew up in the Oklahoma City area).

Although writer Thomas Wolfe said you can't go home again, you really can. For Kerry, seeing the red dirt and the rolling plains of her childhood transported her back to a time of wide-open spaces, wheat fields rolling to the gentle waves of the wind, and the sapphire, smog-free skies. It was easy for her thoughts to turn inward, as they would for you if you return to your roots and homeland.

■ **What are some other benefits to family reunions?**

Obviously, you're going to find out more about your family's background, but you're going to gain a sense of belonging, which every person needs. Every family has a story, and that was no different for Kerry. Her ancestors were Mennonites who came to America from Europe to escape military service and religious persecution. As pacifists, Mennonites refuse to bear arms or take oaths, and they spoke a peasant German dialect called *Plattdeutsch*. Kerry learned that her grandfather, David Reimer, was a conscientious objector during World War II, which didn't sit well with others. Kerry's mother was mocked cruelly by other schoolchildren, who made fun of her German heritage and her father's decision not to enlist.

Going back even farther, Kerry's great-great-grandparents were David and Henrietta Karber, pioneers who left Eastern Europe in the early 1870s. They met in Kansas and were married in 1877. A few years later, with the help of other Mennonite immigrants, they built a new church and called it *Hoffnungsfeld*—Field of Hope. They built their field of dreams, and people came.

Henrietta Karber endured incredible hardships when her young family moved from Kansas to Oklahoma by covered wagon train. That first summer, the Karbers lived in a tent while David worked the land. Their first home had so little room that the chairs had to be placed on the table in order for people to walk by. They ate a steady diet of corn bread and prips (roasted barley coffee).

At the reunion, Kerry met relatives she never knew—a flight attendant, a university vice president, a lawyer, an accountant, a missionary, an elementary school principal—and *lots* of farmers. But through it all, Kerry discovered a sense of pride in *her* family. Their courage and determination over the years strengthened her values. She felt gratified for the risks her ancestors took for religious freedom. It felt good to belong to a family that placed a strong faith in God.

■ **We've never had a family reunion, and I'm thinking that it would be fun to do it once. If I'm actually going to jump in with both feet, what do I need to know to plan one?**

Family reunions take a lot of hard work, but it's worth it. Here are a few pointers to keep in mind from Kerry:

▶ **Start small.** Family get-togethers don't have to number in the hundreds. Begin with a dozen or so relatives who live within a day's drive.

▶ **Plan early.** Remember, it takes at least three to six months to pull off a large reunion. Set up a committee to make the major decisions, such as location and time of year. Most family reunions are in the summer, when the days are long and most people take their vacations.

▶ **Go for the "old country."** Family reunions can be held anywhere, but often the most memorable are held in small towns and rural areas—far from busy cities. It helps if a local committee can handle the arrangements by booking a city park, church fellowship hall, or community center.

▶ **Build a mailing list.** Send out a mailer with the dates, lodging arrangements, and cost of meals (so family members can begin planning and saving). Be sure to consider financial limitations. Ask for addresses of hard-to-locate relatives.

▶ **Find ways to celebrate your family's unique heritage.** You might visit old family homes and farm areas, as well as grave sites. Country museums are also worthwhile.

▶ **Try to overcome geographic and generation barriers.** To help people get acquainted, give everyone a sheet of paper with blank boxes for each branch of the family. The object is to get signatures for each of the boxes—a painless way to meet lots of family members. Color-coded name badges with a different color for each branch of the family can help things run smoothly.

▶ **Showcase the talents of as many people as possible.** For instance, have family members dress up in period costumes and perform a play on how the ancestors took a wagon train before settling on their homestead.

▶ **Provide activities of interest to everyone.** Entertain the children with horseshoes, riding a small train, or taking old-fashioned hay rides.

▶ **Involve as many people as you can.** From day one, volunteers will be needed. Ask family members to sign up for at least one task, be it kitchen duty, busing tables, or planning games.

▶ **Communicate clearly to avoid mishaps.** Upon arrival,

hand each family member a detailed registration packet containing information on all of the weekend events. That way, everyone will know exactly where they should be, and when.

▶ **Keep a record of all your arrangements for the next reunion.** After your first get-together, you'll have so much fun that you'll probably want to do a reunion every few years.

▶ **Finally, create memories that will live past the reunion.** For Kerry, that happened one Sunday morning when the Karber family choir sang the "Doxology" *a cappella* at the church service. One of the Karber descendants, Rev. Linden Unruh, delivered a moving sermon. After church, they ate Sunday dinner in the fellowship hall, where each table centerpiece held a bunch of brightly colored balloons.

Following the meal, the entire extended family, several hundred strong, walked outside. Standing in the balmy Oklahoma breeze, they released their balloons. As the multi-colored balloons soared into the heavens, they softly sang, "God Be with You Till We Meet Again." There weren't many dry eyes to be had.

■ **Whatever happened to that thirteen-year-old girl who accepted the Lord in 1945?**

That young girl was Evelyn Kunkel, a first cousin of Kerry's mother. This is the "rest of the story" that Kerry heard:

The thirteen-year-old girl grew in the Lord. On Sundays, she could walk down the dirt lane to the main road to catch a ride to church. On the days when her ride didn't come, she waited, waited, and then walked home alone.

When she was eighteen, she left home to attend a Christian college. The encouragement of her Christian cousins buoyed her during difficult times, and she tried to support herself and go to school at the same time. She met a fine young Christian man, Eldred Kunkel, and they married. The young couple settled in San Jose, California, where Eldred became a successful building contractor.

When Kerry heard Evelyn, in her late sixties, tell her story, she was there right next to her on that country road more than a half century ago. Kerry had more than a record of a common past but also a gift to the future. Give that gift to your family members.

Kerry Veale lives with her family in Huntington Beach, California.

2

Drawing a Family Circle

. . . .

■ **My extended family "extends" for thousands of miles.**
What are some ways we can close that distance?

In Lonny and Beverly Borts' living room in Syosset, New York,
aunts and uncles, first, second, and third cousins sit together and
enjoy cake, coffee, and each other's company. Reminiscing, laughter, and lots of news are being swapped: a recent graduation, two
weddings, and the birth of a seventh-generation baby. Photographs
of cousins from a trip to New Zealand are passed around.

This is no ordinary Saturday night party; it's the Littman Family
Circle gathering, which meets five times a year. From its earliest
beginnings in 1936, the Littman Family Circle has "strengthened
the ties that bind us together as relatives and friends," says its president, Marilyn Brenner of Teaneck, New Jersey. The Littman
Family Circle has kept the family in contact through picnics,
anniversary dinners, a regular newsletter, and even a book of family
history and genealogy written by Mrs. Brenner.

Besides meeting socially and sharing news, Family Circle members also help each other out: writing letters of recommendation
for a son's first job, rounding up volunteers to visit a great aunt in a

nursing home, and collecting money for a "Sunshine Fund" to help a family in need.

In Upstate New York, the Podolny Family Circle has members whose ages range from ten months to eight-six years. "Our Family Circle brings a great feeling of belonging, closeness, and family unity," says Blanche Liebman of Hartsdale, New York. "Because everyone lives fairly close to each other, we meet every month. When my husband had bypass surgery, family members called and visited. They also sent us gifts."

■ How did family clubs get their start? This sounds interesting.

Many immigrants came to this country between 1881 and 1914, and they all lived close to one another. When the grandchildren of immigrants left for the neighboring suburbs, many still desired to keep in touch through Cousins' Clubs and Family Circles.

As a child growing up in Philadelphia, Rabbi David Packman of Temple B'nai Israel in Oklahoma City, Oklahoma, attended his mother's Cousins' Club monthly gatherings. "We had Sunday brunch in an aunt's or uncle's home and then stayed to visit through the afternoon and evening. By then you were filled in on everyone's news. If a relative was sick, money was collected. If a need for child care or personal help arose, someone volunteered," says the rabbi.

In today's get-up-and-go society, the splintering of the family has not gone unnoticed. "I think what is happening is that the family has gone from something people took for granted or found burdensome to something that is like sand slipping through your fingers," said Ira Wolfman, author of *The Kids' Book of Genealogy: A Guide for Ancestor Detectors.* "If you don't hold on to what you've got, you suddenly discover that it's gone."

Family Circles were the backdrop to a 1990 Hollywood movie, *Avalon*, the story of a Jewish immigrant from Poland, Sam Kachinsky. "I came to America in 1914," he tells his grandchildren often. "It was the most beautiful place I'd ever seen."

As *Avalon* demonstrated, many Family Circles fell by the wayside following World War II. "I thought it would be interesting to show the evolution of a family over a fifty-year period—how the structure changes and the extended family disappears," said writer/director Barry Levinson. "I grew up with my grandparents and parents, and aunts and uncles came through the house all the time. We had a real sense of family, but now that's part of vanishing America."

Bringing back Family Circles, even if members live thousands of miles away, is one way to stem the tide. "One of the great benefits is regaining the continuity people are lacking," says Tully Plesser, part of the Schreiber Family Circle, which has members far and wide: Los Angeles, Toronto, New York, Florida, Israel, and Europe. "Children develop a sense of belonging. They realize they have ties to different sizes, shapes, and kinds of people, not just their little family unit."

As a child, Mr. Plesser was inspired by the different qualities and achievements of relatives he met in Family Circle gatherings: a concert pianist, an author, a physician, among others. "I was exposed to excellent role models," he said, "and achievement became more attainable because these people were close to home. It motivated me to say, 'People from my family can do that, and so can I!' "

■ If I decide to start a Family Circle, how should I start?

Here are some tips:

▶ **Make the first step.** You can be the catalyst for your family to grow closer. Gather names and addresses of family members living near you and choose a time to meet. Send out invitations and a short letter explaining why you want to start a Family Circle. Even if only three or four people show up, your circle will grow. You've got to start somewhere.

If you're isolated from other relatives, you might schedule a Family Circle meeting at a family wedding. Remember, it's too hectic to meet before the wedding; shoot for the day after, usually a Sunday.

"Don't be too structured at first, locking people in too tightly," says Tully Plesser. "Being flexible and keeping ground rules to a minimum helps people feel more comfortable."

▶ **Divide up responsibilities.** One family can volunteer to have the next gathering at their home. Another committee can bring food and refreshments. Several couples can help gather names and addresses for the roster, an important part of the Family Circle.

"If you're traveling, the family roster is invaluable for making connections," says Ira Wolfman. "If we're going to San Diego, for example, we look in our directory to see if we have distant cousins there. Then we give them a call and get together."

▶ **Make sure you have fun too.** At your first meeting, plan a social time to visit and swap news. Says Ann Davis of Lake Worth, Florida, "I think you'll find as you're sitting close to each other, much is shared. Gatherings generate a lot of warmth and spontaneity. In the family circle, relationships have a head start."

At Ann's "Cousins' Club" gatherings, relatives fill in missing pieces of the puzzle of family history. With the different impressions and stories coming from sisters and cousins about their parents and grandparents, they all learn a lot about their heritage.

Taping oral histories at gatherings is a great way to value both the older people in the family and the history. With the different impressions and stories coming from sisters and cousins about their parents and grandparents, they all learn a lot about their heritage. "Taping is a wonderful thing to do," says author Ira Wolfman. "It affects people deeply and teaches you about your own origins."

Some Family Circle gatherings include an informal business meeting to plan a future reunion, make announcements or discuss needs within the group. Others include a simple worship service.

▶ **A newsletter is essential.** Distance is a problem for many families, but a report such as *The Littman Log* or *The Jordan Journal* is a wonderful tool to keep everyone in touch. "The newsletter is a major factor in helping families stay connected," says Tully Plesser. A newsletter can be handwritten or typed into a computer and printed out. It should include everything from news of the family to anecdotes from the past. Some even include copies of old documents discovered in an attic.

You can also share information about births, graduations, and military service in a "General Family News" section. Some families list birthdays and anniversaries for the
next few months (so members can send greetings).

As your Family Circle grows, the newsletter could have
headings or columns such as:

- ▶ Three Cheers for You! (achievements, graduations,
  etc.)
- ▶ Wedding Bells (engagements and upcoming nuptials)
- ▶ Welcome to the Family! (birth and adoption announce-
  ments)
- ▶ Notable News (interesting trips, promotions, career
  changes)
- ▶ I Remember When (anecdotes about the "good ol'
  days")
- ▶ New Addresses and Corrections

At the bottom of the newsletter's last page, you could
have a tear-off-and-mail section with an RSVP for the next
Family Circle gathering.

- ▶ **Share your faith.** Being in a Family Circle is also a great
  way to share your faith and provides many opportunities
  for ministry. What can be more rewarding than bringing a
  family member into the kingdom!

*This chapter is adapted from writings by Cheri Fuller, an author and writer living in Oklahoma
City, Oklahoma.*

3

A Thanksgiving to Cherish

. . . .

Editor's note: Have you ever asked yourself, "Why do I always have to be the one to cook Thanksgiving dinner for everybody?" Then you will identify with this fictional story written by Elaine Schulte.

Lisa Barnett basted the brown turkey and pushed the enormous bird back into the oven. *To everything there is a season . . .* she thought as she quickly closed the oven door on the twenty-five-pound tom . . . *and a time to every purpose under heaven.*

Why were the words so persistent, so haunting this Thanksgiving afternoon?

Pulling off her oven mitts, Lisa surveyed the warm kitchen. Turkey giblets simmered in a stainless steel pot; on the next burner, in her heavy iron pot, peeled potatoes began to boil. On the countertop, a glass casserole dish held brown-sugared yams. Lisa realized she was preparing Thanksgiving dinner just as her mother always had, and her grandmothers before that, and probably her great-grandmothers.

To everything there is a season. The Scripture swirled in her head as she opened the refrigerator and checked the carrot salad and celery sticks. No one had touched them, nor the two pumpkin pies she'd baked that morning. *Everything's under control,* she thought, *so why is something bothering me?*

The resentment came from deep within: *This is the twenty-fourth year in a row you've cooked Thanksgiving dinner for the family!*

It couldn't be helped, she told herself, closing the refrigerator a bit too hard.

Lisa stepped into the dining room for a quick inspection. Her married daughter, Amy, had set the table with an ecru lace table-cloth inherited from Grandmother. Crystal goblets sparkled over gleaming china and silverware. The table's festive centerpiece was a rattan cornucopia spilling apples, oranges, grapes, and nuts.

It's nice to see Amy has learned to set a formal dinner table, she thought as she returned to the kitchen. Lisa looked out to the back yard and spotted the grandchildren playing with her husband, Jon, who was raking up the last of the fall leaves. Each time Jon created a mound, the grandkids somersaulted into the pile.

I wish I had my camera, she thought as she watched Jon rake the leaves onto the giggling kids. The fading sunlight reminded her that Josh and his family would arrive soon. As she began to wash pots and pans, she recalled Thanksgivings past, and her mind began to wander . . . .

Lisa remembered as a young girl helping her mother cover the stuffing-filled turkey with strips of bacon, rolling dough for the pie crusts, and setting a nice table.

"Thanksgiving isn't just a day," her mother had said as she mashed potatoes. "It's an attitude, a condition of the heart that's thankful no matter what happens in life."

One year, her mother had invited a dozen widows and widowers from church for Thanksgiving dinner. Everyone sat where they could—and didn't mind at all. *Neither had Mom minded all the work it took to feed all those people,* Lisa thought.

Then she recalled the time she came home from college in love with Jon. She'd flung open the front door and dropped her suitcase in the entry.

"Mom!" she called out. "Mom!"

She found her mother in the kitchen, dicing celery and onions for the homemade stuffing.

"You're home early Lisa!" she said, hugging her. "Has something happened? Something exciting?"

"How do you know, Mom?"

"You're glowing, child."

"I'm in love," Lisa blurted. "I mean, I'm really and truly in love."

"I thought so," her mother replied, wiping her hands on her apron. "Let's have tea," she said, gesturing to the small breakfast table. "Tell me about him. Is he in one of your classes?"

Lisa swallowed. "Well, Jon is a little older."

"How old?" her mother asked. "Seventy? Eighty?"

"Oh, Mom," Lisa answered. "He's a twenty-eight-year-old graduate student. Only six years older."

"That's perfect. Just perfect for you."

Lisa sat back in surprise. "Do you really think so?"

"I hoped and prayed you'd marry a mature man. Tell me more about him now that I know he's ancient."

Relieved, Lisa laughed. "Well, he's tall, blond, and handsome. He's thoughtful and kind and . . . ." How could she describe the most wonderful man in the world?

"Romantic?" asked her mother.

Lisa's cheeks reddened. "Yes, very."

"I love him already," Mom said. And so did her father, who accepted Jon as if he were his own son.

Lisa's mind moved to two Thanksgivings after the wedding. She and Jon had just learned she was pregnant. After they arrived at her parents, she was so excited she pulled her mother into the kitchen.

"Guess what, Mom?"

Her mother's eyes widened in speculation, then filled with delight. "If it's what I suspect, I don't want you to tell me. Just announce it to all of us at the table, so we can all share in the first telling."

"Oh, Mom, why didn't I think of that?"

"Because we're all still growing," she replied, patting Lisa on the shoulder.

Then, two years later, Lisa was eight months pregnant with Josh. Because of Mother's failing health, it was the last time she had hosted the big dinner. That's when the Thanksgiving meal had fallen into Lisa's lap and stayed there for twenty-four years. . . .

The resentful day came two years ago. Lisa had resumed her teaching career since the nest was empty. *Why do I always get stuck making Thanksgiving dinner for the whole family?* she thought as she worked over the hot stove that afternoon.

Trying to juggle the demands of the classroom and keep the house running smoothly exhausted her. "If you can make it to the Thanksgiving break," another teacher told Lisa, "you'll be all right."

Lisa had clung to that assurance.

Drying a pot, she glanced through the kitchen door to the long dining room table. She remembered the seating arrangement from two years ago. Dad was at the head of the table at the far end; Amy and Josh with their young families beamed as they sat next to Grandpa. Mother had been next to Josh, but her face was as pale as her body was frail.

When Lisa had finally rushed the last steaming dish to the table, she sat down wearily. Bowing her head, she heard her husband pray: "Heavenly Father, we come to You with thankfulness in our hearts for the many blessings You have bestowed on us in the last year. . . ."

When they looked up, her mother's brown eyes sparkled with happiness. "Thank you, Lisa, for making such a wonderful Thanksgiving for us again. I know how much work it is, and I want you to know how much your father and I appreciate it."

Lisa smiled at the curly-haired woman whose salt-and-pepper hair topped a smiling face, whose brown eyes danced with an indomitable spirit. *I guess I do have much to be thankful for,* she thought.

Her father had glanced up and down the table at everyone. "I hope we'll all be together next year."

A pang of fear flickered through her.

"Of course, we will," Lisa cut in, hoping to change the direction of the conversation.

Jon came to her rescue. "My new business should be going so well next year that we'll hire caterers to cook for Thanksgiving," he joked.

She laughed with everyone else. Just one month later, however, Lisa received a phone call from her father. She sat down weakly when she heard the quiver in his voice.

"It's bad news, honey," he began. "It's your mother. She wasn't feeling well and. . . ." His voice trailed off.

"Is she in the hospital?" she asked, as if the question might forestall her sudden fear.

The phone was silent. Lisa was just about to speak again when her father said, "I called an ambulance," he sobbed. "It was too late. There was nothing I could do."

Not my mother! Not my mother!

Somehow, the family made their way through the funeral arrangements and the days of loss. Last year's Thanksgiving—the first since Mom's death—was difficult. It was as if everyone waited for Mom to join the family at the last minute. Jon had rushed through the blessing, and nary a word was voiced about her during the meal. Afterward, Jon had showed some travel slides to keep painful memories at bay. It was not a joyous Thanksgiving, but they had endured.

Lisa wiped the last of the pots and pans. Everyone was due in an hour. It was Thanksgiving again. *The holidays always come around,* she thought, *no matter what happens in life.* Dad would be here, and Amy and Josh would bring their spouses and small children with them. The house would be full again.

Lisa hung up the dish towel and gathering her courage, stepped into the dining room. Closing her eyes, she could still see her mother. *Oh, Mom, we miss you.*

She heard her mother's words: "Thank you, Lisa, for making such a wonderful Thanksgiving again." And suddenly, Lisa was weeping uncontrollably at the pain of her passing, facing something—she didn't know what—that she'd never faced before.

When she finally caught her breath, her heart flooded with gratefulness that she and Jon had hosted the Thanksgiving dinners for so many years. *It has been a privilege, an absolute privilege.*

Then words from the third chapter of Ecclesiastes came into her heart:

To everything there is a season, a time to every purpose under heaven: a time to be born, a time to die; a time to plant, and a time to pluck what is planted . . . a time to weep, and a time to laugh; a time to mourn, a time to dance.

How long did it take to learn the old truths? How long had it taken her and her mother and grandmothers and great-grandmothers to understand the seasons? *Oh, Mother, thank you for showing me!*

With a knot of love in her throat, Lisa glanced out the kitchen window again at the grandkids tumbling in the piles of leaves near

Jon. She made a vow. She'd make this Thanksgiving another occasion to mold memories, to carry on the tradition so her children and grandchildren would always celebrate Thanksgiving in their lives.

Elaine L. Schulte lives in Fallbrook, California.

4

The Yellow House on Eighteenth Street

. . . .

Editor's note: Have you ever taken a nostalgic trip to your childhood home with your children and grandchildren? Have you ever revisited neighborhoods from yesteryear? In this poignant story by Kathleen MacInnis Kichline, she recalls how, during a cross-country drive, her father made a sentimental stop along the way. What unfolds is a wonderful story of family love and treasured memories. Don't forget to share your memories with your loved ones.

The summer I was thirteen, I discovered the kind of love rarely found in a romance novel. I didn't learn about love from a new boy in town or a bronzed lifeguard, but from a fortyish father of eight—my dad.

The family was moving from the East Coast to Arizona. Mom flew ahead with the baby to Tucson. The rest of us piled into the station wagon for the long cross-country drive. I tried to "mother" my six younger sisters and brothers from the front seat. After four days of turnpikes and highways, we arrived, punchy and tired, in Sioux City, Iowa, my mother's hometown.

We were all ready for a break. Visiting and playing with our cousins for a couple of days was just what we needed. On the last afternoon of our stay, Dad took me aside. "Let's go for a ride," he said. "Just you and me." He didn't have to ask twice.

Every landmark absorbed his attention. We drove slowly past the block buildings of downtown Sioux City. We passed the famous stockyards and headed north to the suburb of Leeds. Dad seemed to know where he was going as we wound through the quiet, residential streets.

Dad pulled up to a rambling, two-story yellow house and switched off the motor. Like all the homes in the neighborhood, this one was set back from the wide tree-lined avenue.

"The house used to be gray back then," Dad said, peering through the windshield.

"Back when?"

"A long time ago. That's the house your mother lived in when I first met her," he mused. "I sent a lot of letters to 610 Eighteenth Street."

We stepped out of the car and stood for a moment. *My mother really lived there?* I thought. Then I remembered a story Mom told me about her father planting a vegetable garden during World War II. Even the front lawn was sacrificed for The Effort. No signs of a garden existed now.

Dad motioned to me, and we began to walk. Each of us was lost in thought. I was still trying to imagine my mother, as a young girl, walking on this sidewalk.

"Was this street the same when you met Mom?" I asked.

"Pretty much," replied Dad. "Only it was spring when I met your Mom at the USO. You know how budding trees are a kind of bright green that only lasts for a couple of weeks? Well, that's how it was back then—everywhere. I remember lots of tulips and big bushes full of white flowers."

"Why were you here, Daddy?"

"I was stationed out at Sgt. Bluff Army Air Force Base. That's before I joined the paratroopers and went to Europe. I'd take the bus into town and get off back there on Fourth Street. I used to run all the way. I never got winded."

I remembered a picture of Dad in his army uniform—his khaki trousers tucked into shiny black boots, a jaunty look creasing his youthful face.

We spent a few more minutes gazing at the yellow house. "Your mom and I used to go for a treat a couple of blocks away," said Dad. "If it's still there, I'll buy you an ice cream."

We made a game of stepping over the sidewalk cracks. Roots from the giant elms thrust the concrete upward, forming an obstacle course. The summer sun flickered through the shade of our leaf canopy.

"It's still there," he said triumphantly. We crossed the street to a large Victorian building facing the intersection. Gallantly, Dad stepped in front of me and opened the arched door. We laughed as my "date" waltzed me into the Green Gables Ice Cream Emporium.

In a booth by the window, I pondered the delicious dilemma of flavors. "What kind did Mom used to get?" I asked.

He thought for a minute. "It was usually chocolate chip."

"Then I'll get chocolate chip too," I said. He grinned like the paratrooper in the picture.

"And I'll order my old favorite: pistachio." He set the menu aside with a flourish.

Dad's stories flowed freely while we savored our ice cream. It seems Mom wore a red dress on their first date: Easter Sunday, 1943. He had just turned nineteen, and Mom invited him to meet her folks.

Dad told me about concerts in Grandview Park, and the time Mom got off work to wave good-bye at the train depot the day he was shipped out to Fort Benning, Georgia. When Dad won a three-day pass for marksmanship, he used it to ride the rails all the way back to Iowa. Of course, he was late getting back to the fort and had KP duty for weeks.

I listened transfixed. My thirteen-year-old imagination re-created every scene. As he spun his tales, his face took on a faraway look.

He really misses Mom. The thought was a surprise to my adolescent understanding of parents. I'd never realized how hard it was for them to be apart. It touched me that he could remember every detail of their courtship and share it with me. For the first time in my young life, I saw that Dad loved Mom in a deep, emotional way. He not only loved her, but fifteen years of marriage and eight children had not diminished his love for her at all. He brightened just at the thought of her.

To him, Mom would always remain Patty Davis, a girl he met in a Midwestern town and fell in love with.

In that moment, a father gave his thirteen-year-old daughter a priceless gift. I glimpsed how real and romantic married love can be. I had no clue something like this existed.

Having seen the Real Thing in the clear green eyes of my father, I knew I'd never want to settle for less. On the threshold of my teen years, I learned a beautiful truth when the years melted away and a young soldier asked me out to the Green Gables for ice cream.

Kathleen MacInnis Kichline met her husband, a cadet at the U.S. Coast Guard Academy in New London, Connecticut, at an Admiral's tea. She and her family live in Mount Lake Terrace, Washington.

5

Leave Behind a Tree

. . . .

Have you ever thought about another family tradition or legacy you can leave behind? As a mother of seven children, including several young adults in their twenties, our family stumbled into a great tradition that any family can incorporate. It's also one that grandparents can begin with their grandchildren. It's called planting trees.

My interest in trees began when I (Margaret Nyman) was nine years old. My dad and I were driving in the family car and chatting about life when he pulled over at a construction site. We got out of the car, and he led me to a felled tree that the workers had recently cut down.

A massive stump, about four feet across, was still in the ground, and Dad thought it might be fun to count the growth rings in the wood. He saw a nice opportunity to point out how many years it takes for a tree to reach such a mammoth size. After both of us took a turn at counting the many rings several times, we finally agreed that the tree was eighty-seven years old.

"See how some of the rings are thicker than others?" he asked me. "During the years when this tree had lots of water and good weather, it grew nice and fat."

Seeing my fascination, he went on. "The thinner rings grew during the years that were harder on the tree. It had to rest more then and couldn't grow much."

We climbed back into the car, and Dad described how trees give off the kind of air people need to breathe, and how we do the same for them. "Wasn't God clever to set it up that way?" he asked. We had a good time thinking and talking about trees and about God until we reached our destination. That night before falling asleep, I pondered the world of trees, especially the big ones, wondering how many rings the biggest tree in the world had, how big-around the trunk was and how tall it was. I also thought about my dad's appreciation for trees and for their Creator.

By the time I was all grown up and married, my husband and I got a chance to plant some trees of our own. A group of friends had presented us with two small flowering crab apple trees as a house-warming gift, and we watched in amazement as lush flowers appeared like magic the very next spring. We were hooked. Eventually we had seven children picking the flowers and crab apples off of those first two trees and climbing them often to check their birdhouses for feathered families.

One day when all of us were on vacation, a woman looked criti-cally at our trail of children and asked me if they all belonged to us. "Yes," I said, beaming with pride. "All ours."

I shouldn't have smiled so broadly, because she followed her question with a quiet comment, "They're breathing more than their share of air."

After recovering from such an insensitive judgment, I thought back to Dad's description of people and trees providing air for each other and wondered, *Maybe we should plant one tree for each of the kids.* At least I'd have a scientific rebuttal if I ever saw that woman again.

In time, the tree-planting idea took root. *Wouldn't it be valuable for the kids to key in on one growing thing and see what happens as the seasons pass?* We decided to invite each of them to choose and then plant their own tree in our yard. We'd already missed the chance to do it as they were born, which would have been unique, but how about just before they left home for college at about eighteen years of age?

And so it came to be. When our first son left home for a university, he chose to plant a weeping willow tree, having enjoyed swinging on the vine-like branches of a willow in a neighbor's yard.

We bought a tree for $11 at the local discount store, and he carefully chose a sunny spot in the back of the yard to plant it.
The trunk of the tree was only the diameter of a child's finger, and our son towered above its tallest branch, but it looked like a healthy specimen. He dug a hole and set it in the ground with high hopes. That was seven years ago. Today, his tree has grown to be twenty-one feet tall and has a trunk eight inches thick. As we had all hoped, it has thrived.

When our second boy was eighteen, he settled on planting a cherry tree, the kind that produces tart red cherries for baking pies. Although much slower growing than a willow tree and less than half the size, the cherry tree has had a tidy crop of fruit each year with the promise of enough cherries for a pie in the near future.

Our daughter, now twenty years old, chose to plant a golden delicious apple tree because of her love for apples, and she decided to give it a home right in the front yard. There are four more children in our family who are looking forward to planting trees, and occasionally I will overhear animated discussions between them about what kind of tree each will plant. The possibilities range from walnut ("I could sell the wood!") to maple ("We could make pancake syrup!") to a California redwood ("Do you think it matters if we plant it in Illinois?").

Maybe the day will come when we will need to move. Although we would leave our special trees behind, they would continue to grow, remaining, at least psychologically, the property of their planters. One day, our kids may have spouses and children of their own who might want to come to the old neighborhood and visit the trees, while their parents recall memories of turning eighteen.

Our son might say to his wife, "Can you believe this huge tree was shorter than I was when I planted it?" While she studies the tree, he might ponder the passing of time and all that can be accomplished as it is spent. Our daughter might bring her children to admire her tree and reminisce for them, "I made applesauce with the apples from this tree, way back when I was young." As her children run off to play, she might find herself thinking about those long-ago years and the path she's taken since her tree was planted.

The critical lady we met on vacation, who we never saw again, might be impressed with our plan to plant seven trees. But more importantly, our children are continually gaining a greater appreciation of nature and its Master, just by watching the trees grow. Although we can't see the wooden rings inside of their trunks, we all know they are there, some thick, some thin, all a testimony to God's faithfulness toward the things He has made.

All of our children have, at one time or another, memorized Psalm 1, and that might come in handy if one of their trees dies or needs to be cut down. Although it will hurt a little, I know that as they count the growth rings in the wood, Psalm 1 will provide gentle comfort.

"Blessed is the man . . . [whose] delight is in the law of the Lord. . . . He is like a tree planted by streams of water, which yields its fruit in season and whose leaf does not wither. Whatever he does prospers" (Psalm 1:1-3).

Maybe, as they meditate on these verses, my children will even plant a few more trees.

Margaret Nyman lives in Prospect Heights, Illinois.

THE BEST MEDICINE OF ALL

"A cheerful heart is good medicine," reads Proverbs 17:22, but many Bible teachers suggest the correct translation could be, "Laughter is good medicine."

How long has it been since you've had a good, hearty laugh? A real belly launcher? How long has it been since you laughed so hard that tears came to your eyes?

For those fifty years and up, a cheerful heart and laughter can help lower blood pressure and reduce stress, which in turn helps you have a healthy heart.

Laughter also reduces worry, which contributes to better mental health. Laughter can cause you to forget frustration, disappointments, and anger. A good laugh can slow you down and let you enjoy a relaxing dinner with your family. It can help you battle depression.

Since laughter is relaxing, it can help you sleep better. Best of all, it's nonfattening, nontaxable, and contains all natural ingredients.

Laughter is also contagious. Have you ever been funny around your grandchildren and watch them catch a case of the "giggles"? Do you remember the joy you felt watching those little ones laugh so hard they threatened to burst?

The next time you're gathered at the dinner table at a big family occasion, share Psalm 68:3 with everyone: "May the righteous be glad and rejoice before God: may they be happy and joyful."

And then encourage everyone to be as funny as he can.

6

The Lamp

. . . .

Editor's note: Tom Wagoner, the police chief of Loveland, Colorado, grew up in the 1950s with Davy Crockett hats and cap guns. In this touching story, Tom shares how a family heirloom taught an unexpected lesson—a lesson that we can apply to our children and grandchildren.

The 19th-century lamp stood proudly on the living room end table, a crown jewel in an otherwise plain household. To Dad, it was a mother pearl—the one priceless object in a home of hand-me-down furnishings.

The lamp had been passed down through my father's family for generations. Before the turn of the century, it had been an oil lamp, sporting a large aqua crystal ball globe and a gold-painted ornamental steel base. At some point, a family member must have adapted it to electricity.

The lamp's shade made you think you were in the middle of a mountain forest with its awesome scene of woods and waterfalls. It was one of the most beautiful things I'd ever seen.

Dad took great pride in showing the lamp to all our visitors, carefully detailing its long family history. That lamp not only lit our home, but it brought light to my dad's heart. It also taught me an important lesson about life.

Child's Play

One day, when my brother and I were young, we were rough-housing in the family living room. He was the cowboy, and I was his bucking bronco. Cowboys have ropes, you know, so to tame this wild bronco, he lassoed me. Then he tied me to the tall end table that displayed the Wagoner family lamp.

The bronco reared. The rope grew taut. The table tipped over, and the priceless heirloom came crashing to the floor. I remember the look of horror on Mom's face when she came running and found the shattered crystal globe on the thin and worn rug.

Instantly, my brother and I started crying. We had broken the most precious possession of the most precious man we knew. Our anguish grew into fear as Mom, with tears in her eyes, cleaned up the broken pieces. She tenderly put the large shards of broken glass and the crinkled lamp shade in a box, as if somehow God would heal it through the skilled hands of a miracle craftsman. But that would never happen. You can't glue together slivers of glass.

Mom scolded us for our carelessness, and she warned us of the consequences when Dad got home. My brother and I knew we deserved a punishment. We cowered in our rooms, wishing over and over that we could turn back the clock and make the lamp whole again.

Time of Reckoning

When Dad walked through the front door, terror rose in my throat. My heart trembled as I overheard Mom tell him about the shattered lamp.

Minutes passed like hours, and after what seemed like forever, he walked into my room. I burst into tears again—half in shame, half in stark fear. I could see the hurt in his eyes. Between sobs, I told him I was sorry.

"I didn't mean to do it, Dad," I wailed. "I'm sorry, I really am." Then I turned away to receive my well-deserved punishment.

But instead of a spanking, I felt a pair of gentle arms surround me.

"Tom," he said in a sad, soft voice, "I'm not going to spank you. Your mother told me it was an accident."

"But I broke the lamp," I sobbed. "It's ruined."

"Yes, it's ruined," said Dad softly. "But it's just a lamp. Someday, a long time from now, you may have a son or even a grandson. He will probably break something that's very important to you. And when that happens, I want you to remember this day. I want you to know that he didn't mean to hurt you. He will love you, just as I love you." Dad hugged me again and then walked out of the room.

Something More Precious
The lesson from my father on that awful yet wonderful day was a lesson of love and forgiveness.

Dad taught me that his family was more precious than his physical possessions, even his best ones. I was reminded of this when Jesus said in Matthew 6:19-21: "Do not store up for yourselves treasures on earth, where moth and rust [and boys] destroy, and where thieves break in and steal. But store up for yourselves treasures in heaven, where moth and rust do not destroy, and where thieves do not break in and steal. For where your treasure is, there your heart will be also." (The bracketed material was added by me.)

Another passage that spoke to me was: "Therefore, there is now no condemnation for those who are in Christ Jesus. . . . The Spirit himself testifies with our spirit that we are God's children" (Romans 8:1, 16).

There was no condemnation that day I broke the family lamp, though I deserved it. My father's love and forgiveness were greater than the value of his prized possession. And today, when our adult children forget their promises or break our hearts, or grandchildren tip over lamps, how I react will stick with them for a long time. Perhaps for eternity.

These days my wife, Brenda, and I enjoy browsing through antique stores, looking out for a family lamp similar to the one I broke. My father is in his late seventies, and it would give me the greatest pleasure to find a lamp just like the one he loved. I doubt I'll find a replica, but that's all right. I experienced the real thing—a father's love—and that's something neither of us will ever be able to fix with a price tag.

Epilogue
Shortly after this story was published in *Focus on the Family* magazine, Brenda Courtney, a mother of three living in the Midwest,

read the article to her three small children. She told them that my father's forgiveness of me is what Christianity is all about. Then Brenda remembered that she had recently received an antique lamp from her aunt, and she noticed that her lamp looked exactly like the drawing used to illustrate the story. She called me at the Loveland Police Department and asked for the address of my father, Jack, who is still pastoring a church.

One cold, snowy morning in Danville, Illinois, my father's doorbell rang, and there stood Brenda with her lamp. She had driven over 100 miles with her little children to give the lamp to my father. You can imagine how this brought tears to my father's eyes, and Dad later told me that he couldn't help but praise God for His love manifested in the hearts of one of His children.

Brenda's lamp was practically identical to the one my brother and I had broken forty years earlier, and never in his faintest dreams did my father expect the Lord would use that incident to bring honor and glory to Himself.

Tom Wagoner lives in Loveland, Colorado.

3

You and
Your God

When Commitment
Crosses the Line

· ·

■ My husband and I are deeply committed to ministry, which has led to our involvement in a fledgling church-plant. My husband leads Bible studies, prayer meetings, and times of individual counseling. I have busied myself with mentoring women and hospitality. Our schedule teems with obligations, rarely giving way to leisure or recreation.

One day, an opportunity for a brief respite presented itself: a four-day trip to the local mountains. We packed up our bags and headed east for the two-hour drive, but not without this proviso from my husband: He would drive back home the next evening, lead the Bible study, and then rejoin me and my grown daughter late that night.

I put my foot down, and when it came down, a hootin' and hollerin' argument ensued. He ended up leaving me for the day, but was I right to go ballistic?

Your husband probably saw his actions as loyal and responsible. But was he legalistic? Probably. To those who benefited, leaving a vacation was a noble act. No one questioned your husband's devotion to duty; rather, they commended him. But what of those who didn't benefit? That would be you and your adult daughter.

Elaine Minamide of San Diego says the above scenario is not a fabrication, nor is the family a composite. In fact, she knows them well. It's her family—a family who for years, barring the occasional flu or head cold, never missed a church meeting and rarely took a day of rest. It was Elaine's husband, Perry, who left her in the mountain cabin during their vacation to lead a Bible study. Why did they overburden themselves so? As Perry put it, "When other people went on vacation, I stayed home and minded the shop. I *liked* minding the shop."

Her husband may have liked minding the shop, but he was unaware of the damage such loyalty was exacting. At the time of the mountain vacation incident, they were both on the verge of a breakdown. Like a runaway train heading for collision, they didn't know how to stop. It never dawned on them to ask God about vacations; the Minamides simply didn't take them. It didn't occur to Perry to find someone else to lead the Bible study. It was his responsibility, period.

■ Were the Minamides being legalistic?

Yes, according to the Minamides. They say they were caught up in a less obvious, more insidious form of legalism: a performance-based lifestyle that led to resentment, anger, and despair. This kind of legalism manifested itself in a not so much "thou shalt" as "I must." Not only did it lead to hopelessness, but it had a disastrous impact on their family life.

For instance, midweek meetings and semiannual conferences automatically went on the calendar. Perry and Elaine scheduled nothing on Sundays except church or church-related activities. Once, when an aging relative's birthday party was planned on a Sunday, they politely declined and sent flowers and a card instead. They passed up many opportunities to spend vacation time with family due to previously scheduled church commitments—something Perry, who recently lost his father to a sudden heart attack, now deeply regrets.

Perry and Elaine didn't view themselves as legalistic. Rather, they considered themselves deeply committed, faithful—even exemplary. They didn't see themselves as trapped in anything but their own honorable choices. They failed to acknowledge their rules for living eclipsed any other possibilities, even those laid out in Scripture.

Eventually, those rules wore them down, and something had to give: their marriage and their family. By the time their runaway train crashed, personal relationships had degenerated to the point where they were living a façade. Perry and Elaine went to church smiling, but returned home bitter.

Personally, Elaine began to resent every obligation their self-appointed commitment to ministry demanded. At one point, she quietly began to rebel. When it was time to go to another meeting, she had a ready excuse: *Leah isn't feeling well. I have a headache. You go on without me tonight.* A wedge drove its way into their family: he went to church, she stayed home with the kids. Something was radically wrong, but they had no idea how to fix it.

■ **Our family often gets caught up in procedures and sticking to a schedule. Is Elaine saying that's a bad thing?**

Of course not. All families need structure. In their case, they went overboard with following a schedule, which gradually ate away the vitality of their marriage relationship. At some point, service for God had become all mixed up with duty to "man," and they didn't know who they were serving any more.

■ **Why are some Christians driven by unrealizable standards?**

Peter Jones, Ph.D., professor of New Testament studies at Westminster Theological Seminary, thinks it all boils down to a false perception of both God and ourselves. "It's true that God is 100 percent holy, and that He expects us to be holy," he says. "But that is attenuated by the fact that He loves the 100 percent sinner 100 percent."

Is there hope for performance-based couples who tend toward overcommitment and burnout?

Sure, there is. The secret is learning to adopt a healthy attitude toward commitment, while at the same time balancing that attitude with an awareness of our limitations. Here are a few suggestions:

1. Maintain a close walk with the Lord. If we're in touch with the Lord, He'll be able to let us know when enough is enough. God is such a perfect, loving Father. Can't He tell us to take a break when we're doing too much?

2. Pray about everything. When someone comes to you and asks you to do something, don't automatically assume it's the word of the Lord. Pray about it, even if it means you have to wait. Let the Lord confirm whether this is how your time and gifts are to be spent. We burn out because we see a need and automatically assume we're the one to fill the need. But God didn't call us to do every single thing that comes down the pike.

3. Pay attention to warning signals of overcommitment. One of the telltale signs that we're doing too much is when our relationships at home are tense and unhealthy. We need to consider the totality of Scripture—*serve the Lord, yes,* but also, *husbands, love your wives.* The bottom line is that God blessed us with the institution of marriage and family, but along with that blessing comes the responsibility of caring for and nurturing that family.

■ What ever happened to the Minamides?

When Perry and Elaine finally owned up to the fact that legalism was making their marriage very difficult, they were on the brink of despair. But God showed them a way out. They recognized their destructive tendencies and were able, by His grace, to move toward healing. They stepped down from leadership, a difficult decision. They cut back on other commitments and gradually reexamined their priorities: which is *really* more important—dashing off Wednesday night right after supper for a church meeting or helping children with homework? They actually began planning vacations—and sticking to them.

"I can't say we're completely disentangled, but I believe we're on our way," Elaine says. "We're back on track. We're learning to accept the fact that there's nothing we can do to change God's mind about us: nothing we can wear, say, think, accomplish, or perform. The matter is settled. We're grateful that God is rebuilding that foundation out of surer, stronger stuff: the quiet assurance that comes from knowing He is God."

This chapter is adapted from writings by Elaine Minamide of Escondido, California.

2

The Rediscovering Christian

. . . .

I (Maurcia DeLean Houck) never considered myself very religious. To be honest, I didn't want to be. It felt comfortable to know there was a God. What was the point in figuring out all of the whys and hows?

Don't get me wrong. I have always been a believer who prayed. Especially when it came time to ask for favors. But that's where my religious expression began, and that's where it ended: in the knowledge that I was a Christian.

That's the way I felt until I began attending a new church with my husband. He went as a servant to the Lord. I went to meet new friends. Only something unexpected happened. Along with those new friends came new feelings and a glorious new understanding. I became excited. I became thirsty. And slowly but surely, I became saved.

That realization was a surprise to some who knew me. Especially an old friend I met for lunch one day. We hadn't seen each other in some time. Trying to catch up that afternoon, we chatted about our jobs, spouses, and eventually, my newfound love of the Lord.

As I finished, my friend leaned back in her chair and chuckled. "I don't believe it," she said. "You of all people have become a born-again Christian."

I was stunned. No, not me. I wasn't born again. That sounded too fanatical . . . too open . . . too religious. "Oh, no," I told her. "I'm not born again, I'm. . . ."

It was there that I faltered. *What am I again?* I wondered. I left my friend that day searching for an answer.

For weeks I pondered the question: *Was I born again and didn't even know it?* I decided not. The phrase "born again" seems to denote a death and resurrection of sorts. My faith hadn't really died. It had never really had the chance to be fully born in the first place. What I had experienced seemed to me to be more of an eye-opener. I had the basics of faith, it just needed to be discovered. Or maybe rediscovered.

That's it! My heart screamed. You're not a born-again Christian, you're a rediscovering Christian. My journey had take me on a rediscovery of the world of Christ and all that it has to offer me. Even now, the more I learn, the more I seem to realize that there is much more to discover . . . and even more to rediscover.

I also know now that I'm not alone. At one time or another we're all rediscovering Christians. Just when things get comfortable—I mean really comfortable—God has a way of shaking us up. Suddenly there's a change in our lives. It may be something drastic like a death or an illness, or maybe it'll be more subtle like going to church to meet new people. Regardless of what it is, that change is what sets our minds and hearts on a new path. The path to rediscovery.

Suddenly new meanings are brought to old words, and the same old parables are given the breath of life, offering a freshness never before experienced.

Don't be like I once was. Never settle for the ordinary. Open yourself up to rediscovery . . . in yourself . . . in your church . . . but especially in our Lord, Jesus Christ.

I did, and I've never regretted it.

3

A Niche for the Woman Alone

. . . .

■ I became a believer after my marriage, and I'm grateful that my husband, who doesn't attend church, is not against my attendance each week. The problem, though, is that I don't fit in any of the Sunday School classes.

Recently, the pastor asked the congregation to complete a survey. Traditionally, we've had the genders split during the Sunday School hour—men in their class, women in their separate class—but the church is planning a new mixed class for "in-betweeners"—those older than the college and career class but younger than the senior citizens' group. He said the planning committee thought the group coming out of the survey will be for singles, but that perhaps something also will be developed for the married couples in that same age-group.

I looked at the form he had given us. There were boxes to check to indicate age bracket and marital status—single, married, widowed, divorced—as the basis for the new classes. But no box for someone like me. In that moment, I felt my aloneness deeply. Now what?

Too bad you can't be introduced to Karen, who attends a large suburban church and found herself in the same position as you. She wasn't comfortable in the couples' class but didn't belong with the singles' either. So, she met with the pastor and gently suggested that she teach a class for women, like herself, who sit alone Sunday after Sunday. He was surprised as she named individuals who would benefit, and confessed with embarrassment that he hadn't considered that group since they quietly slipped in and out of each week's service. The class Karen started is still going strong more than a decade later, and deep friendships have grown out of their mutual concerns. By the way, the pastor did check to see if there were any *men* in the congregation who were attending without their wives and who would like a separate class. No takers.

■ **Well, that's great for Karen, but I'm not a teacher, and I'm not going to start a class. Any other suggestions?**

We're assuming that you're praying about this—just as you would over any challenge. After you've prayed, you may want to meet with your minister. He, like Karen's pastor, may be unaware of those who would benefit from such a class, and you may get his creative juices flowing. Or perhaps another woman has already approached him about wanting to teach adults, but he isn't sure what to suggest. Remember, if you don't ask, the answer is always no.

■ **It's situations like this that make me long for the "good ol' days" when families did things together.**

Actually, situations like this have been around for quite a while. Just look at Joanna in chapter 8 of the Book of Luke. If she could speak to you, she'd say something like, *You're like me! You're in church without your husband. I know what that's like. It's difficult to be alone, but I served Jesus to the fullest of my abilities without my husband by my side.*

Luke 8 begins: "The twelve disciples went with him, and so did some women who had been healed of evil spirits and diseases: Mary (who was called Magdalene) from whom seven demons had been driven out, *Joanna, whose husband Chuza was an officer in Herod's court,* (emphasis ours), and Susanna, and many other women who used their own sources to help Jesus and his disciples."

Chuza's boss, you will recall, was the one who cohabited with his sister-in-law and also murdered John the Baptist. We can only imagine what kind of personality it must have taken to serve on his staff.

Meanwhile, perhaps Joanna was sensitive to some of the "other women" who served quietly. Perhaps she sought out those with problems similar to her own. Perhaps she watched for newcomers to the group, welcoming them and helping them feel less awkward.

■ **Okay, so I'm a modern-day Joanna. But how do I apply that fact to my situation?**

First, know that Christian fellowship is important—even when one has to overcome obstacles to find it. Joanna undoubtedly played an important role in nurturing and stimulating meaningful fellowship for the women who followed Jesus, just as you can watch for and welcome other women who worship alone. Later, after the Lord's death, Joanna was part of the group who prepared spices and lovingly took them to the tomb. While Luke 24 doesn't give details of that early morning trip, we can imagine the comfort their shared sorrow provided.

Second, the Lord is with us all the time, no matter how isolated we occasionally feel. He knows our needs, and we can feel His presence. Yet that sense of His presence doesn't excuse us from following His command to assemble with other believers (Heb. 10:25).

■ **Well, your pep talk has helped some. Any other thoughts?**

Just this: A woman alone can follow, listen to, learn from, and serve the Lord to the fullest of her own abilities and over the long term. She's not doomed to second-class discipleship. She is not an awkward extra. In fact, Joanna was among the first to realize the Lord had risen. Never again would she have to wonder if He were the Lord and Friend of the woman alone.

Nor do you.

This material is adapted from a Christian Herald *magazine article written by an anonymous wife.*

I ASKED GOD

I asked God to take away my pride. God said, "No, it is not for Me to take away, but for you to give up."

I asked God to make my handicapped grandchild whole. God said, "No. Her spirit is whole. Her body is only temporary."

I asked God to grant me patience with my cranky husband. God said, "No. Patience is a by-product of tribulations; it isn't granted, it is earned."

I asked God to give me happiness in my sunset years. God said, "No. I give you blessings; happiness is up to you."

I asked God to spare me pain in my joints and muscles. God said, "No. Suffering draws you apart from worldly cares and brings you closer to Me."

I asked God to make my spirit grow. God said, "No. You must grow on your own, but I will prune you to make you fruitful."

I asked God to help me love others, as much as He loves me. God said, "Ah, finally you have the idea!"

4

A Grandchild's View of God

. . . .

Editor's note: Danny Dutton, an eight-year-old from Chula Vista, California, was asked to "explain God" for his third-grade homework assignment. Here's how he did (and you can read this to your grandchildren):

One of God's main jobs is making people. He makes them to replace the ones that die so there will be enough people to take care of things here on earth. He doesn't make grown-ups, just babies. I think He does it that way because they are smaller and easier to make. That way, God doesn't have to take up His valuable time teaching them to talk and walk. He can just leave that to mothers and fathers.

God's second most important job is listening to prayers. An awful lot of this goes on, since some people, like preachers and things, pray at times besides bedtime. God doesn't have time to listen to the radio or watch TV on account of this. Since He hears everything, not only prayers, there must be a terrible lot of noise in His ears, unless He has thought of a way to turn it off.

God sees everything and hears everything and is everywhere, which keeps Him pretty busy. So you shouldn't go wasting His time by going over your parents' heads and asking for something they said you couldn't have.

Atheists are people who don't believe in God. I don't think there are any in my hometown. At least there aren't any who come to our church.

Jesus is God's Son. He used to do all the hard work like walking on water and performing miracles and trying to teach the people who didn't want to learn about God. They finally got tired of Him preaching to them, and they crucified Him. But He was good and kind like His Father and He told His Father that they didn't know what they were doing and to forgive them.

God said. "Okay."

His dad (God) appreciated everything that Jesus had done and all His hard work on earth, so God the Father said He didn't have to go out on the road anymore and that He could stay in heaven. So Jesus did.

And now He helps His dad out by listening to prayers and seeing things that are important for God to take care of and which ones He can take care of himself without having to bother God. Kind of like a secretary, only more important, of course.

You can pray anytime you want, and They are sure to hear you because They got it worked out so one of them is on duty all the time. You should always go to church on Sunday because it makes God happy, and if there's anybody you want to make happy, it's God.

Don't skip church to do something you think will be more fun, like going to the beach. This is wrong. And besides, the sun doesn't come out at the beach until noon anyway. If you don't believe in God, besides being an atheist, you will be very lonely because your parents can't go everywhere with you, like to camp, but God can.

It is good to know He's around you when you're scared in the dark or when you can't swim very good and you get thrown into real deep water by big kids. But you shouldn't just always think of what God can do for you.

I figure God put me here and He can take me back anytime He pleases. And that's why I believe in God.

A CHILD'S VIEW OF WISDOM

by Marjorie Lee Chandler

Our granddaughter Sarah and her younger sister had just been with us for Vacation Bible School. Coming from Ohio to California just for the week, she didn't have instant friends as pals. With the VBS western theme of "Circle of Friends Ranch," there was hope. Monday morning, I dropped Sarah off in her designated "white scarf" group.

The days went merrily along—until the Thursday evening potluck and musical performance for parents. The Family Center was bulging with excited kids and parents trying to track them. We brought up the rear of the single buffet line and had scant grub on our tin plates. Sarah didn't complain.

After gulping down a few bites, Sarah ran up front to sit on her group's designated hay bale. First there was a long slide show, complete with snapshots of everyone—except Sarah. She didn't complain.

Noisily, the children funneled through the outside door to put on their western costumes. It was pandemonium! Sarah motioned for us to come with her, but she didn't complain.

When Sarah filed back inside with her group to sit on their hay bale, we chose to stay near the back where it was more peaceful. When Sarah looked out and saw our empty seats, fear took over, and she lost her prior composure.

With more than a hundred children, we didn't miss Sarah until we took our original seats near the end of the performance. Our eyes searched to and fro, but Sarah was not among the white scared buckeroos. Where was she? How long had she been gone? What could I do?

A grandmother's heart took over. I marched right up front and whispered to her leader, "Where's Sarah?"

She hadn't been missed! Suddenly Sarah appeared at my side. "I couldn't see you," she said. Assured that we were still there, Sarah sang the last song. It was a "grab your partner" song, and Sarah didn't have a partner. She didn't complain. Her composure had returned.

When I tucked Sarah in later that night, I told her how proud I was of her during a difficult evening. Sarah's comments revealed wisdom beyond her scant six years:

"I just decided to toughen up and pray to Jesus!" explained Sarah. "When I was standing alone and there was no one—just a lot of air around me—I knew that Jesus was still with me. He's my best friend of all. He's with me everywhere, to comfort me, to help me, to keep me from harm. It doesn't matter how bad it is, He will always be there."

Sarah had learned a lot more that night than just singing songs in a crowded room. She had learned the wisdom of the ages that will be with her forever.

4

. . . .

You and Your Older Children

Discovering the
Classic Books

· ·

■ Patrick, my high school senior, came home this afternoon and told me that his English teacher ordered the class to read the first two chapters of Dickens' *Great Expectations* and be prepared for class discussion and a quiz tomorrow.

Patrick tried to read it, but after staring at the first page for a while, he came out of his room and said, "This book looks boring. Can you take me to the library so I can check out some *Cliff Notes?* The chapter summaries will tell me everything I need to know."

"Don't you think you should try reading the book first?" I asked.

"Nah, it will put me to sleep," he replied. "But we better hurry. Everyone in the class will be going to the library to get those *Cliff Notes.*"

I ended up taking him to the library. Did I do the right thing?

At that late date, probably. Many young people—even students in college preparatory classes—are turned off by the classics. Unfortunately, they never allowed themselves the privilege of discovering great literature.

Mothers can have a significant influence on their teens' reading habits. If you want them to develop a love for the classics, encourage them to start with the Bible.

Patrick Henry said it well: "The Bible is worth all other books which have ever been printed." The Bible has been called a complete library because it contains adventure stories, romances, history, law, philosophy, and poetry.

In the early days of our country, the Bible was the only book available, and readers immersed themselves in its pages. Many of our nation's leaders read the Bible regularly, including John Quincy Adams, the sixth President, who made it a practice to read the Bible cover to cover every year.

What a contrast to our modern society! Today, nearly all teens recognize Dennis Rodman and Madonna, but don't know who Abraham, Moses, and Paul were. You can help your teens set up a schedule for reading the Bible each day.

■ What if my high school kids say the Bible is too boring?

Then suggest they read the books that contain familiar stories, such as Genesis, Exodus, Ruth, Samuel, and one of the Gospels. From a literary standpoint, it is important for your teens to become familiar with the Bible because many great works of literature contain biblical allusions.

■ I have to confess to something: I like to read romance novels. Not a whole lot, mind you, but I find them entertaining. Should I hide those books from my kids?

If you only read romance novels, you're not exposing your teens to quality reading. If you feel inadequate about choosing classics for yourself or suggesting them for your teens, consult resource guides such as Clifton Fadiman's *Lifetime Reading Plan* or Mortimer J. Adler's *Great Books*. English teachers and librarians usually recommend lists of classics grouped according to age levels.

You might also peruse the classics section of a bookstore or library. Students bored with assigned reading of classics at school may have a different perspective if they see their parents reading classics—or other thoughtful literature—at home for recreation and enjoyment. If teens grow up in a home where parents normally turn to books, chances are they will learn to like reading.

■ Ah, but I didn't grow up in such a home. So what do I do?

Start by building your own home library, and it can be done with very little expense. Look for books at used bookstores, garage sales, and community events. You can anticipate your public library's semi-annual book sale, where hardbacks go for 50 cents and paperbacks cost a quarter.

Keep books in convenient places in your home. You can have books in every room of your house—even the kitchen. Give your teen a place to store his own books. Talk about books that influenced you while growing up.

■ What can I do to help my teens cultivate their own interests? Join a book club?

No, you don't have to do that. If your seventeen-year-old son enjoys adventure stories, suggest that he read Defoe's *Robinson Crusoe* or Wyss' *The Swiss Family Robinson*. If your eighteen-year-old daughter is fascinated with mysteries, suggest that she read du Maurier's *Rebecca*, a story of romance and mystery set in an English country estate. After you have discovered books that interest your teens, give them similar ones as gifts.

Keep in mind that your teens may never enjoy the books you cherish. Your daughter may not like Twain's *Huckleberry Finn* as much as you do, but you can share a love of Remarque's *All Quiet on the Western Front* and Buck's *The Good Earth*.

Sometimes movie and television adaptations of classics stimulate interest in them. Books such as Stevenson's *Kidnapped*, Dickens' *A Tale of Two Cities*, and Dumas' *The Three Musketeers* have been vividly brought to the screen. After watching Humphrey Bogart and Katherine Hepburn in *The African Queen*, your daughter may ask to read the C.S. Forrester novel on which the movie was based.

■ **But I have a son who's one of those "reluctant readers." He's going to be a tough one to get reading.**

Then a good abridgment of a classic may be the answer. Classics such as Melville's *Moby Dick* and Scott's *Ivanhoe* can be enjoyed by reading the condensed editions.

Books can also be "heard" these days on audiocassette tape. Bookstores have classics such as *Alice's Adventures in Wonderland* and *Treasure Island* readily available on cassette. You can also check them out at some public libraries. Because many teens enjoy listening to tapes, this may be one way to expose them to the classics. Tapes can also help to improve listening skills.

Final thoughts: Mark Twain may have had high school students in mind when he said, "A classic is something that everybody wants to have read and nobody wants to read." A teen who is made to read a book and dislikes every page of it will probably associate reading classics with boring and unpleasant activities.

Classics can play an important role in helping teens reach maturity. Literature confronts young people with basic eternal problems of human beings and helps them better understand themselves and their world. Good books can soften loneliness, eliminate boredom, and enrich a teen's life.

As a parent who values the classics, you must use your intelligence, time, and imagination to encourage your teen to read. Who knows? Soon the tables may be reversed and your son or daughter may say to you, "Mom, you mean you haven't read *Pride and Prejudice?* I thought everyone had read it. Let me tell you about it and maybe you'll want to check it out at the library. . . ."

This chapter is adapted from writings by C. Joanne Sloan of Northport, Alabama.

2

Parents and Teen Employment

. . . .

■ **To work or not to work? I'm not talking about whether I should return full time to the workplace, but whether my teens should work during the school year. I'm all for a part-time job during the summer months, but I'm wary of letting them work when they have so much homework and extracurricular school activities. Where do I draw the line?**

When our grandparents were growing up, teen employment was usually the domain of those destined to work blue-collar factory jobs, young folks who weren't going to—or weren't able to—further their education. As St. Louis Cardinal pitcher Dizzy Dean said during the Great Depression, "Those who won't say ain't, ain't working."

These days, times are a-changing regarding adolescents in the work force. Teens are now twice as likely to work as they were in 1950, according to Simmons Market Research Bureau. The proliferation of McDonald's and Wendy's on every street corner has created an unprecedented demand for cheap labor—one that high school-age students can easily fill. Teenage Research Unlimited, another market research firm, estimates that by their junior year, more than 40 percent of high school students will have jobs, and that the average teen has $60 a week in spending money from jobs and allowances. In addition, school-time jobs are predominantly held by middle-class students, the organization notes.

■ **Is the research showing that part-time jobs affect school performance?**

Psychologists Ellen Greenberger and Laurance Steinberg addressed this subject in *When Teenagers Work*, a book that demonstrates how teen jobs hurt academic performance and do not provide more family income. Instead, the authors demonstrate, the modest paychecks are tossed into a sinkhole of car payments, lavish dates, designer clothes, stereos, and TVs. Only 10 percent of high school seniors said they were saving most of their savings for college, and just 6 percent said they were chipping in to help pay family living expenses.

As for school performance, high school students in California and Wisconsin who worked more than twenty-one hours a week did much poorer in school (average grade-point-average: 2.66) than teens who worked ten or less hours a week (grade-point-average 3.04). The students working long hours were so tired (many high schools start at 7:15 these days) that they struggled to keep their eyes open during class. Study hall was a coveted class period: a place where students could lay their heads on the table for fifty minutes of interrupted shut-eye.

Homework? Public schools have become less demanding since the 1960s because they can't enforce the higher standards. The average high school student has one hour of homework. That leaves enough time to put in a shift at Burger King, and if the students don't get around to what little homework they have, well, the teacher can't do anything about it anyway. So teens learn less.

"Everybody wonders why Japanese and German and Swedish students are doing better than us," said author Laurance Steinberg. "One reason is that they're not spending their afternoons wrapping tacos."

■ **We believe a moderate amount of work during the teen years can be beneficial. Are you saying don't let them work at all?**

Of course not. It's up to you to ask yourself these tough questions: Why is my teen working? Is it to learn how to work? To learn responsibility? To pay for necessities I can't afford? To augment his college fund? Or is it to make monthly payments on that gleaming Mustang sitting in the driveway?

Forty percent of teens seventeen and under have their own cars or trucks. Coincidentally, this matches the number of teens who have jobs by their senior year. If your teens say they *must* have cars because everyone else does, point out that 60 percent of their peers *don't* have their own cars. Tell them they can borrow yours, or do what this New Hampshire mom did:

"My husband and I know that a lot of kids work to have cars," said Patricia Witters. "It can be the most important thing in life to have wheels. We decided that if we provided a car, our kids could concentrate on other things, like their studies. So we bought used cars, usually old Suburbans because they're built like tanks. At one point, we had three kids in high school. Having one car taught them to share. They had to learn to work things out."

The Witters said their children learned to appreciate the well-used Suburbans. "These weren't fancy cars," said Patricia. "They were used for getting from point A to point B. What we instilled in them was, 'You can't have an accident.' Anyone who had an accident had to pay for it with his or her own money. One of the boys slid on ice one winter and busted up the light assembly. It cost a couple of hundred dollars to fix it. Even though the car was a junker, he had to learn to be responsible."

■ **What are some reasons for teens not to work during the school year?**

Don't forget that high school is a stressful time for youngsters dealing with adolescence, peer pressure, dating, and learning to be independent. Adding work to the equation can push some teens over the edge mentally. They won't have time to pursue outside interests, which means bidding adieu to football, track, drama, and the French Club.

No time for church activities—who has spare hours for the youth group? And finally, no time for family. Don't expect your working teens to be home for dinner when they're washing dishes during the evening "rush." Parents need to count *all* the costs before allowing their children to join the work force while their values are still forming.

Working teens are also likely to shy away from tough classes. In a public television documentary on U.S. education a few years ago, the filmmakers featured a student named Tony, who was a senior at American High School in Fremont, California, a San Francisco suburb. Tony said he wanted to become a computer technician; "That's where the money is," he added with a grin.

"Well," asked a reporter, "are you taking calculus or any difficult math courses?"

"It's my senior year," replied Tony. "I think I'm going to relax."

Will you allow your teens to skate through high school? Instead, explain that no "senioritis" is allowed in your home. Then walk through the reasons why (or why not) they're taking each class. Encourage excellence. Explain that tough classes mean more work at the front end (college being the back end), but that now's the time to get a head start on science, math, English, and foreign language.

Also point out that they will need good study habits in college, and that if they're used to cracking open the books in high school, studying will become as natural as breathing by their senior year of college.

■ What if my teens want to work or believe a part-time job could help them down the road?

If your sons or daughters really want to work, let them do so on Saturdays. Everyone must realize, however, that this means your teens will probably be sacrificing youth group activities and time to "mess around" with friends.

Another option is to let them work during the summers, when they can really get into a job and learn some skills. The goal is to do your best to raise happy, well-adjusted kids, and to do your best to get them through college.

This material is adapted from writings by Mike Yorkey and Greg Johnson.

3

When Does Parenting End?

■ **I am a mish-mash of emotions. We are facing the dreaded "empty nest" when our last child leaves for college in the fall. What can we do to emotionally brace ourselves?**

A house without children is bittersweet. Yes, you will have more privacy, perhaps even a new life, but you will have a hole in your heart the size of a VW Beetle. You will miss what's going on in your children's lives. Your phone conversations will be unsatisfying as well, and listening to one-word answers while music blares in the dorm room will leave you feeling even more left out and distant.

Buy a notebook to keep a record of your phone conversations. It's hard to remember unfamiliar details in your child's new environment. Jot down the name of his college's sport team, and if he goes to a football or basketball powerhouse, follow the team in the newspaper or on the Internet. Ask about favorite professors or friends at work. Don't miss noting pressure points coming up in their lives. The next time you call, he'll be surprised and delighted that you're up to speed with things in his life.

In between phone calls keep a six-by-nine envelope handy to stuff with interesting clippings from your hometown newspaper. When the envelope is full, add a little note of love and send it off.

Your college-age son or daughter will smile knowing you were thinking of him or her so often, especially during the first quarter of the freshmen year, when homesickness is at its strongest.

And if your teen has an e-mail account, cyberspace is the way to stay in touch! You can peck a couple of sentences each day and stay involved in his life. By making an extra effort to stay "close" to your college-age child, you'll have a forever friend.

■ **They say that parenting begins when a child is born. But does it ever end? Should it? If so, when? My husband and I are grappling with these questions as our oldest son nears high school graduation. I know that at some point parents need to "let go" of their children when they become young adults, but I'm not sure where that line is.**

Author Marjorie Chandler interviewed an expert on this subject: Dr. James C. Dobson, host of the "Focus on the Family" and founder of the family ministry with the same name. "The process of letting go of our offspring should begin shortly after birth and conclude some twenty years later with the final release and emancipation," says Dr. Dobson, who agrees that "letting go" is the most difficult assignment parents face.

"The release is not a sudden event," he says. "In fact, from infancy onward, the parent should do nothing for the child that the child can profit from doing for himself. Refusal to grant appropriate independence and freedom results in rebellion and immaturity, whether during the terrible twos or later in adolescence."

A strong advocate of loving discipline during the early years, Dr. Dobson contends that there comes a time when the relationship between generations must change. "By the time children are eighteen or twenty," he notes, "parents should begin to relate to these offspring more as peers." This liberates parents from the responsibility of leadership and children from the obligation of dependency, he says.

■ **What do you do when your late teen or young adult child makes choices quite different from what you had hoped for?**

Parents often feel frustrated and embarrassed at the inability to influence the child they thought had been "trained up in the way he should go," but who is now "departing from it."

"It is especially difficult for us as Christian parents to release our children into adulthood because we care so much about the outcome of our training," says Dr. Dobson. "Fear of rebellion and rejection of our values and beliefs often leads us to retain our authority until it is torn from our grasp. By then, permanent damage may have been done to family relationships."

■ **I worry about my adult child choosing a mate that, I hate to say it, I would not approve of. I know I can't dictate that choice—nor do I want to—but I want to save my child from a lifetime of regret. What's Dr. Dobson's advice?**

One of the most difficult times for parents to remain silent is when their young adult offspring chooses a mate they disapprove of. "Though it is painful to permit what you think would be a marital mistake," Dr. Dobson warns, "it is unwise to become dictatorial and authoritarian in the matter. If you set yourself against the person your child has chosen to marry, you may struggle with in-law problems for the rest of your life."

■ **But what about those rare cases when there are grounds for opposing a potential marriage, such as a young man with a criminal record?**

"If there are good reasons for opposing a potential marriage, a parent can be honest about those convictions at an opportune moment and in an appropriate manner," replies Dr. Dobson. "But that does not entitle the older generation to badger and nag and criticize those who are trying to make this vitally important decision."

For example, Dr. Dobson suggests that in such a situation a parent might say: "I have great concern about what you're doing, and I'm going to express my views to you. Then I'll step aside and allow you to make up your own mind. Here are the areas of incompatibility that I foresee. . . . I'm going to be praying for you as you seek the Lord's will in this important matter."

The most critical ingredient, Dr. Dobson says, is to make it clear that the decision is "owned" by the offspring, not by the parents.

■ What are the consequences of not handling these crises properly?

"Unresolved conflicts during late adolescence have a way of continuing into the adult years," Dr. Dobson cautions. Many letters that he receives at Focus on the Family in Colorado Springs, Colorado, speak about long-term strained relationship with parents. These hurting people often mention that their parents never set them free or granted them adult status.

Dr. Dobson adds that the letters may tell incredible stories to back up the accusations. One was from a twenty-three-year-old woman who was regularly spanked for misbehavior. Other persons in mid-life still don't feel accepted and respected by their parents. "Clearly," he said, "letting go is a very difficult process for most parents."

■ What can Christian parents do when their son or daughter willfully takes part in sinful behavior that violates everything they stand for? And how should we react, for example, if the grown children forsake family ties and join a cult-like religious group?

"I don't recommend that parents keep their concerns and opinions to themselves," says Dr. Dobson, "especially when eternal issues hang in the balance. There's a time to speak up. But the manner in which the message is conveyed must make it clear that the parents' role is advisory, not authoritarian.

"The ultimate goal is for parents to assure the young person of their continued love and commitment, while speaking directly about the dangers that they perceive. And I repeat, it must be obvious that the responsibility for decision-making ultimately rests with the offspring."

Referring to Proverbs 22:6, Dr. Dobson believes that these maxims are presented as probabilities, not promises: "Even if we train up a child in the way he should go, he sometimes goes his own way! That's why we parents tend to experience tremendous guilt that is often unjustified. Our kids live in a sinful world, and they often emulate their peers, despite our teaching to the contrary. God gives each child a free will and He will not take it from them, nor can we," says Dr. Dobson.

Citing several environmental and inborn factors that parents do not control—individual temperament, peer-group pressures, and the innate will of the child—Dr. Dobson noted that these combined forces are probably more influential than parental leadership. "It is simply unfair to attribute everything young adults do good or bad to the skill or ignorance of the parents. A hundred years ago when a child went wrong, he was written off as a 'bad kid.' Now, any failure or rebellion in the younger generation is blamed on the parents, supposedly reflecting their mistakes and shortcomings. Such a notion is often unjust and fails to acknowledge a young adult's freedom to run his own life."

■ **What if my adult son asks to come for the holidays with his girlfriend in tow? I have no problem with her coming, but he told me that they could take the basement bedroom. My jaw nearly dropped to the floor, and I mumbled something about it being all right, but now I'm having second thoughts.**

You are right to have second thoughts. You should call back and reiterate your invitation, but mention that you and your husband talked over the situation, and you do not feel comfortable having them sleep in the same bedroom under your roof. Be firm, yet don't go ballistic. State calmly that you're glad to make another bedroom ready for the girlfriend and that you're looking forward to meeting her (or renewing acquaintances).

■ **What attitude, then, should a parent have toward a twenty-four-old offspring who insists on living with someone of the opposite sex?**

"It is difficult to force anything on a person that age, and in fact, a parent shouldn't try," Dr. Dobson warns. "But Mom and Dad certainly do not have to pay for the folly."

The father of the Prodigal Son, symbolizing God's patient love, permitted his son to enter a life of sin. But he didn't send his servants to "bail out" his erring youngest when times got difficult.

"It was the son's choice to go into a sinful lifestyle, and the father permitted both the behavior and the consequences," Dr. Dobson observes. "An overprotective parent who continually sends money to an irresponsible offspring often breaks this necessary connection between sinful behavior and painful consequences."

A parent's goal should be to build a friendship with his or her child from the cradle onward. "When the parent-child relationship is secure, both generations can enjoy a lifetime of fellowship after the child has left home and established a family of his own," Dr. Dobson says.

Parents who once looked with awe and wonder at their newborn bundle of life may find the delivery of that same child into adulthood two decades later no less a marvel. Just as parents cannot keep their newborn child in the safety and protection of the womb, they cannot keep the child from passing into the adult world at the end of childhood.

In the pilgrimage of children "coming of age," prudent Christian parents will prayerfully try to influence but not prolong control over their maturing children. The rest they leave in the hands of the Creator.

■ **An older couple told us in our Bible study that they unwittingly "overparented" in a misguided attempt to help their adult children determine the best choices in life, marriages, finances, and parenting style. How can we avoid being the "Parents From Hell"?**

When all is said is done, when the children have moved out for good and are well on the way down the roadway of life, the parent's role is to be a friend to their adult children. A friend cares but does not interfere, manipulate, or threaten to withhold love.

Here are some areas to avoid that will help us parents of grown children maintain an appropriate role:

▶ **Avoid controlling.** Impulsive parents want to rush in and set things right. One frequent reason adult children do not discuss their ongoing problems is that parents are "fixers," not listeners. We need to accept our child's situation and learn to simply listen.

▸ **Avoid treating your adult like a child.** Parents demean their adult offspring by saying, "When will you ever grow up?" Or, this favorite chestnut: "You don't seem to know how to handle anything! I thought I taught you better." Rather than focusing on the mistakes of either your adult child or his or her spouse, we need to spend our energy in prayer and in strengthening our own marriage. Being a good role model is a sacred calling.

▸ **Avoid heaping on personal and spiritual guilt.** It doesn't do much to further the family cause when you say, "How can you let us down like this?" Or, "God will surely punish you if you don't shape up fast." Adult children with problems want parents to believe in them, not tear them down. Our role is to encourage our children and the members of their family.

As a parent-friend, we can urge our children to find appropriate counseling and/or seek nonfamily mentors to guide them through a tough time. Tell your adult children you are "cheering for them," and don't forget to tell them that you are praying for them.

■ **Thanksgiving and Christmas aren't like they used to be when our kids lived at home. One is married; two aren't. No grandkids yet. My wife gets very emotional when it comes to the holiday season, and I want to do what I can to help manage the situation. What track should I get on?**

The track that says, "Proceed With Caution!" The holiday times are fraught with emotional difficulty in the best of situations, and if you and your wife have been experiencing a roller coaster of emotions in past years, the track will have its share of bumps.

Before the "season of giving thanks and being merry" arrives, go out for dinner with your wife and discuss your goals for celebrating. Consider asking your adult children to tell you (honestly) how your goals mesh with their needs and desires. The results of this informal "poll" may cause you to modify your original agenda, especially if you are tradition-minded parents who tend to idealize the holidays.

Gathering together to celebrate the holidays as you have for the last twenty years may be difficult for several reasons. Now that your children are grown and gone, they have responsibilities to their professions, their own families, and their in-law families. You may have to consider going to where *they* live.

If you extend an invitation to "come home" for the holidays and several of your children accept—go for it! Concentrate on having a good time with those who come, not being critical of those who do not. Thoughtful parents will suggest that their not-yet-married child may bring a guest to the holiday table. But don't fret if they don't; they're building a life on their own terms.

With God's grace, look for ways to accept and adapt to realistic holiday expectations. You can help stitch new patterns of love into an ever-changing family tapestry.

This chapter is adapted from writings by Marjorie Lee Chandler of Solvang, California.

4

Filling the Empty Nest

. . . .

Editor's note: As we learned in the previous chapter, the kids may leave the house, but we never stop being a mother or father. In this narrative account from a mother who's experiencing the empty nest, Henrietta Bos describes the emotions swirling around inside her. She and her husband run a family farm outside Twin Falls, Idaho.

So this is an empty nest, I thought, looking around me. Wrinkled clothing and an ironing board decorated one corner of the family room, compliments of Michelle's weekend at home. The coffee table, littered with empty cups, had the unusual texture of oatmeal cookie crumbs, the result of an impromptu visit by her old church youth group.

The telephone rang. Funny how the phone can sound lonely. That's because of the missing sounds of Cheryl, Larry, Michelle, and Jim scrambling to tackle the receiver.

I don't think I've sat down since Jim left for college last September and left me with this so-called empty nest. Maybe the best way to cope with an empty nest is merely to fill it, I thought. No, too simplistic.

Thinking of the kids brought back a flood of memories. When they were learning to play softball, their attention spans were hardly the length of an inning. They were trying their best to play the game, but the umpire gave up and quit calling balls. We parents sat in the stands and cheered as though it were the seventh game of the World Series.

Most of those games were called on account of darkness because no one could get anyone out.

At the time, the subject of the empty nest seldom crossed my mind. I probably should have been more perceptive. "From the moment of conception," said pediatrician Lendon Smith, "everything is aimed at getting the child out of the house."

When Michelle graduated from high school and moved 120 miles away, I cried when I walked by her bedroom—the bedroom I used to nag her to clean. Suddenly, I hated its perfectly organized neatness. True, the first two children had already left home, but they had relocated nearby. And in barely two more years, I would go through the trauma of saying good-bye to my very last child. I'm not sure I realized it at the time, but I was being challenged to deal with life in a brand-new way.

A Time to Look Backward

At first with all the children gone, I spent a lot of time worrying about the inane. I convinced myself that my youngest son would never manage laundry without me. One summer I sent Jim off to summer camp with a pile of clean clothes. When he came home he was wearing the same pair of filthy jeans he had worn all week. The truth is I wasn't worried about the state of my children's dirty clothes. I simply missed the children.

I raised my children to be independent, responsible. When they left home, they were ready to go. So why was I spending so much time thinking about the "good ol' days," the days when they couldn't cross the street without me?

One father wrote a newspaper story about his children's growing-up years. As each child advanced to a new stage in life, this father discovered a strange truth: Wiping the jelly off the last child's face is not nearly as much trouble as it once was.

"We want him to grow up, of course," the father wrote of his youngest. "It's just that it doesn't seem as urgent as it once did."

After Jim left home, I found myself praying at odd times during the day. "Please protect him from the peer pressures of the college campus," I pleaded. "After all, God, I really did do a lot of things right, didn't I?"

My children certainly retained my favorite sayings, like, "A job worth doing is worth doing right." I also worked hard to make sure my home was founded on my favorite Bible verse, 2 Thessalonians 3:16: "Now may the Lord of peace himself give you peace at all times and in every way."

When the kids were teenagers, we saved enough money to install a swimming pool so they could congregate in the backyard with their friends. I strove for family togetherness in other ways. I'm sure I'm the only woman in the world who ever remodeled a kitchen and said no to a dishwasher. All of us washed dishes together, using the time to talk about the events of our day.

We still vacation together. Last winter, the whole family rented a condo in Sun Valley, Idaho, and bundled up for family sleigh rides. When we are apart, the kids call twice a week and visit once a month. So why do I still worry about them?

Many people assume that surviving your children's teenage years is enough to prevent you from feeling lonely during the empty-nest years. Comedienne Carol Burnett was once told by a psychologist that she should treat her teenage children like outpatients from a mental hospital. Anyone who behaves like adolescents should be locked up. But even my children's teen stages didn't stop me from missing them when they finally left.

I once heard a radio DJ announce an upcoming national BB gun competition. "With no mothers to tell you you'll shoot your eye out," he laughed. There it is in a nutshell. Though I have enough trust—both in my children and in God—to move beyond any feelings of grief in the empty nest, I will always be a mother.

My Identity Today

Parenting is like sustaining one loss after another, psychologists say. One day at a time, a mother is constantly working herself out of a job. In some ways, this is still true. But even now there are many days when I still feel like my motherly role is just as important as when the kids were in diapers.

When my husband, John, and I make the three-hour trip to Oregon to see Jim play college baseball, the whole team calls us

Mom and Dad, and they assure us they could never pass their finals without the home-baked goodies we bring them. I continue to cook Sunday dinner too—pot roast and potatoes—for the children and their families who live nearby.

My first grandchild was born six months before Jim left home. The second will arrive soon. And yet, there is more to me than being a mother and grandmother. With the children gone, new challenges presented themselves; some were expected, others were not.

With John working long hours on our farm and Jim no longer around to help out, I could see who was going to take on the lawn-mowing chores. To my surprise, the extra exercise was a Godsend. I spent that first empty-nest autumn picking sweet corn at 6:30 A.M. to sell at a roadside stand. All of it added up to an aerobics workout extraordinaire—a great stress reliever.

Some women use their extra time and energy to return to school or to launch a new career. I worked part time as a retail store manager while my children were in their teens, but my major incentive was financial. Two incomes became necessary after words like "orthodontist" and "10-speed bike" crept into our family vocabulary. John always supported me in my decision to reenter the work force at different stages in our life together.

Today, I run a part-time housekeeping business and keep the books for our farm operations. We also have a couple of side businesses: a Northrup King seed corn dealership and a carpet company. I have come to believe that each woman must search for the life that is right for her. All the while knowing that your children will probably never "rise up and call you blessed" in your lifetime—and your husband will probably never learn how to do 50 percent of the housework.

Life Goes On

Occasionally, I run across one of those magazine burnout charts, the kind that rank your life experiences during a one-year period. These stress charts make me feel like everyone else must be worse off than me. Recently though, I began to notice how many of life's stressful events deal with marriage and family life.

Getting married is a chart-topper at fifty points. Bringing a new baby into the family clocks in at thirty-nine. Son or daughter leaving home equals twenty-nine points. Since I've been married for twenty-eight years and have raised four children, I figure I should have had at least four nervous breakdowns by now.

I know there are couples in the world who wave good-bye to the last child, walk back into the living room, sit down and cringe at the thought of a future alone together. I thank the Lord that John and I are not like that. We miss the kids, certainly, but we enjoy each other. We take time to attend a weekly Bible study for couples. In the evenings, we have more time to spend with one another. Summer days are quieter without kids splashing in the pool, but our new life together is bringing us closer. Life without children has its advantages.

If we want to take off for the weekend, we do it. When the kids were at home, one of us always stayed with them. John and I couldn't slip out of town when the entire student body of the local high school knew our teenagers would be alone in the house for three days.

A month after Jim left home, John and I took a two-week trip to our childhood homes in Minnesota. We had just turned fifty, not old enough to qualify for those "senior" discounts, but the change of scenery put us at ease.

John and I aren't the only couple in the world to enter the empty-nest years with our marriage intact. According to the Census Bureau, 19 out of 100 couples will be divorced by their fifth anniversary, with 14 more splitting up before the tenth anniversary. Only 7 more couples out of the 100 will be divorced by the fifteenth year, 7 more by the twenty-fifth and 3 more by the fiftieth.

Where do the answers to a happy, meaningful married life in the empty nest lie? Should you think back to the low days, the times when you felt like you were raising the kind of kids you didn't want your kids to play with? Or should you remember the good ol' days, when the kids made you proud? Life has a way of dismissing the painful memories.

It probably makes more sense to accept the fact that life in the empty nest is both good and bad, like much of the rest of life. Life simply goes on.

In today's world, there are classes to teach children how parents will act when they prepare to leave home. In truth, when my children come home to visit, they are the ones who feel the pressure of re-adjusting to the changes that have taken place in their home.

I'm far from unhappy in my empty nest, and I don't think anyone has to be. I loved the years when the children were home, but deep down, I knew all along that those children were loaned to me by God, that they belonged to Him before they came to me. God has always been with my children, even when I couldn't be. He's with John and me too, in this so-called empty nest. The way I look at it, it would be pretty silly to stop trusting Him now.

This chapter is adapted from writings by Henrietta Bos of Twin Falls, Idaho, who was assisted by writer Denise Turner.

A HUMOROUS LETTER TO A COLLEGE FRESHMAN

Dear Son:

I'm writing this letter 'cause I know you can't read fast. We don't live where we did when you left home. Your dad read in the newspaper that most accidents happen within twenty miles from home, so we moved.

I won't be able to send you the address because the last family that lived here took the house numbers when they moved so that they wouldn't have to change their address.

This place is really nice. It even has a washing machine. I'm not sure it works so well though: last week, I put a load in and pulled the chain, and I haven't seen the clothes since.

The weather isn't bad here. It only rained twice last week; the first time for three days, and the second time for four days. About that coat you wanted me to send you. Your Uncle Stanley said it would be too heavy to send in the mail with the buttons on, so we cut them off and put them in the pockets.

Your brother John locked his keys in the car yesterday. We were really worried because it took him two hours to get me and your father out.

Your sister had a baby this morning; but I haven't found out what it is yet so I don't know if you're an aunt or an uncle. Also, Uncle Ted fell in a whiskey vat last week. Some men tried to pull him out, but he fought them off playfully and drowned. We had him cremated, and he burned for three days.

Oh, you should know that your friends went off a bridge in a pickup truck. Ralph was driving. He rolled down the window and swam to safety. Your two other friends were in back. They drowned because they couldn't get the tailgate down.

There isn't much more news at this time. Nothing much has happened.

Love,
Mom

P.S. I was going to send you some money, but the envelope was already sealed.

5

Giving It the Old College Try

. . . .

■ **Oh, boy. We have two children in high school, and in less than two years, our oldest child will enter college. This, of course, will be a formidable financial experience for us, but at the same time, my husband and I believe the greatest gift we could give our children is a four-year college degree. My husband said, "When we're dead and gone, what good will their inheritance do them? Let's spend it now on their college educations."**

Those are our intentions, but at the same time, we have very little savings to dip into. How are we going to pay for it?

You're right: College educations *can* cost $64,000 for four years, and tens of thousands more if your child attends a top private university like Harvard, Yale, or Stanford.

How to pay for it? We'll share some strategies later in this chapter, but you should be reminded of just what a difference a college education means in the labor market. Fifteen years ago, the typical college-educated worker made 38 percent more than a worker with a high school diploma. Today, the typical college-educated worker makes 73 percent more.

There's another issue at work. You want your daughter to marry a college-educated young man who can earn enough to allow her to be a stay-at-home mom when the grandkids arrive. At the same, you want your sons to be able to adequately provide for their families. A college education greatly increases the chances of that happening.

■ **Yes, but at what price? I can't believe parents are falling over themselves to pay $120,000 to send Johnny to an Ivy League school for four years. Why are they so willing to pay so much?**

Prestige, and because many parents have decided that the more expensive the tuition, the better the degree. But you know what? Anxious parents seem too willing to pay anything, and educators and college admission officers have caught on to this phenomenon. (This may help explain why college tuition has risen at more than *double* the increases in the general cost of living.) From their ivory-tower perch, college administrators figure parents are willing to pay through the proverbial nose for prestige.

Let's be honest about most college degrees: *where* your children go to college mainly helps with their *first* job interviews. Afterward, advances up the promotional ladder are determined by how well your children perform in their jobs.

Granted, prestigious colleges are important for medical school admission, grad school, law school, and careers in higher education. Other professions? Not so important.

■ **Even paying for a state university at $10,000 a year is going to financially strap us. What can be done to pay for our children's college bills?**

Every family that has gone on before you can tell a different story of how God met their needs and how they scrimped, borrowed, or reduced their tuition and housing bills. Here are some general principles that you and your family can employ:

▶ **Don't believe the sticker price.** Many private universities charge $20,000 and up for one year of tuition, room, and board. Yet these same colleges have large "endowments," which means generous alumni contribute to the old alma mater—especially after a winning football season. At any rate, these endowments enable the college financial aid office to offer a small number of incoming students "merit grants," or financial aid that doesn't have to be repaid. Quite frankly, you can bargain with schools and say, "We can't afford $15,000 a year, but we think we can handle $11,000. Will that work for everybody?" You'll see them come off their price.

▶ **Check out college aid.** Most institutions will loan students a couple of thousand dollars a year, but that amount must be repaid by the time they graduate. The university will also offer a "work-study" program in which a student is paid for working in the dorm cafeteria or the college bookstore.

▶ **Check out the federal government.** Parents can apply for a variety of loans from the federal government. Most students can receive between $2,000 and $5,000 annually. The biggest loan provider by far is the U.S. Department of Education, which administers seven different financial aid programs. Loan decisions are based on four major factors:

 ▶ parents' income
 ▶ parents' assets, such as savings accounts and investments
 ▶ student's income
 ▶ student's assets

An eighteen-year-old isn't likely to have much in the way of income or assets, so the determination will rest largely on your financial resources. In most cases, these federal student loans must be repaid within ten years of graduation. Unfortunately, parents who have sacrificed expensive vacations and the purchase of a bigger home in order to save for those college expenses may end up being penalized for planning ahead. If your financial income and assets are above a certain amount, your child may not qualify for a federal loan.

For a complete description of federal loan programs, write the Federal Student Aid Information Center, P.O. Box 84, Washington, DC 20044, or call toll-free (800) 433-3243. Be sure to ask for a complimentary copy of *The Student Guide.*

▶ **Check out your company.** Many large companies, as well as labor unions, have college loan programs for children of employees. If you or your spouse are a military veteran, check with your local Veterans Affairs office. It never hurts to ask.

▶ **Check out philanthropic foundations.** Community organizations and civic groups such as the American Legion, YMCA, 4-H Clubs, Kiwanis, Jaycees, Boy Scouts, as well as fraternities and sororities, offer grants and loans.

■ **What if all these avenues turn out to be dry holes? What do I do?**

You can always refinance your home or take out a home-equity loan to help get their kids through college. (Interest payments on these type of loans are tax-deductible, which means you can probably receive a 15 percent or 28 percent "rebate" back from the government.)

Of course, doing so eats into your hard-won equity—equity that can be used to finance your retirement, for example. As for retirement plans, you're not allowed to tap into them without a major tax penalty until you reach fifty-nine-and-a-half. But some retirement plans allow you to "borrow" your pre-tax dollars before then, if the "loan" is repaid with a certain time (usually five years). Be sure to check out all the ramifications before taking this route.

■ **My daughter, who's a high school senior, says she wants to go a private liberal arts college in the South—an expensive one—but not once has she asked how her college will be paid for. In other words, I'm sure she's thinking, *Oh, Mom and Dad will pay for it.***

Anyone who is college-bound should know exactly what she is expected to contribute, and you should outline what sacrifices you are willing to make to cover the high cost of college tuition. If that means you're going to foot 100 percent of the bill, explain why. If that means you will pay 100 percent of college but she is expected to finish in four years (in other words, no taking a year off to "find yourself"), discuss the situation. If that means you're willing to pay most of the bills but your daughter will have to pay her living expenses, talk it through. If the only way to send your daughter to Yale is if she works a full-time summer job and/or a part-time student job, then talk about what that means.

■ **I'm in a quandary. My daughter, Andrea, is quite a good tennis player, and although she probably won't win Wimbledon, I think she is good enough to play in college. How much do I push her?**

If your child is an excellent athlete, musician, student, actor, or actress—and has a solid chance of parlaying that talent into some sort of scholarship or grant, then you should "encourage" your talented teen to practice or study as much as possible. If you have an exceptionally talented athlete, you might tell her to look at the extra time practicing as a part-time job. Would she rather be hitting her backhand or taking orders at McDonald's? More and more athletic scholarships are available for teens, especially young women, thanks to Title X laws.

■ **What about these advanced placement tests I hear about? Do you really receive college credit?**

You sure do. Almost as an afterthought, I (Mike Yorkey) took several advanced placement tests in high school, and I passed them all. Coupled with a community college political science course I took during my senior year, I entered the University of Oregon with forty-two credits—nearly a year's worth. Although I had to hustle my final year, I graduated from college in just three years, saving my parents 25 percent of my education costs!

More and more school are offering three-year degree programs to students even without advanced placement credits. Drury University in Springfield, Missouri, and Albertus Magnus in New Haven, Connecticut, are among those institutions making it possible to graduate in three years. Check your local bookstores or libraries for a copy of the *College Board Index of Majors and Graduate Degrees* to learn more about this option.

GOOD-BYE, FIRSTBORN; YOU'RE OFF TO COLLEGE

by Margaret Nyman

This morning, we said good-bye to our oldest child, Nelson, and left him at his new home 1,000 miles from ours. He will be living under the influence and care of Christian professors and administrators, taking Bible courses, and attending mandatory chapel with the other students.

So why am I full of reservations about leaving him? I suppose my reluctance is simply the result of losing my son. I know I'm not really losing Nelson, but as my child, I know he is gone.

The professor who led devotions in the campus dining hall this morning gently informed the parents that our children will be different when they return to us. How hard was that to swallow! The water in my eyes threatened to betray my resolve to be cheerful when our moment of separation finally came.

In the chapel, my son was seated directly in front of us with his new dorm roommate. I studied his manly size, his fresh haircut, his muscular shoulders. Nelson shifted from side to side, no doubt antsy for us to finally drive away and leave him to his new freedom.

Maybe he too was experiencing his own sense of uneasiness. Atop his head was perched the yellow and blue beanie that identified him as a college fresh-man. It surprised me that he wore it so willingly. The one hat he had hung up for good, however, was the hat of childhood, and I'm glad he did.

As the professor continued his devotional comments, he described how to properly say good-bye to our sons and daughters that morning. As he talked, my thoughts returned to the miraculous moment when Nelson was born and I curled him into my breast as I held him for the first time. Then came the day he learned to give me deliciously wet, nine-month old kisses.

I remembered the fear in his eyes on his first day of nursery school, and then his glee at learning to ride a motorbike when he was only eight years old. Connected to that memory was the day seven years later when he broke all five toes in a motorcycle accident.

More painful was the morning we discovered that, at age sixteen, he had secretly bought his own car after we had told him he wasn't ready, and the four hellish days that followed when he ran away from home in subzero temperatures.

My husband and I have a valuable history with our man-child. He has brought us happiness and misery, anger and delight. Yet I know that you can't back up on the freeway of life. Whether I object or not, our firstborn is on his way toward adulthood. Although I will not be closely involved from this day

continued next page

forward, I hope that this fine young man will sometimes call upon me as a consultant. Such a thought is full of bright promise.

A few minutes after the professor concluded his remarks, my husband and I stood with our son in his dorm room. I handed him our gift of a leather-bound study Bible with his name engraved in gold on the cover, along with two bags of peanut-butter cookies. It was time to say good-bye.

Nelson leaned toward me and let me kiss that chiseled cheek and hug those hardened shoulders.

"I love you, Honey," I whispered, smiling as best I could, dabbing at my eyes. His father shook his hand, patting his back firmly. "I love you, Kid."

As we turned to go, Nelson said, "Thanks a lot, Mom, Dad."

We weren't sure exactly what he was referring to, but we decided he meant "Thanks for getting me this far."

We walked out the door, drove away, and made a vow to pray for our son every single day. Although we can no longer parent him in the way we have known for eighteen years, we can trust God to parent him in our absence with a perfection that we could never hope to achieve. We couldn't leave him in better hands.

■ **Looking over our family finances, I don't see any way to afford a state school or a private university. Is my only option junior college?**

Probably. If your college-bound son or daughter can't qualify for grants—which is what you want since loans have to be repaid—then set your sights closer to home. Tuition at a community college or local JC is *much* cheaper than a state university. In either case, in-state tuition costs far less than out-of-state tuition at state universities. This may not be the ideal situation, of course, since part of the college experience involves cutting the so-called "apron strings" from you—Mom and Dad. Remember, your son or daughter can always *finish* the last year or two at a prestigious school, which means the diploma will say he or she graduated from that excellent institution of higher learning.

Anyway, parents often debate the pros and cons of deciding in favor of a local college. If your son or daughter remains home, remember that he or she will probably need a car, which can cost several thousand dollars a year. At an out-of-town university, most students live on campus and can get around on a bike. But having your son or daughter imagining life without a car could be a traumatic experience. Be prepared to deal with it.

■ What about savings bonds for college?

Unless you were buying savings bonds before your newborn came home from the hospital, this is probably not a good option. Government EE bonds are currently paying around 4 percent, but if you use them to pay for college tuition, they are tax free. They are not a wise investment for the long haul, as least compared to mutual funds.

■ What about the prepaid tuition plans for state colleges?

You're talking about programs in which the parents pay, let's say $200 a month when the child reaches middle school, and guarantees that when the child reaches college age, he can attend ol' State U and not pay a penny for tuition and room and board.

That's not a bad option, but it's not a great one. Investment planners say you get a bigger bang for your buck by taking the same money and investing it in a blue-chip mutual fund and letting it "grow" over the years.

■ My son wants to go to Wheaton College, a private Christian university just outside of Chicago with a sterling reputation. The cost is daunting: I've been told that we can expect to pay more than $25,000 a year, but I'm well aware of the benefits. So do we hold on tight and go for it?

Private Christian colleges cost more than state universities, but you must consider the benefits—perhaps eternal—of having your son or daughter taught by Christian mentors and role models during this crucial time of transition.

Dr. James Dobson has said on the "Focus on the Family" broadcast how much he values Christian colleges, and in one of his monthly newsletters, he wrote, "The single greatest influence during the college years does not come from the faculty. It is derived from other students! Thus, being classmates with men and women who profess a faith in Jesus Christ is vital to the bonding that should occur during those four years."

This material is adapted from writings by Mike Yorkey and Margaret Nyman.

6

Here Comes the Bride . . . and Her Mother

. . . .

■ Not long ago, my church had a "let's all model our wedding dresses" program. The two women who could still fit into their wedding dresses showed up. One of them, my friend Joan, was really proud of the way she looked in hers. That is until her nineteen-year-old daughter walked in and said, "Don't feel bad, Mom, but I hope you won't ask me to wear *that* when I get married."

The comment made me suddenly realize that the day my college-age daughter, Alexia, *could* wear a wedding dress—even mine—isn't so far off. When that day comes, how much say will I or *should* I have in Alexia's wedding?

Ah, therein lies the rub, doesn't it, for on that special day, who makes the decisions: Mom, or the bride-to-be?

Before we discuss this further, a little background. According to recent statistics, 95 percent of today's Americans will eventually marry. Some of these people may start out thinking that planning a wedding is easy, partly because they have never before planned one, and partly because their parents have.

One writer conducted a poll to find out what words of wisdom mothers pass along to their daughters. A primary example was this:

"You can do anything you want with a boy, but I'll be sitting on your shoulder and you won't enjoy it." This may go double when it comes to planning a wedding.

Thus on one side of the wedding cake, we have the prospective bride. "Who is this wedding for, anyway?" she asks. "This is my special day, and I, not my mother, should be the one making the decisions about it."

One the other side of the cake stands the mother of the bride. "I've dreamed of this day since my baby girl was born," she replies, "and I am determined to give her the kind of wedding memories she will treasure for the rest of her life."

Denise Turner, a fiftysomething mother whose own wedding took place thirty years ago, often thought about writing her mother a letter of clarification, of gratitude, maybe even of apology. If Denise were writing that letter today, she said she would say something like this . . .

Dear Mom,

Remember my wedding? As if you could forget it! You were so devastated when I came home for spring break during my junior year in college and told you I had decided to get married. It was too soon, you said. I didn't yet have the "teaching degree to fall back on," which was so important to women of your generation. "You can't get married without one," you told me.

Mom, I wasn't even majoring in education.

Still, you have always been the type of mother who "comes around" when given a little time. One minute you were vowing to disown me if I ruined everyone's holiday by getting married during Christmas vacation, and the next minute you were deciding that the brides-maids should wear furry muffs. You were deciding a fair number of other things too, Mom.

When I began making wedding plans, I was amazed at the difference in our tastes. Especially since overnight you became much more extravagant than me, when through the years, you had always been such a savings account buff. I guess I had given you the perfect reason to spend the nest egg.

Remember that day when you told me to stop considering such tacky looking wedding veils? Then you said, "I'll find you the one you really want."

I went back to college and recounted that conversation to my friend Meg, who had just gotten married. Meg's parents had sent her off on her honeymoon with an elaborate gift box of the best champagne and two very expensive goblets. "Phil and I would much rather have had a bottle of Pepsi and two Styrofoam cups," she sighed.

Then there's that wedding cake we chose. Just last week, a bakery employee was telling me about all the brides who have fought for the right to have chocolate wedding cake, while their mothers insisted on virgin white batter. The bakery now makes lots of wedding cakes with one layer of white and one of chocolate, he said. He thinks this means mothers and daughters are getting better at communication and compromise.

Mom, I had a white wedding cake.

Still, I'm not complaining. Even thirty years ago, I knew that the decision of who holds the veto power in wedding planning is somewhat dependent upon the bride-to-be's age and status in life. I was very young and, in general, willing to defer to you.

And so when I hinted that I might like a small wedding, you reminded me that you never got to have a large one. You assured me that I would someday appreciate the beautiful pictures in my wedding album.

I wasn't convinced. It sounded a bit like an instant replay of the thirteen years I spent taking dance lessons because you loved to dance. But I figured it wouldn't hurt to comply. That was before I heard about your plans for my pre-wedding parties.

I still remember one of those showers so clearly, the one where I hardly knew any of the guests. All of the people there were your friends. I felt like I had crashed my own party that day, Mom, though I must admit that I did get some great gifts—especially the Tupperware!

I guess both of us will remain eternally grateful that I chose a husband who shared our family's religious background. At least we didn't have to argue over which church to select, like Aunt Ethel and Cousin Betty. Remember how we had to talk Ethel out of wearing black to her daughter's wedding? "It makes me look thinner," she kept saying, "and, besides, I am in mourning."

I think we were lucky that you liked your prospective son-in-law from the beginning, even though you didn't approve of his hairstyle, his choice of clothing, the music he listened to, and a few other minor facets of his lifestyle. Or, as they say, the parents give their daughter away to someone who is not nearly good enough so that the couple can have grandchildren who are better than anyone else's.

So many times in the weeks preceding my wedding, I wanted to talk to you, Mom. "I know you want this to be perfect for me, and I do love and appreciate you," I wanted to say, "but . . . ."

I never said it, though. I'm not sure why. Perhaps, down deep, I could see that most of the disagreements between us were the results of ordinary tension: tension for me, because I was preparing to leave behind the remnants of my childhood, and tension for you, because you were quickly working yourself out of a job.

At the time, Mom, it was hard for me to see the complex sets of emotions enveloping both of us. You knew—didn't you?—that after the wedding, you and Daddy wouldn't be the most important people in my life anymore. You would still be extremely important, of course, but not the most important.

I was never able to "go home again" after my wedding. Not in the same way. Because home was in a different place after that. Even though I had already lived away from you for three years before I got married, the wedding really did symbolize the final breaking away, didn't it?

In the years to follow, my new husband and I built our own family unit. We added our own children—your grandchildren—into the mix. A son named Stephen, and a daughter named Rebecca.

■ **Denise Turner did a wonderful job expressing the emotions that she felt getting married thirty years ago, and I think I have a handle on this delicate dance between mother and daughter. What will Denise do when her daughter announces her engagement?**

Denise is anticipating that day, and when it comes closer, she says she will write a letter to Rebecca that goes something like this . . .

Dear Becky,

You are growing up so fast. It seems like only yesterday when you were singing "Sesame Street" and begging for that red tricycle and throwing a temper tantrum. (Oops, the temper tantrum was yesterday, wasn't it?)

In just a few short years, Becky, you will be ready to marry. You will be combing the newsstands for bridal magazines—magazines that contain whole glossaries of bridal bouquet terms and tips on choosing the correct lace gloves. Yet these magazines do not explain how to handle an overly assertive mother of the bride—a mother who may someday be asked to come through with a loan for a down payment on a house.

In truth, there may be no way to banish the mother/daughter wedding planning blues and also remain faithful to the Christian principles of family love and honor. No way short of elopement, that is.

I know. Not only because I have played the role of the blushing bride, but also because I am now a mother.

When the time comes for you to plan your wedding, Becky, I suppose we will begin by talking about the expenses involved. I am well aware of the fact that many parents feel they have the right to plan a daughter's wedding because they are footing the bill. With the average wedding now costing over $10,000, these parents have a point.

"Today's parents should start saving for their daughter's wedding the moment the ultrasound confirms it's a girl," your Aunt Carol once told me. "By the time the child can say the words 'I hate boys,' it is already too late."

I hope I won't be a pushy mother of the bride. I hope I will never suggest a menu for your reception dinner and mention the cost of the banquet hall in the same sentence. If I do, I am sure you will remind me as you have many times before, that a gift with strings attached is not really a gift at all.

I don't think I will insist on my own preferences when you are selecting your guest book, napkins, or wedding attendants. I know that some mothers do try to appease friends or relatives by picking certain children to be flower girls or ring bearers, but I also know a few such mothers who have risked the success of the entire wedding by selecting children whose nap times coincided with the time of the ceremony.

I will try to stay quiet when you are choosing your wedding music too, since people of different generations could hardly be expected to agree on a Top 10 countdown. I learned that one from Janet, who used to live down the street. She overruled her mother and made her favorite song, "You Light Up My Life," the featured solo at her wedding, and told me her mother never let her forget that the local newspaper account of the wedding listed the song as "You Light Up My Liver."

I know a lot of couples have been using Celine Dion's "My Heart Will Go On" from the *Titanic* movie, but I would recommend that you don't go there. Something about ships sinking isn't a good metaphor for marriage.

You may be glad to know that I have been reading up on the subject of wedding planning, Becky, and I have discovered that there are two sides to everything. I have learned that psychologists now advise prospective brides to clarify their expectations, to work at talking with their mothers about the wedding without putting anyone down, and to remember that no one lives in a vacuum. They advise mothers to examine the difference between interfering and offering suggestions, to hold tight to their sense of humor, and to concentrate less on things that will not matter ten years into the future. This is good advice for both of us, Becky; but who listens to advice when there is a wedding to plan?

I didn't when I was the bride, and my wedding day arrived anyway. Then a short time afterward, everyone returned to real life—a life filled with mortgage payments and car repairs and "What's for dinner?" Eventually, in the midst of all that real life, I gave birth to a daughter of my own.

Now I'm the one who cries whenever I hear the song "Sunrise, Sunset." And I'm the one who is ready to say to you, "I did my best, but I made some mistakes."

Thirty years later, my most vivid memory of my own wedding is the memory of an event that took place after the ceremony. It is my memory of the moment when I left for my honeymoon—and left your grandmother mopping up the floor of the church basement, which had been flooded by a broken water pipe during my reception. It is the memory of a scene that is both so normal and so touching that it almost makes me cry.

I kissed my mother good-bye when I left the church that day, Becky, and I am glad I did. But if I had it to do over, I would leave her with more than a kiss. I would leave her with some carefully chosen words too.

"We didn't need to worry so much about planning this wedding, Mom," I would tell her, "because you had already planned the important parts of my wedding long before the actual day of the ceremony—by giving me the blessing of a Christian home where I came to know the Lord, and being the kind of wife you were for Dad." You came from a good heritage, Becky. A heritage of love.

When you get married, I fully expect to be left behind at the church, mopping the floor if need be. I might gripe about it a little, but don't take my complaints too seriously. For I will feel very lucky, and completely satisfied, if you give me nothing more than a good-bye kiss before you go.

Love,
Mom

This chapter is adapted from writings by Denise Turner of Twin Falls, Idaho.

A WONDERFUL SURPRISE

by Mike Yorkey

My wife, Nicole, is Swiss, and she graduated from the *Kaufmaennische Berufschule* in Baden, Switzerland, which is the equivalent of graduating from a four-year university here in the States.

Following that event, Nicole did office work for a manufacturing company, but she still lived at home. Her father, Hans, began charging her 300 francs a month—around $150—for room and board (a hefty part of her paycheck and a sizable amount back in the 1970s). There was some grumbling on Nicole's part, but her father told her it was time she started paying her own way.

Several years later, Nicole traveled to the United States to learn English and teach skiing, and we met in California. We fell in love, I proposed, and we made plans to get married—in Switzerland, of course, where all her family was.

The wedding was like a fairy tale, taking place in a fourteenth century chapel that was part of an old castle. I discovered that Swiss weddings were a bit different: the crowd outside the church threw bits of wrapped chocolate instead of rice. In all, we had a great time. At the wedding reception dinner, Hans joked that he was losing a daughter but gaining a bathroom, a wry observation since the family lived in a home with only one bathroom.

At any rate, late in the reception when nobody was looking, Hans told us that he had a little wedding present for us. He handed Nicole a bank book, and inside were several dozen 300 Swiss franc deposits that he had made over the years. Nicole burst into tears when she realized that her father had been putting all that "room and board" money into a savings account for her. Said Hans, "You couldn't expect a father to do anything else, could you?"

The bank book was a great little nest egg for Nicole, and it all happened because a father had the foresight—and courage—to initiate a savings program for his daughter.

Parents: The Best Role Models of God's Love

. . . .

■ **My husband and I became Christians after our two children left the nest. When they visit, they go to church with us sometimes, but I have to be frank: I often lay in bed at night and wonder if they will really take the Christian faith to heart. What should I be doing to make sure they become part of God's kingdom?**

Christian parents—even those who came to a knowledge of Jesus Christ late in life—long for their offspring to share their belief in God. Why? Faith is bonding glue, and the best way to convey theology is through healthy relationships. As wise parents, you will value your adult children more than you value an issue.

Sometimes parents and adult children misunderstand each other's motives. For example, consider the differences in these interchanges:

Parent: "We're going to nine o'clock church tomorrow. Would you like to come with us?"

Adult son: "No, that's the only time I can see Josh."

Parent: "It seems to me you could spend just one hour a week in church."

Adult son: "Don't make me feel guilty, Dad."

The son's real reason for declining is that he feels he doesn't know anyone at his parents' church. The parent thinks the son is finding excuses. The son thinks his parents want to tell him what to do. Keep inviting your grown children to join you in church—especially if there is a special speaker who may appeal to them. Issue your invitation with love and a smile, and if you get turned down, don't turn it into the Biggest Rejection You've Ever Received.

■ **I get so discouraged because my twenty-four-year-old son hangs out in sports bars and cheers for his teams all weekend long. What can I do, short of grabbing him by the scruff of his neck and dragging him to church?**

Don't do that! We know you're not being serious, but you have to be prayerful and patient about matters of faith. Deep spiritual growth comes from within and in its own time. Gen Xers are usually more concerned with how people live, not what they believe.

Do be encouraged. Many young adults see themselves as spiritual seekers who gravitate to "journal theology"—a metaphor for personal growth. Just because your children don't relate to traditional worship doesn't necessarily mean they have turned away from God. They're looking for an interactive faith. Maybe you can point them to a "seeker" church with upbeat music backed by a drum beat.

Whatever you do, know that your grown children are looking at you, their parents, to see how your faith in Christ is lived out in the real world.

■ **My husband loses his temper when our adult son, who moved back in with us, doesn't try hard enough to get a better job. I think being an assistant manager at Burger King is all right for a twenty-four-year-old; my husband says he should be "doing something better with his life." When he blows up, I tell him that it's Steve's life. What am I up against?**

You certainly have the right attitude. It *is* your son's life, and if he wants to spend it in the fast-food restaurant industry, then that is up to him. As for your husband, he will have to learn how to manage his anger, or it will manage him. Sure, it's easy to get ticked when grown children do foolish things. For example, parents may feel their adult kids are exasperating them on purpose—like working at Burger King. Maybe so. But the truth is, we choose to be angry.

A closed mind, unhealthy prejudices, and personal pride are kindling for fiery anger. We easily find fault and become frustrated and angry when values collide with our emerging adult children.

To keep conflict at bay, some parents deny it exists ("Our family is as happy as most"); brush it off ("Things only get out of hand now and then"); or wallow in guilt ("I guess I'm just not a good parent").

You will have to be a skilled negotiator with your angry husband. In resolving conflict, you are trying to make peace. You are trying to break down the wall between him and your son.

■ **We have gone through the emotional wringer in the last year—too many details to describe here, but bailing my son out of jail was about the lowest we could go. We are seeking professional help, but in the interim, what should we do?**

After trauma in the family circle, raw emotions may flood in and fracture precious links. Whatever caused the break—a criminal charge, a bad debt, a collapsed marriage—has the entire family feeling the vibra-

LOVING OUR CHILDREN THROUGH A LIFETIME

Once parents, forever parents. Family was God's idea from the beginning of Creation, as we read in Genesis. God chose families as the best place to teach us how to love one another. But from the beginning, parents found they had to work at loving their children through tough times. (Cain was not exactly an exemplary son when he killed his brother.)

Children grow up and make poor life choices. Choices that parents have no control over. Like the Prodigal Son, problem children may "come to their senses" and come home again. Then again, they may not. Yet children who are out of relationship with their parents will not feel loved at arm's length. Parents' love—a reflection of God's love—can only be felt through sincere words and gracious actions.

A summary of the four most effective things parents can do to love their children through a lifetime are:

► Accept your children as individuals
► Listen without fixing their problems
► Work to strengthen your own marriage
► Never stop praying

tions.

Dealing with family disappointments and trauma can deepen dependence on God. Through prayer, God connects us to the "bigger picture" of life. When we see needy family members in God's perspective of love, we can let go of past regrets and bring healing into our relationships. After all, our past and present is the unfolding story of God working in our lives. It is His-story, as well as our story.

■ **My son, Ian, is in his early twenties, two years out of school, and living in another state. He took a job with a major insurance company. A mother can tell when a son has veered off-track, and besides, he's even told us that he doesn't go to church much. We still have a relationship, but I feel like it's lessening with each month. What can I do to reverse this?**

As a parent, any loss of connection to a adult child who has left the nest is distressing. Although we may never "disown" a child we truly love, our ability to express love may get sidetracked because of anger, fear, and disappointment. You're in the "disappointment" camp.

Loving our children begins with a deliberate decision to model kindness in our families. Sometimes we have to put aside our impulses and, instead, choose to love. The gift of love is not based on what our child does or doesn't do; it's based on our consistent desire for relationship. In other words, no matter what happens with your son, keep the relationship going. Find reasons to visit and do things together, or even send him plane tickets to come home for the holidays. Continue to be part of his life.

Parental love is a matter of the heart. It is knowing your adult child isn't there yet. Keep in mind that parents depend on love to link the generations, and Christian love can bind up the broken links in a family circle. The oft-quoted message of love in 1 Corinthians 13 guides us: "Love does not delight in evil but rejoices in the truth. It always protects, always trusts, always hopes, always perseveres. . . . And now these three remain: faith, hope and love. But the greatest of these is love."

This chapter is adapted from writings by Marjorie Lee Chandler of Solvang, California.

8

When the Vow Breaks

. . . .

■ Our daughter's voice on the other end of the telephone line sounded desperate. In a voice rough with tears, Beth poured out her heartache. Apparently she and Mark were barely speaking, not sleeping together, and contemplating divorce.

"Can I come home for a while?" she sobbed.

Filled with anxiety, I fought the temptation to make hasty decisions or rash promises. Instead I responded, "Let Dad and me pray about this overnight. We'll call you tomorrow morning."

That evening my husband and I shared our deep disappointment that a seemingly stable marriage had soured. We remember Beth's joy in meeting Mark, whom she called "the man of her dreams." Had we not prepared her to be a wife? To understand that marriage means sacrifice?

My husband and I wondered whether we could have done more to encourage Beth and Mark's marriage bond. We knew Beth didn't like being alone when Mark traveled and that he had little time for shared hobbies. Maybe we should have sent them on a weekend getaway. Had we been involved enough in their lives? Or too involved at times? As we talked, we shed tears both for our daughter and for the son-in-law we loved dearly.

After a night of prayer, discussion, and very little sleep, we called Beth with our answer: "We've decided to invite you for several days on the condition that Mark can come too."

Beth was noticeably silent. Fully expecting a "Welcome home," she was caught off guard. For the next few minutes we gently but firmly explained our parenting position. On their wedding day two years earlier, we determined to support both Beth and her husband. Marriage unites two people into one; we wanted to uphold both parts of the whole.

Did we do the right thing?

After seeking the Lord's guidance and praying about it, who could disagree? Besides, parents who've been through similar stories and hastened to "help" their son or daughter through a marital crisis may have thoughtlessly created an unhealthy triangle. By too quickly seeing their child as the victim and their in-law child as the villain, they may have unwittingly fanned the flames of the fire they had hoped to put out.

Obviously if the situation seems dangerous—such as spouse or child abuse—your response should be quite different. But in most situations, a knee-jerk reaction siding with your own child only serves to reinforce feelings of resentment against the very person with whom the shattered son or daughter needs to reconcile.

Tim Kimmel, speaker for Family Life Ministries and author of *Powerful Personalities*, sees husband-wife-parent triangles as a "deflection of intimacy" because they keep the couple from "engaging in the face-to-face conversations so badly needed." Parents who long to see reconciliation should be careful not to take sides in disputes.

■ **But that caution leaves me wondering what we as parents can do to help our children through the inevitable rough spots of marriage. No loving mother will feel comfortable sitting idly by while her beloved son or daughter suffers through a**

troubled relationship or makes choices that could destroy their marriage.

There are several ways we can support our children's marriages without crossing the line into interference. Here is what some experts and parents say:

1. Simply listen. When Walt and Marilyn's son Kirk telephoned to tell them his five-year marriage to Janis was breaking up, they quickly rearranged their schedules and headed north. As they drove, Walt and Marilyn prayed for wisdom in dealing with two distraught adult children.

When they arrived, Janis tearfully revealed her feelings that the marriage had been a mistake. "We just don't have much in common," she said. Walt and Marilyn carefully and deliberately conveyed love and concern for both Kirk and Janis, expressing their hope that the two would commit to working through this.

"Mostly," Marilyn said later, "we just listened that weekend. I held Janis' hand as she expressed her disappointment in not yet having children. We sympathized with Kirk who, without medical explanation, felt guilty for not becoming a father. We asked open-ended questions which allowed them

> ### BREAKING THE NEWS OF A DIVORCE
>
> Sons or daughters whose marriages are breaking up often won't tell their parents their marriage is over. Why? Although they are adults, children don't want to look like failures in their parents' eyes.
>
> Consequently, most parents are shocked to learn that their child's marriage has dissolved. They had no warning. No chance to help! Disappointment turns to anger because sacred marriage vows were not kept. Parents are fearful for their son or daughter who will be single in a broken world.
>
> Research shows that the most important factor in the recovery of divorced persons is affirmation from their family. Parents are one-of-a-kind friends who can give unconditional love. Divorced children want their parents to believe in them, no matter what.
>
> Divorce ends marriage; it does not end a family. God may not always redeem a marriage, but He does redeem persons. God's grace, shown by a family's care and concern for one another, brings healing and hope. Adopt 1 John 4:7 for your family banner: "Let us love one another; for love is of God."

to explore ways to make their marriage more fulfilling. Kirk later told his dad that he appreciated how our nonjudgmental approach had enabled him and Janis to cut through hostile tension."

By loving and listening, these parents walked alongside their emotionally hurting adult children.

"The best way to keep lines of communication open is to put yourself in your children's shoes," says psychologist Les Parrott, who along with his wife, Leslie, directs the Center for Relationship Development at Seattle Pacific University. "The more empathy you bring to the relationship—with both people in the couple—the better the communication will be."

We need to remember that hurting people rarely expect friends and family to "fix" a situation; more than anything they need an opportunity to vent their feelings in a safe setting.

2. Resist the urge to help. As mothers, we often feel frustrated because we want to "do" something for the couple, but our children will only resent unsolicited help or advice. Consider a midlife twist on an old adage: Parents should be seen, but not heard. This, however, comes with a caveat. When adult children ask for advice, parents can indicate what they would do while being careful not to take control.

You should know that when young marrieds are willing to discuss their problems, they tend to omit key issues. "Parents seldom have the whole picture," says Irene Kelly, a marriage and family counselor in private practice in Columbia, California. "A lot of damage is done when parents are too judgmental or when they give poor advice."

A better solution, suggests Irene, is for parents to graciously encourage couples to choose objective mentors they trust or recommend a Christian marriage counselor.

3. Strengthen your own marriage—and pray. Parents are lifelong role models. As our adult children struggle in their marriages, they may be watching ours even more closely. For this reason our own bonds need to be in good shape.

"One of the best things you can do for your child is to love your spouse," says Leslie Parrott. "Take stock of your marriage relationship; do you need specific goals to make it better?"

One important commitment for parents is to be faithful in

prayer when they see warning signs in their children's marriages. Praying for adult children can reset hope in their hearts—and in yours. However, as we all know from experience, prayer doesn't guarantee the outcome for which we hope.

Several months after Marilyn and Walt's quick trip to their son's home, Kirk announced that a legal divorce was in progress. These caring parents had hoped that the distraught couple's earlier agreement to seek counsel would turn things around. It didn't. Deeply disappointed, they had to learn to accept the choice that was not theirs to make. Marilyn, especially, grieved over the loss of Janis as a daughter-in law.

No one said parenting would be easy—at any stage. It's especially difficult when our married children are going through stormy waters. We took care of their hurts when they were little, and our impulse is to rush in and rescue them from the grown-up pain of marital crises. Instead, our best hope for our adult children is to pray that God will direct their lives.

■ **In our case, the night Beth and Mark arrived at our home, one of them plopped a suitcase in the den, making an obvious statement. I felt my heart pound as I asked if there was anything I could do to help. My husband and I momentarily wondered if we had been too optimistic. Despite our concern, we gave no directives, allowing them the space to be comfortable.**

On the third day of their visit, when Beth packed a picnic lunch for two, we were encouraged. We still don't know the specifics, but a breakthrough was obvious on their return. During dinner, we listened as our newly revived couple planned a potential business venture. That night the den was empty.

We felt like we didn't do much, but it must have been the right thing.

Sometimes the best things that parents can do in those situations is not much at all. Just being there or being effective "behind-the-scene" parents means you're willing to serve as pillars, supporting an adult child in the midst of marital storms. Through prayer and a carefully selected course of action, you can create an atmosphere that encourages your adult children to cope with their own marital problems, knowing you will love them no matter what.

This chapter is adapted from writings by Marjorie Lee Chandler, author of After Your Child Divorces *(Zondervan).*

5

You and Your
Grandchildren

1

A Grand Holiday

. . . .

Two decades ago on September 6, 1979, President Jimmy Carter signed an important proclamation officially declaring the first Sunday after Labor Day to be Grandparent's Day.

If two generations follow you in your family tree, you have a special role. A role to take seriously—and to celebrate. Because Grandparent's Day isn't as well-known as Mother's Day and Father's Day, you may need to take the initiative. You don't want to beat your chest and say, "Hey, look at me," but Grandparent's Day should be a day for the entire family, if you live close enough to that second and third generation.

If your grandchildren live too far away, you can mark the occasion by sending them something that's unique about you. Here are some ideas:

► Ask your grandchild to make up a list of ten things you could do the next time you are together. Agree on the top three choices and make specific plans.

► Make a videotape of your day-to-day routine with descriptive commentary about your workplace or hobbies. End your "show" with a staged phone call to your grandchildren.

► Create a useful wood craft and a promise to build something together before Christmas.

► Design a personalized quilt, robe, or tote bag offering to teach your grandchild basic needlework skills.

► Sort through your old photos and put together a little album with captions that highlight past family celebrations.

Longer-range projects might include:

► Begin a diary about your grandchild, noting his or her interests, dreams, likes, and dislikes. Someday this will be a one-of-a-kind graduation gift.

► Propose a "Family Home Page" on the Internet to keep your family circle in touch.

► Research and reproduce your family crest, or design one to usher in the new century.

This year, make Grandparent's Day a fun-filled, memorable family holiday. If you do, your grandchildren will surely conclude that the senior members of their family are truly "grand."

2

Spare the Rod?

. . . .

■ When I was raising my children, my husband and I didn't fail to give them a good spanking when they directly disobeyed us. We followed Dr. Dobson's advice found in his first book, *Dare to Discipline*, and we were careful not to spank out of anger and only when other punishment alternatives had been exhausted. Our kids came out wonderfully, I might add.

Now it's our children's turn to have toddlers and preschoolers running around the house. Sometimes I've noticed that they've gotten out of hand and needed a smack, but when their parents did nothing, I bit my lip and didn't say anything. Later, when my daughter-in-law and I happened to discuss disciplining the kids, I could tell that she would never spank them. "I don't believe in hitting kids," she told me.

I don't want to cause a family rift, but well-behaved grandchildren are a delight to have around our house. Undisciplined grandkids, on the other hand, are little monsters, if you catch my drift.

I'm thinking about buying a copy of Dr. Dobson's revised book, *The New Dare to Discipline*, and giving it to my daughter-in-law as a present. Is that a good idea?

By all means, you should purchase *The New Dare to Discipline* since it's the best book on the subject. But you may want to discuss that option with your son first since you will want the book to be well-received—and read—once they receive it. This is also a good time to arm yourself with a greater knowledge of where spanking is at these days.

For instance, opposition to parents spanking their children has been growing significantly in elite circles over the past fifteen years. No doubt much of this opposition springs from a sincere concern for the well-being of children. Child abuse is a reality, and stories of child abuse are horrifying.

■ **Is spanking as accepted as it was in my days as a young mother?**

According to a research poll commissioned by the Family Research Council, 76 percent of the more than 1,000 Americans surveyed said that spanking was an effective form of discipline in their home when they were children. These results are made all the more impressive by the fact that nearly half of those who answered otherwise grew up in homes where they were never spanked. Taken together, more than four out of five Americans who were actually spanked by their parents as children say that it was an effective form of discipline.

In addition, Americans perceive lack of discipline to be the biggest problem in public education today, according to a recent Gallup poll. Several studies show strong public support for corporal punishment by parents.

■ **Why do critics claim that spanking a child is abusive?**

These allegations arise from studies that fail to distinguish appropriate spanking from other forms of punishment. Abusive forms of physical punishment such as kicking, punching, and beating are commonly grouped with mild spanking. Furthermore, the studies usually include, and even emphasize, corporal punishment of adolescents, rather than focusing on preschool children, where spanking is more effective. This blurring of distinctions between spanking and physical abuse, and between children of different ages, gives critics the illusion of having data condemning all disciplinary spanking.

■ **My daughter-in-law always comes up with several arguments against disciplinary spanking, saying she favors "time out." How do I respond to that?**

Any form of discipline (time-out, restriction, etc.), when used inappropriately and in anger, can result in distorting a child's perception of justice and harming his emotional development. In light of this, let us examine some of the unfounded arguments promoted by spanking opponents that your daughter-in-law may use:

Argument #1: Physical punishment establishes the moral righteousness of hitting other persons.

Counterpoint: The "spanking teaches hitting" belief has gained in popularity over the past decade, but it is not supported by objective evidence. A distinction must be made between abusive hitting and nonabusive spanking. A child's ability to discriminate hitting from disciplinary spanking depends largely on the parents' attitude with spanking and the parents' procedure for spanking. There is no evidence in the medical literature that a mild spank to the buttocks of a disobedient child by a loving parent teaches the child aggressive behavior.

The critical issue is *how* spanking (or, in fact, any punishment) is used more so than *whether* it is used. Physical abuse by an angry, uncontrolled parent will leave lasting emotional wounds and cultivate bitterness and resentment within a child. The balanced, prudent use of disciplinary spanking, however, is an effective deterrent to aggressive behavior with some children.

It is unrealistic to expect that children would never hit others if their parents would only exclude spanking from their discipline options. Most children in their toddler years (long before they are ever spanked) naturally attempt to hit others when conflict or frustration arises.

The continuation of this behavior is largely determined by how the parent responds. If correctly disciplined, the hitting will become less frequent. If ignored or ineffectively disciplined, the hitting will

DO'S AND DON'TS FOR SPANKING

The following are guidelines that Dr. Den Trumbull has developed about spanking.

1. Spanking should be used selectively for clear, deliberate misbehavior, particularly that which arises from a child's persistent defiance of a parent's instruction. It should be used only when the child receives at least as much encouragement and praise for good behavior as correction for problem behavior.

2. Milder forms of discipline, such as verbal correction, time-out, and logical consequences, should be used initially, followed by spanking when noncompliance persists. Spanking has shown to be an effective method of enforcing time-out with the child who refuses to comply.

3. Only a parent (or in exceptional situations, someone else who has an intimate relationship of authority with the child) should administer a spanking.

4. Spanking should not be administered on impulse or when a parent is out of control. A spanking should always be motivated by love for the purpose of teaching and correcting, never for revenge.

5. Spanking is inappropriate before fifteen months of age and is usually not necessary until after eighteen months. It should be less necessary after six years, and rarely, if ever, used after ten years of age.

6. After ten months of age, one slap to the hand of a stubborn crawler or toddler may be necessary to stop serious misbehavior when distraction and removal have failed. This is particularly the case when the forbidden object is immovable and dangerous, such as a hot oven door or an electrical outlet.

7. Spanking should always be a planned action, not a reaction, by the parent and should follow a deliberate procedure.

   ► The child should be forewarned of the spanking consequence for designated problem behaviors.

   ► Spanking should always be administered in private (bedroom or restroom) to avoid public humiliation or embarrassment.

   ► One or two spanks should be administered to the buttocks. This is followed by embracing the child and calmly reviewing the offense and the desired behavior in an effort to reestablish a warm relationship.

8. Spanking should leave only transient redness of the skin and should never cause physical injury.

9. If properly administered spankings are ineffective, other appropriate disciplinary responses should be tried, or the parent should seek professional help. Parents should never increase the intensity of spankings.

likely persist and even escalate. Thus, instead of contributing to greater violence, spanking can be a useful component in an overall plan to effectively teach a child to stop aggressive hitting.

Argument #2: Since parents often refrain from hitting until the anger or frustration reaches a certain point, the child learns that anger and frustration justify the use of physical force.

Counterpoint: A study published in *Pediatrics* indicates that most parents who spank do not spank on impulse, but purposefully spank their children with a belief in its effectiveness. Furthermore, the study revealed no significant correlation between the frequency of spanking and the anger reported by mothers. The mothers who reported being angry were not the same parents who spanked.

Reactive, impulsive hitting after losing control due to anger is unquestionably the wrong way for a parent to use corporal punishment. Eliminating all physical punishment in the home, however, would not remedy such explosive scenarios. It could even increase the problem.

When effective spanking is removed from a parent's disciplinary repertoire, he or she is left with nagging, begging, belittling, and yelling, once the primary disciplinary measures—such as time-out and logical consequences—have failed. By contrast, if proper spanking is used with other disciplinary measures, better control of the particularly defiant child can be achieved, and moments of exasperation are less likely to occur.

Argument #3: Physical punishment is harmful to a child.

Counterpoint: Any disciplinary measure carried to an extreme can harm a child. Excessive scolding and berating of a child by a parent is emotionally harmful. Excessive use of isolation (time-out) for unreasonable periods of time can humiliate a child and ruin the measure's effectiveness.

Obviously, excessive or indiscriminate physical punishment is harmful and abusive. However, an appropriately administered spanking of a forewarned disobedient child is not harmful when administered in a loving controlled manner.

Argument #4: Physical punishment makes the child angry at the parent.

Counterpoint: Any form of punishment administered angrily for purposes of retribution, rather than calmly for purposes of correction, can create anger and resentment in a child. Actually, a spanking can break the escalating rage of a rebellious child and more quickly restore the relationship between parent and child.

Argument #5: Spanking teaches a child that "might makes right," that power and strength are most important, and that the biggest can force their will upon the smallest.

Counterpoint: Parental power is commonly exerted in routine child-rearing, and spanking is only one example. Other situations where power and restraint are exercised by the average parent include:

▶ The young child who insists on running from his parent in a busy mall or parking lot.

▶ The toddler who refuses to sit in his car seat.

▶ The young patient who refuses to hold still as a vaccination is administered or as a laceration is repaired.

Power and control over the child are necessary at times to ensure safety, health, and proper behavior. Classic child-rearing studies have shown that some degree of power, assertion, and firm control is essential for optimal child-rearing. When power is exerted in the context of love and for the child's benefit, the child will not perceive it as bullying or demeaning.

■ **When my daughter-in-law talks about "hitting" the children, I can tell she doesn't know the difference between spanking and "hitting." How can I distinguish the two for her?**

Corporal punishment is often defined broadly as *bodily punishment of any kind.* Since this definition includes spanking as well as obviously abusive acts such as kicking, punching, beating, face slapping, and even starvation, more specific definitions must be used to separate appropriate versus inappropriate corporal punishment.

Spanking is one of many disciplinary responses available to parents intended to shape appropriate behavior in the developing toddler and child. Child development experts believe spanking should be used mainly as a back-up to primary measures, and then independently to correct deliberate and persistent problem behavior that is not remedied with milder measures. It is most useful with toddlers and preschoolers from eighteen months to six years of age, when reasoning is less persuasive.

Moreover, child development experts say that spanking should always be a planned action by a parent, not an impulsive reaction to misbehavior. The child should be forewarned of the spanking consequence for each of the designated problem behaviors. Spanking should always be administered in private. It should consist of one or two spanks to the child's buttocks, followed by a calm review of the offense and the desired behavior.

■ **What about the argument that spanking leads to physical child abuse?**

The abuse potential when loving parents use appropriate disciplinary spanking is very low. Since parents have a natural affection for their children, they are more prone to underutilize spanking than to overutilize it.

Surveys indicate that 70 to 90 percent of parents of preschoolers use spanking, yet the incidence of physical child abuse in America is only about 5 percent. Statistically, the two practices are far apart. Furthermore, over the past decade reports of child abuse have steadily risen while approval for parental spanking has steadily declined.

Teaching parents appropriate spanking may actually reduce child abuse. Parents who are ill-equipped to control their child's behavior, or who take a more permissive approach (refusing to use spanking), may be more prone to anger and explosive attacks on their child.

For instance, the Swedish experiment to reduce child abuse by banning spanking seems to be failing. In 1980, one year after this ban was adopted, the rate of child beating was twice that of the United States. According to a 1995 report from the government organization Statistics Sweden, police reports of child abuse by family members rose fourfold from 1984 to 1994, while reports of teen violence increased nearly sixfold.

In conclusion, there is no evidence that mild spanking is harmful. Indeed, spanking is supported by history, research, and a majority of primary care physicians.

This material was produced by Den A. Trumbull, M.D. and S. DuBose Ravenel, M.D. Dr. Trumbull is a board-certified pediatrician in private practice in Montgomery, Alabama. He is a member of the Section on Developmental and Behavioral Pediatrics of the American Academy of Pediatrics. Dr. Ravenel is a board-certified pediatrician in private practice in High Point, North Carolina. A longer, more detailed version of this chapter originally appeared, with full references, in "Family Policy," a publication of the Family Research Council. For more information, write the Family Research Council at 801 G Street, N.W., Washington, DC 20001, or call (202) 393-2100. Or you can go online and find the report at www.townhall.com/frc.fampol/fp96jpa.html.

3

Table Manners for the Very Young

. . . .

■ **I grew up in a home where Dad would point to the salt shaker and wait for someone to pass it. And he'd protest if you included the pepper!**

I thought of that story as I noticed how our grandkids nearly stood up in their chairs and grabbed the salt shaker. I know my daughter is trying to be Miss Manners with them, but kids will be kids. What can I do to back her up *and* teach the grandkids some good dinner-table manners?

Manners, and the civility underneath it, are certainly a lost art today. Folks chew with their mouth open, letting the whole world see what they have in their mouths; prop both elbows on the table and point at you with their knives; and yawn without covering their mouths. Some even belch at the dinner table—or worse.

Anything you can do to teach your grandkids not to do any of those things—plus lick their fingers, talk with their mouth full, slurp their soup, and point to the salt shaker—will give them a head start in developing character. Let's face it: What they learn as children will stay with them into adulthood, and old habits are not soon forgotten. That's why it's crucial to introduce grandchildren to manners while they're young, rather than waiting until they've developed bad habits that are difficult to break later in life.

Besides, you want holiday gatherings to be pleasant and relaxed—especially if this is the only time of the year you get to spend with your adult children and grandkids. You don't want the grandkids relegated to card tables in front of the TV. No, you want them around your table (provided it's big enough) so everyone can enjoy turkey and all the trimmings with linen and fine china.

■ At what age should we start making a big deal about manners with the grandkids?

Tiffany Francis, who specializes in teaching manners to the very young, says, "When they're young, they're interested." Her program, "Manners and More," located in Phoenix, Arizona, welcomes children as young as five to learn the finer points of etiquette.

The night before Thanksgiving isn't the time to start teaching manners. Worse, don't wait until they're ten or eleven. According to some experts, even very young grandchildren are capable of learning basic rules of etiquette. For example, by the time they are five years old, they should be able to:

▶ sit up straight
▶ keep their hands in their lap
▶ chew with their mouth closed
▶ place their napkin on their lap
▶ hold a fork correctly (like a pencil)
▶ cut soft meat or vegetables with a knife

■ What are some ways to make manners-training fun?

Learning table manners doesn't have to be drudgery. Many experts suggest incorporating games and songs into manners-training. One idea is letting your grandkids "play restaurant" when they come over to your house. You can be the "waitress" and serve them while they "practice" their manners. Another idea is to set out the nice dishes and linen tablecloth for your grandchildren.

If you're willing to experiment, you can use incentive games to teach manners. One called "I Caught You" involves placing five coins in front of each grandchild's plate. Children are told which table manners they will be practicing. Whenever a rule is violated, a coin is removed. Whenever a rule is observed, the coin is replaced. Another game is called, "Who Gets the Surprise?"

There's another game that's ideal for small children just learning to count. Whenever anyone at the table is caught violating a rule of etiquette—and that includes the adults—he or she has to leave the room and count to twenty. Preschoolers especially delight in catching adults talking with their mouths full so they can banish them to the counting corridor. Along the same lines is "Napkin, napkin on the lap, who can I catch?" Children are encouraged to "catch" anyone who has forgotten to place his napkin on his lap, adults included.

■ **How big a deal should we make about manners when we are in restaurants?**

A visit to a nice restaurant is an excellent tool for teaching grandchildren manners. Restaurants serve several purposes:

1. Restaurants provide children with an opportunity to practice what they've been learning at home.

2. Restaurants represent a welcome treat to reward good behavior.

3. Restaurants familiarize children with dining in formal settings. Such familiarity will help them when they begin attending more formal social settings where proper dining etiquette is a must.

In her still-relevant book on etiquette, Amy Vanderbilt wrote, "Children are beginners. They are starting a job in life." As beginners, they have the privilege of being taught early in life that "good manners" are more than rules to learn. It's a lifestyle that reflects a fundamental Judeo-Christian principle: Do unto others as you would have others do unto you. The quaint notion of "acting like ladies and gentlemen" is as relevant today as it ever was. As grandparents of small children, you have a chance to instill in your grandchildren the habit of good manners, a habit they will carry well into adulthood and pass on to their children—and their children's children.

This chapter is adapted from writings by Elaine Minamide of Escondido, California.

4

Picking Up the Pieces

. . . .

■ **We are nearly sixty and planning to enjoy our golden years, but we have a prodigal daughter who has a child out of wedlock, and it just grieves our hearts to see how that precious child is being raised. My husband and I are waiting for the other shoe to drop; in other words, we may become parents all over again. I hear more and more grandparents are raising second families. Is that true?**

Yes, it is. Nellie Morse (a fictitious name) remembers the time her three-year-old granddaughter Emilie was sitting on her potty chair, rolling a piece of toilet tissue into a cigarette-shaped form.

"Whatcha doing?" asked Nellie as Emilie worked her little fingers around the tissue.

"I'm rolling a joint," she replied.

"Who taught you how to do that?"

"My mamma and her friend. They taught me."

That's when Nellie knew she had to confront her twenty-four-year-old daughter, Marilyn, who had traded life as a hardworking single mom for the fast lane of bikes, booze, and drugs. For months, Marilyn had been hanging out with a motorcycle gang and a succession of long-haired boyfriends.

"I know you're fooling with drugs," Nellie told her daughter when she came to pick up Emilie.

"Who told you that?" Marilyn asked.

"The baby."

"Oh, Mother, she just made that up."

"Babies don't lie. She wouldn't know *how* to make up something like that. If you're not going to straighten up and raise her right, why don't you just leave her with us?"

Marilyn slowly nodded. Within a few weeks, she appeared before a judge to sign the necessary adoption papers, granting her parents custody of young Emilie.

Those legal proceedings happened nearly nine years ago, and today, Nellie, and her husband, Grant, count themselves among an increasing number of grandparents who are being recycled—as parents to their children's children.

■ How many grandparents are parenting a second time?

According to 1990 Census Bureau figures, nearly 1 million grandparents are raising grandchildren by themselves, and another 1.5 million grandparents have opened their homes to grandchildren and a son or daughter, as well. Thus, approximately 5 percent of American families represent a grandparent raising a grandchild.

"I don't think many of us understand how serious the problem is," says Irene Endicott, a grandmother of twelve and author of *Grandparenting Redefined*. "At a time when older people are supposed to be enjoying the fruits of their labors and thinking about retirement, they are chasing four- and five-year-olds around and using up all their retirement funds in the process."

Grandparents raising grandchildren is not a new phenomenon. For centuries, grandparents have stepped in and raised children orphaned through disease or war. Closer to our era, President Bill Clinton lived as a young boy with grandparents while his mother studied nursing in Louisiana. But in the last decade, the number of grandchildren living with grandparents has shot up 37 percent, a rise paralleling the swelling numbers of single parents and out-of-wedlock births.

■ **Why the sudden increase? You told us that grandparents have had to step in for thousands of years.**

Blame it on the four D's: drugs, divorce, desertion, and death of a parent. "Substance abuse is by far the number-one cause of grandparents' legal custody of their grandchildren," says Mrs. Endicott. "Young single mothers, already addicted or unable to cope with their situations, turn to drugs for a way out. It's the children—malnourished and emotionally neglected—who suffer the most."

One of my neighbors told me that her doorbell rang at 10:15 one night, and she opened the door, and it was her daughter. She had her little baby in her arms and she was crying. "He's gone, Mom. He left me," she cried. "Can we stay with you?"

Who could refuse such a request, especially when flesh and blood are involved? Nor can grandparents deny Scripture. In 1 Timothy 5:8, Paul writes, "If anyone does not provide for his relatives, and especially for his immediate family, he has denied the faith and is worse than an unbeliever."

■ **What are some of the difficulties that grandparents face?**

Grandparents in their fifties and sixties know they don't have as much stamina for middle-of-the-night bottle feedings or keeping tabs on energetic youngsters. Others are at an age where their bodies are starting to break down. Fifty-six-year-old Nellie Morse, for instance, survived two bouts of cancer. Five years ago, doctors informed her she had a year to live, but she was determined to beat that prognosis. "I'm still

WHAT CAN GRANDPARENTS DO?

When grandchildren come to visit, don't just entertain them. Many times when grandkids arrive, grandparents run them all over the city, catering to their every wish. Consequently, the kindly grandparents end up exhausted. When grandchildren visit, require that they participate in some things that interest you too.

Also, get to know the world of your grandchildren. Start conversations that focus and enlarge upon your shared experiences. Don't reject their tastes in favor of your own, but instead, share your differences.

alive," says Nellie, "but I'm scared to death that I won't live to raise Emilie."

Taking in grandchildren usually resigns grandparents to a penny-pinching retirement. For many, their high-income earning years are a memory, and they are living on a modest pension or fixed income. Many must dip into savings or sell their homes—nest eggs they expected to tap later in life. But grandparents who do make the sacrifice know they are doing it "for the least of these."

"Pete and I have suffered, but not like the children have," said Peggy Jackson, who is raising two toddlers. "We were looking forward to wherever the Lord wanted us to go, never thinking we would have to raise a family again. But God has taught us the valuable lesson that we can serve Him through these kids, and we're determined to do exactly that."

■ **I am not a grandparent raising my grandkids, but last week, I was invited for dinner at my son's home. When I walked in, my nine-year-old grandson, Kenny, didn't notice my presence. In fact, his attention was fixed on another rerun of "America's Funniest Home Videos."**

"Kenny, aren't you going to say hello to your grandfather?" his father asked.

"Hello, Grandpa," Kenny responded like a trained parrot, his eyes never leaving the television set.

Why don't kids have respect for their elders?

Yes, the young boy's manners need sprucing up, and when you get a quiet moment with your son, you should express your disappointment with Kenny's behavior. You'll have to speak carefully, however, since your son is apt to be defensive about any shortcomings in Kenny.

■ **I've also noticed that my grandson and I don't seem to have much to say to each other. When I try to start up a conversation with Kenny, it seems like we are on different wavelengths. Is it just me, or is it the difference in ages?**

Robert D. Strom, Ph.D., a college professor, has found that

there is an ever-widening "generation gap" between the young and the elderly of our culture. Dr. Strom has examined some of the trends that have made it difficult for the generations to see eye-to-eye, and he has some creative solutions to this growing problem.

"When the older people of today were children," Dr. Strom explained, "the world was changing less rapidly. Consequently, in those days, a grandfather might reasonably say to his grandson, 'Let me tell you about life when I was your age. . . .' "

In this type of society, the grandfather's advice was relevant because he had already confronted the situations his grandchildren would someday have to face. Because of the slow rate of change, children could see their future as they observed the day-to-day activities of parents and grandparents. The Amish and Mennonites are examples of "past-oriented" societies that still exist today. In these religious communities, grandparents are viewed as experts and authorities by all age-groups.

But something happens when modern technology is introduced to a society. For one thing, the rate of social change increases. Therefore, successive generations of grandparents, parents, and children have less in common.

This means that children today are having experiences that were not part of even their *parents'* upbringing. AIDS, life in a single-parent family, and the World Wide Web are just some examples. So recalling your own childhood as the basis for offering advice ("When I was your age . . . .") has become less credible.

■ **But I've gained a lot of experience over the years that I want to pass along. Are you saying that my experiences are no longer relevant?**

Certainly they are, but keep in mind that when you were in school, you spent most of your time memorizing events that had already happened, and your teacher asked you to figure out what could have been done differently. Every student heard the warning: *Those who do not understand the mistakes of the past are destined to repeat them.* For this reason, subjects like history and literature were given special priority.

However, in today's present-oriented culture, schools emphasize subjects that prepare students to excel in a highly technological society and to make decisions concerning the future. A subject like penmanship, for example, does not receive the attention it once did because personal computers have diminished the need for hand-writing.

Another significant result of rapid change is the development of a "peer culture," in which both adults and children prefer to learn from people whose experiences are similar to their own. The popularity of self-help books and support groups is one manifestation.

Despite these trends, you're to be saluted for wanting to be part of your grandson's life. Hang in there. You'll do just fine if you adapt to the changing world without compromising your moral values and standards.

RESERVOIRS OF KNOWLEDGE

Grandparents, whether they are being "recycled" as parents or acting in their God-given grandparenting role, are reservoirs of knowledge and experience. We should invite them lovingly to share and enrich our lives and the lives of our children.

The next time you see your parents, tell them that you would like to record some of their memories for posterity. Turn on the camcorder (borrow one, if you must) and ask questions.

For example, have them talk about their recollections of their parents and grandparents, where they went to school, what it was like growing up during World War II or the 1950s, and places they have lived. If appropriate, ask them to share their testimony and what God has meant to their lives. Telling how faith has impacted their lives can leave a tremendous impression on the grandkids.

5

Growing Tenderhearted Grandchildren in a Tough World

· ·

■ When our children were small, I used to say to them, "It's more blessed to give than to receive, isn't it?" And they would almost always reply, "No, it isn't . . . getting is better!"

On their last visit, I asked two of our little grandchildren if it was more blessed to receive, and they replied just like their father did thirty years ago. I laughed, but at the same time, I wondered, *How can I teach them to care for others?*

Learning to care for others—that it is more blessed to give than to receive—is a spiritual discipline that requires constant nurturing. Our responsibility as grandparents and parents is to help those little ones become tender toward the less fortunate, especially those who still don't know the Lord Jesus Christ as Savior.

To illustrate this, Pat Palau, wife of internationally known evangelist Luis Palau, had the joy of visiting with a good friend from university days. For nearly thirty years, Diane has served as a teacher of missionary children at Faith Academy in the Philippines. Because Diane has worked with children for so long, Pat asked her, "What kind of children do you have nowadays?"

Diane replied, "The children's self-esteem is higher. Even five-year-olds are more confident than they used to be. But there's a flip side to it. Children have also become more selfish."

■ But doesn't the Bible teach us that we are special?

Yes, God's Word does, and our grandchildren need to hear that. But that's not all. We also need to care about other people and learn to put them first, just as Jesus Christ did.

■ How is that done? What ideas can you share?

Here are seven strategies that Luis and Pat Palau have found effective for raising tenderhearted children.

1. Sponsor a child, especially a needy boy or girl living in a Third World country. When Luis and Pat first thought about sponsoring a child years ago, they discussed it with their sons and suggested "adopting" a boy from Mexico. They thought that was a great idea because they used to live there. Since then they've sponsored children through several organizations, but one of the best is Compassion International (P.O. Box 7000, Colorado Springs, CO 80933).

Several years ago, Luis took his youngest son, Stephen, with him to a youth conference where Luis was speaking. While there, Stephen saw a presentation on sponsoring children and bought home a picture of an orphan, promising to support this little boy forever. The Palaus pitched in, and their son is still supporting a Compassion child. If your grandchild is willing to sponsor a child, your desire to help financially shows your sensitivity and desire to share.

2. Encourage your grandchildren to pay attention to news via the television, newspaper, or Internet. Learning about cities or nations affected by natural disasters and hearing about other tragedies remind us that we live in a hurting world. If your grandchildren are old enough to discuss current events, talk about what God is doing in those parts of the world.

It's easy to shut off our minds to the needs of the world by saying, *Well, they've lived like that all their lives. They're used to it. They don't notice how bad this really is.* But suffering is suffering.

3. Inform your grandchildren about the world's major religions. You can do this when they tell you about Sunday School.

Becoming tenderhearted involves understanding that the religions of the world inevitably enslave people and often make their lives miserable. Helping grandchildren to see that most people are under the domination of Satan won't make them feel superior or arrogant, especially if you display respect and genuine love for people from all walks of life. By word and example you can communicate to your grandchildren that "We don't ridicule or make fun of people, even in private."

4. Become active in your local church missions program. Invite missionaries into your home and invite your son or daughter and your grandchildren over. Again, if they are old enough, allow them to take part in dinner table conversations. This is one of the best ways they can get to know some of God's servants. By talking about different people and customs, other parts of the world will seem more real to them.

TEACHING GRANDKIDS THE FOUNDATIONS OF THE FAITH

by Luis Palau

The Bible instructs parents to raise children "in the training and instruction of the Lord" (Eph. 6:4).

Grandparents, while not the primary parents, can certainly buttress those efforts to teach the next generation about Jesus Christ and cement in their grandchildren's minds the foundational truths of the Christian faith.

We can do it in small ways that stay with loved ones for the ages. When I was only ten years old, my father died. Yet the impact my dad had on my life has continued to this day. I remember waking up early in the morning, for instance, and tiptoeing out of my bedroom. My dad would often be in his office, on his knees, with a blanket over his shoulder, reading.

One day I went into his office and asked, "Dad, what are you reading?"

He said, "Luis, I'm reading a book in the Bible called Proverbs. It has thirty-one chapters, one for each day of the month. As you grow up, read a chapter of Proverbs every day, and you'll be all right."

The foundational truths my dad taught me about the value of reading God's Word and believing what it says, combined with sincere obedience, have kept me walking with the Lord all these years. Those same truths can bless our grandkids' lives too.

The next time you're with them, read an age-appropriate story from the Bible. Tell the older ones that Proverbs has thirty-one chapters, and that a good habit is reading one chapter each day.

5. Read age-appropriate biographies of William Carey, Mary Slessor, Hudson Taylor, and other great missionaries to your grandchildren. You can find those books in Christian bookstores. Children especially enjoy hearing about George Mueller, whose specialty was trusting God to what some might call an extreme. He took in thousands of orphans from off the streets of England and cared for them, providing the best of everything without asking for financial help.

Several times when Mueller's family was without food, they set the table anyway as if they were awaiting a meal. Once a cart laden with bread broke down in the street right outside their home. The bread man came to the door saying, "I don't know what to do with all this bread because I can't take it any farther. Could you use it?" The lesson the orphans learned was to look to God for everything—even if you possess nothing. That's a good lesson for us today too.

ALL THE TIME IN THE WORLD

While at the playground one day, a woman sat down next to another woman on a bench. "That's my grandson over there," she said, pointing to a little boy in a red sweater who was gliding down the slide.

"He's a fine looking boy," the other woman said. "That's my grandson in the blue sweater on the swing." Then looking at her watch, she called him.

"What do you say we go, Todd?"

"Just five more minutes, Oma, please? Just five more minutes," the boy pleaded.

The woman nodded and Todd continued to swing to his heart's content. Minutes passed and the young grandmother stood and called to her grandson again.

"Time to go now!"

"Can we stay five more minutes, Oma? Just five more minutes?"

She smiled and said, "Okay."

"My, you certainly are patient," the other woman responded.

The grandmother smiled. "My older son Tom—Todd's father—was killed by a drunk driver last year. I'd give anything for just five more minutes with Tom. I've vowed not to make the same mistake with Todd. He thinks he has five more minutes to swing. The truth is, I get five more minutes to watch him play."

6. Deliberately forego something in order to emphasize giving to others. "Live simply so that others might simply live." Let your grandchildren see how what you have given up has helped others. They may think of things they don't need either.

As missionaries living in Latin America, Luis and Pat Palau have been on the receiving end of other children's generosity. One group of children saved their money all summer so Luis and Pat could buy their sons a bicycle. That gift meant a lot to them.

After moving back to the U.S., the Palaus discussed whether to install a deck and hot tub in their backyard or use the same amount of money to take their sons with them to visit several countries. The family decided that the money would be better spent traveling together. Involving their sons in that decision made visiting other mission fields that much more significant.

It isn't easy to cultivate tenderness in the hearts of children, but it's worth the effort. We live in an increasingly cynical, callused society that affects all of us somewhat, and that's the kind of society our grandchildren are growing up in. Why should we feel embarrassed if our grandchildren cry over the sufferings of others? Instead, we should rejoice to see them growing in their care and concern for people.

We must allow our hearts to be broken by the things that break God's heart. Because He dwells in us and desires to work though us, we can become part of the answer to some of the world's most urgent problems.

Together with your grandchildren, discover anew that true happiness and joy are found, as the Apostle Paul says, in not looking "only to one's own interests, but also to the interests of others"— wherever they may live.

This chapter is adapted from writings by Pat Palau, whose husband, Luis, is the founder of the Luis Palau Evangelistic Association in Portland, Oregon.

6

"I've Got Difficult Grandchildren"

. . . .

■ From the moment my first grandson was born he exhibited a classic Type-A personality—demanding, aggressive, intense. When I baby-sit him, he hurls his pacifier across the room, yells when hungry, and throws himself facedown on the carpet when distraught. He's a preschooler now and still learning the fine art of self-control, but what triggers aggression in children?

The most obvious cause is frustration. Consider how many times toddlers are denied permission to carry out some desired activity, how many no's they hear each day, or how often they see a coveted plaything in the clutches of another. Then he appears on your doorstep—ready to go ballistic when deprived of anything he craves.

Besides frustration, other factors play a role in triggering aggression. Physiological disorders such as hyperactivity may cause a child to be "propelled from within by forces he cannot explain," explains Dr. James Dobson in *The Strong-Willed Child*. Stress or anxiety can contribute to aggression, as well. And believe it or not, food allergies actually cause some children to be aggressive, belligerent, or combative.

■ **I know a certain amount of aggression in toddlers is normal, but how do I help them control it and continue the socialization process?**

Here's where grandparents and parents come in. And while daunting, it's not impossible to civilize aggressive toddlers. Some suggestions:

▸ **Establish clear rules-of-play.** Hitting, biting, or grabbing will not be tolerated.

▸ **Reinforce those rules immediately.** No warnings! If a child grabs a toy from a playmate, insist that he return it. If he hits or bites, take him aside, firmly remind him of the rules, and follow-up with a brief time-out.

▸ **Stay calm.** Don't shout, yank, or overreact, especially when dealing with aggression. Role-modeling goes a long way toward shaping our children's personalities.

▸ **Teach alternatives to aggression.** Even toddlers can learn negotiating skills. Demonstrate by holding out your hand and saying "May I have that toy?" Praise a grandchild when she successfully negotiates for what she wants, either in role play with you or while interacting with peers.

▸ **Tune in to the child's emotional or physical needs.** Is he hungry? Tired? Jealous? Frustrated? Some aggressive acts can be thwarted by wise intervention before a crisis occurs. A healthy snack, a short nap, a brief separation from a competitive peer, or soft music in a dimly lit room may be all that's necessary to calm an agitated spirit.

■ **"A child who lies is either afraid of you—or she's four," I recently read in the *Mother's Almanac*. But seriously, I have a little granddaughter who tells fibs, little white lies, and outright falsehoods. I'm concerned, so what should I do?**

Children lie for a variety of reasons. Some children, particularly preschoolers, mingle fantasy with reality and "stretch" the truth. Children also lie because that's what they see grown-ups do.

Besides the fact that "lying lips are an abomination to the Lord" (Prov. 12:22), lying is a personal transgression. Emotionally affronted, we tend to react heavyhandedly. We can offset this tendency by:

▶ **Staying even-tempered.** Rather than yelling, "Who smudged my window?" say, "I see somebody got fingerprints on this window. Shall I get a cloth so whoever did it can clean it up?"

▶ **Rewarding honesty.** Consider minimizing the consequence for the original infraction as a reward for telling the truth.

▶ **Sympathizing.** Let them know you understand how hard it must have been to tell the truth.

■ **When do children know they are lying?**

According to experts, fabrication is a normal part of early childhood behavior. "Most children don't begin to understand truth and falsehood until the age of seven—the age of reason," writes William Sears, M.D. If your grandchild stretches the truth, rather than automatically assuming he's lying, try jogging his memory. For example, if he tells you, "My daddy catched a robber last night," remind him that it was, in fact, the police who caught a robber. You can also remind him about the story of the little boy who cried wolf.

When adults lie, they often justify it as the lesser of two evils. Unfortunately, small children aren't sophisticated enough to differentiate between tactful evasion of the truth and a lie. If for some reason you feel compelled to tell a "white lie," don't do it, especially when the grandkids are in earshot. If you're really committed to teaching your grandchildren the importance of honesty, consider changing your behavior. As always, role models are the best teachers.

Help your grandchildren tell the truth by:

▶ Letting them know you love them no matter what they do.

▶ Talking about times it was hard for you to be honest.

▶ Letting them know they can tell you anything—even "secrets."

▶ Taking them seriously.

▶ Praising them for honesty.

▶ Being truthful yourself.

This material is adapted from writings by Elaine Minamide.

8

What Do I Do about That Music?

. . . .

■ I can remember it like yesterday: Ed Sullivan introducing the Beatles—John, Paul, George, and Ringo—to America. When I was in college, I bought Jimi Hendrix albums because my roommates talked about him all the time—but I hated his music. But what passes for "popular music" today goes way beyond the pale. Not only are the lyrics unintelligible, the beat is relentless. My grandchildren like to listen to that stuff, and they're barely into elementary school. What's happening here?

Who would have thought that today's post-fifties crowd would actually pine for the Beatles and Rolling Stones? Nostalgia aside, however, those groups certainly did their share to promote drug use and casual sex, and society is still shaking off the effects of shattered lives and broken relationships.

Fittingly, thirty-five years later, the musical landscape can be described as "fractured." We've got rock, pop, street rap, country, hip-hop, heavy metal, speed metal, death metal, and urban metal, and new genres are being invented with each new cycle. Fortunately, we also have a fairly recent phenomenon called Christian Contemporary Music, or CCM.

What you need to know is this: If you hit the ceiling every time your children brought home a Doobie Brothers or an Eagles eight-track, you'd absolutely go through the roof if your grandkids pushed "play" on their Marilyn Manson or Madonna compact disk.

Things haven't changed much from the late '50s and '60s. It's been said that teenagers use music to get back at their parents, and there's a ring of truth to that statement. If your grandchildren are in public school, they're probably aware of every group that's getting steady rotation on MTV or hit radio stations. The subtle pressure to fit in and keep up with the lunchroom conversation still pervades middle school and high school campuses.

■ **My husband and I were driving in the car, and the grandkids kept wanting us to turn to the "B-100" radio station. Ed hadn't listened to anything but talk radio in years, so he acquiesced. What came screeching out of the car's speakers was just awful. I'm afraid Ed didn't handle it very well. "Listen to those guys!" he yelled to the back. "I bet they look like girls! And who can understand the words anyway? These guys just have to be evil."**

The kids still clamored for Ed to leave the station where it was, but he punched in Rush Limbaugh, and all communication stopped. What should Ed have done?

All your husband did was reveal his prejudices and age. Such statements may end the discussion, and then you can never have *any* input on your grandchildren's music likes and dislikes.

Now suppose Ed had said: "You know kids, let's drop by the Wherehouse, and I'll buy you a new CD. But I want us to check the lyrics together before we buy because it's important to know about the message that music will be pumping into your brains."

Your husband will probably blow their little minds, and they may initially sense something is fishy. But have him follow through on his idea, which will show that he is fair and open-minded.

■ **What if we look at the lyrics sheet or listen to a couple of the CDs and know the parents wouldn't approve?**

If you should discover that the music is garbage, calmly remind them of your responsibility to God to protect their spirits and their brains. Tell them that one day they'll be making their own choices about music, but that day hasn't arrived yet.

■ **You mentioned Christian Contemporary Music. Should we be pushing that as an alternative?**

Everyone realizes there are diverse opinions on this subject. Some parents don't believe that music can be Christian if it has a 4/4 beat. *In other words, it has to be old or slow if God likes it.*

Don't fall for that logic, no matter how much you prefer good ol' "traditional" music. If your adult children enjoy CCM, praise the Lord. Sure, Contemporary Christian Music wasn't prevalent when your kids were young, but it's a positive alternative today with great Christian artists and groups in every music style imaginable. If CCM music is part of your grandchildren's homes, there's a strong chance the parents won't be fighting about secular rock music with them.

The key is lyrics. Everyone, young and old, should discuss the words of all the kids' music. If there comes a sticky moment when it's apparent that a certain CD runs afoul of the family standard, step in and offer to buy the CD at half-price. Then go with the grandkids to the music store and pick out some good Christian alternatives.

■ **Speaking of alternatives, who are some good ones?**

I (Mike Yorkey) recently took the kids to see Rebecca St. James in concert. Andrea and Patrick are full-blown teens—no longer little kids who used to listen to Psalty sing about Charity Churchmouse. Like most in their age-group, they like to listen to music, so my wife, Nicole, and I are encouraging them to listen to good music.

The first time I heard of Rebecca St. James, a twenty-one-year-year-old from Australia, was when she appeared on the cover of *Brio,*

Focus on the Family's teen magazine for girls. When I popped her "God" CD into my player, I liked her songs—especially her lyrics.

Midway through her concert, Rebecca asked the audience to sit down. "I'd like to tell you about this ring I'm wearing," she said, pointing to a gold band on the ring finger of her right hand.

"It's a Promise Ring, and when my parents gave it to me, they said it was to symbolize my commitment to wait until marriage to have sex. I can tell you right now, I will be waiting for that special person God has planned for me!"

I clapped and cheered like everyone else in the sold-out audience, and then I snuck a look at Andrea and Patrick. *This is great*, I thought. *Rebecca is telling my kids exactly what Nicole and I are saying to them.*

Because Andrea and Patrick are going to listen to someone on their little portable CD players, I want them to listen to Rebecca St. James. I want them to look up to Rebecca as a role model. I want them to learn that living the Christian life can be cool—just like Rebecca.

What I don't want them to listen to are albums by artists like Marilyn Manson, Tupac Shakur, Alanis Morissette, and other secular musicians whose tunes are frontal attacks on everything Nicole and I are trying to impart to our children.

For more on the subject, I sought out Bob Smithouser, editor of *Plugged In*, Focus on the Family's monthly youth culture newsletter. Bob lives and breathes this music stuff, and I figured he would be a good guy to answer my questions. Here's my interview:

Mike: Bob, am I naive, or has all hell literally broken loose in the music industry?

Bob: Not at all. If anything, the naive parents are the ones who refuse to acknowledge the depth of the problem. You mentioned Marilyn Manson. He's a satanic priest who tears the pages out of Bibles on stage. His dark music is unlike anything we've heard in years. Lines like, "I've got abortions in my eyes" . . . "I wasn't born with enough middle fingers," and "I will bury your God in my warm spit" give you some idea.

Rapper Tupac Shakur was gunned down several years ago in a fashion similar to the gangster-style violence he has glorified throughout his career. And Alanis Morissette has sold an amazing 15 million copies of her despairing disc "Jagged Little Pill." The garbage being produced by the mainstream music industry is as disturbing as ever.

Mike: Bob, you were at the same Rebecca St. James concert that I was. She sure seems to come from a different world than the Tupacs, Mansons, and Morissettes. She appears to provide a godly alternative. What is your take?

Bob: I've had a chance to get to know Rebecca some, and I can honestly say she's among the sweetest, most genuine people I've met in the business. "Celebrity" isn't her goal at all. She's a minister of God's Word. If I had a teenage daughter, I'd want her to be as on-fire as Rebecca. You know, Mike, it hurts me to read the statistics of young people suffering from sexually transmitted diseases, drug abuse, and more subtle afflictions such as moral relativism. Rebecca offers purity and a clear vision to an audience that has been told there is no hope.

Mike: I know there have to be other artists like Rebecca that I can plug my kids into. Who are they?

Bob: The list is always growing. I respect artists like Wayne Watson, Geoff Moore, DC Talk, Steven Curtis Chapman, World Wide Message Tribe, Scott Krippayne, Michael W. Smith, and the Newsboys. I recently met Jaci Velasquez, a talented young lady who keeps Jesus at the center of her lyrics. These Christians, and others like them, are on the front lines of what has become a musical war zone for the hearts and minds of young people.

Mike: Are there some Christian artists who *don't* focus on the Lord in their songs?

Bob: Sad, but true. I've noticed that a growing number of artists under the umbrella of "Contemporary Christian Music" have gotten soft with the Gospel message. I heard an album by a band called Aleixa that sounds like the junk played on MTV. There are a number of reasons this is happening, but I think parents and teens need to be selective when buying what's marketed as "Christian music."

Mike: You mentioned DC Talk. My wife and I once took Andrea and Patrick to see DC Talk. They were loud! But what grabbed Nicole and me was how clearly and repeatedly they talked about the Lord.

Bob: DC Talk has been bold and straightforward about their faith. Even Billy Graham has had the guys sing at his crusades because he realizes the open door they have with young people.

Toby McKeehan, the group leader, once told me that they consider themselves "musical missionaries." He compared their job to someone overseas using the language of a foreign culture to reach people with the good news of Christ. Their language just happens to be rock, rap, and hip-hop. I believe their commitment is solid.

Mike: I've heard that a DC Talk's song "Just Between You and Me" received secular radio play and was even played in movie theaters while people wait for the show to begin. That's encouraging. Have any other groups been embraced by the mainstream?

Bob: I get letters from many teens turned on to Jars of Clay. This Christian group has generated a lot of interest, especially in secular circles. The guys have opened for Sting and signed on with Coca-Cola to record a jingle. Now the question is, "What will they do with this platform?"

Mike: Are there dangers in "crossing over"?

Bob: Sure. I was disappointed to see Jars of Clay contribute a song to the soundtrack for the violent action film *The Long Kiss Goodnight*. When I called their publicist, she said they were trying to be a light in a dark place. That's all well and good, but I can't help but believe that some churched kids who follow the band might take Jars' involvement with this project as an indirect endorsement of the film. Artists need to think these things through from a biblical perspective.

Mike: In the past, teens have complained that there haven't been quality Christian alternatives for every style of secular music. Is that true today?

Bob: No. Virtually every genre is represented. This is a big struggle for parents and grandparents. They want to choose their battles carefully and avoid alienating their kids, yet they're not comfortable with certain musical styles, even when the messages are Christian.

Having said that, I think bands like Plankeye, Supertones, and Out of Eden can provide terrific pro-God options for teens already attached to the edgy musical styles of worldly counterparts. But at the same time, I'd be careful about introducing an eight-year-old to styles like rap, punk, or grunge. Why create a taste in young children for genres that could lead to trouble as they're tempted by mainstream equivalents in adolescence?

Mike: What's the story on Michael W. Smith? When my son attended Kamp Kanukuk, Joe White's Christian sports camp in Branson, Missouri, Michael played for the campers, and I understand that he and his family hang out at Kanukuk every summer. But didn't Michael attempt to "cross over" and become a mainstream artist?

Bob: After Amy Grant landed a few pop hits, her peers saw a chance to impact a wider audience. Michael was one of them. Personally, I don't think there is anything wrong with Christian artists "crossing over" if the cross goes over with them.

In recent years, Michael's music and concerts have been as evangelical as ever. His "Live the Life" tour was very impressive. It was nice to see families with young children, as well as teens, enjoying a great time.

Mike: Another artist I like is Steven Curtis Chapman. Is he reaching the teen audience?

Bob: Absolutely. It's easy to assume that all young music fans gravitate to "the hard stuff," but that's just not true. If you go to see Steven or Point of Grace in concert, you'll find the under-twenty crowd well represented.

Christian music is a powerful medium and a burgeoning industry. Chosen carefully, it can also be a great tool for imparting values and an upbeat sense of God's presence in our lives—not just in teens, but in all of us.

GET PLUGGED IN

If you're trying to stay abreast of music and other forms of entertainment so you can stay relevant with your adult children and young teens, then *Plugged In* is the resource for you.

Focus on the Family's youth culture staff monitors the popular media and provides information to help you come up to speed on music, movies, television—you name it. Just write Focus at the Family, Plugged In, Colorado Springs, CO 80995, or call toll-free at (800) 232-6459.

College-age students can also check out their very own "webzine" called Boundless. The Internet address is www.boundless.org.

8

... *And a Little Child Shall Lead Them*

. . . .

■ **I want to leave a legacy with my grandchildren, but not just a legacy of who I was or what I did. I'm thinking about something of impact. Is there anything I could do?**

Florence Turnidge, a seventysomething Seattle grandmother, was wondering the same thing. Then she took her granddaughter to visit a dying man and changed their lives forever.

It all happened the first time Florence took her granddaughter, Jennifer Turnidge, to the nursing home. Jennifer was three years old. Beaming smile. Eyes alive. There in the rest home, the little girl stood erectly with her grandmother next to the man in the wheelchair.

The man was in the twilight of his life. Everette Rao had not smiled in weeks. Eyes that once sparkled now stared into space. Jennifer Turnidge could not see that a brain tumor was slowly ushering life out of his body.

"Brother Everette, I've brought someone to see you," said the grandmother.

Slowly, the fifty-five-year-old, terminally ill man turned his head. Hoping he still had a glimmer of vision, Florence pointed to a small, cherubic face. Everette's eyes responded. A grin crept across his face. All around the room, the feeling was contagious.

"The nurses told me they hadn't seen him smile like that in weeks," said Florence. That day at Seattle's Crista Nursing Center, a child had done what medicine, nurses, and even a trickle of caring visitors had not been able to accomplish—bring a flicker of happiness and hope to a lonely, dying man.

For Florence, Brother Everette represents thousands of ailing or elderly people in America's nursing homes who are living out their remaining days alone. And though many of the nation's aging—including those living in rest homes—enjoy fruitful relationships with friends and relatives, others are forgotten by their families.

■ How did Florence get the idea of taking her grandchildren with her to nursing homes?

It began when her mother became gravely ill and died. She and Florence were inseparable prayer partners, and next to her husband, her dearest friend. After the grief continued for two years, she cried out, "Lord, I've got to do something about this."

The Lord prescribed a large dose of generosity for Florence's hurting heart. "My grief was too great to handle alone, so I decided to walk over to a nearby rest home," Florence remembers. "There, I met several older, widowed women just like Mother, who somehow didn't have a loving family to look after them. I thought to myself, *This is where I belong.*"

At Crista, Florence visited Everette Rao, a Bible scholar from India with whom she had led prayer groups for a dozen years. "For a long time, we were able to converse. Eventually, though, his health worsened. It got to the point where his hollow eyes looked straight through me. One day, I said, 'Lord, I'll keep going to see Brother Everette, but it's going to be awfully hard. I've got to have grace, because I can't stand it.' "

The Lord whispered into Florence's heart that Brother Everette loved little children. That was it! She called her married daughter, described her idea, received permission, and then said to her granddaughter, "Jennifer, I have a friend at the rest home, and you can make him happy. If you make him happy, you'll make Jesus happy."

■ **Were all the visits pleasant ones? And wasn't it a little too soon to expose an innocent grandchild to so much death?**

Confronting death is not an easy assignment, but it can teach children that they will see their newfound friends in heaven. Of course, common sense must be exercised. You don't want to expose small children to someone in their "death rattle" or a menacing, drooling figure who doesn't know where or who he is.

■ **If we pick up on this idea, what could we do to make our first visit to a nursing home with the grandchildren a positive experience? How young can a child be?**

Grandkids can be as young as two years old. Age is not as important as the child's readiness. Hyperactive children, for instance, present more of a risk. They may overreact to an older person watching them and become nervous. It's important to create an atmosphere in which both grandchild and grandparent feel comfortable.

■ **How long should visits be?**

Ten to fifteen minutes is reasonable. Think quality, not quantity. A grandchild and a nursing home resident can experience love and natural acceptance within moments after meeting. Likewise, establishing meaningful rapport often takes only minutes.

■ **Is there anything special we should do in preparation?**

If the grandchild is old enough to understand, explain where and when you'll be going, as well as why you're visiting. Wheelchairs and walkers may seem threatening to small children. Share with them that the Lord has provided older people with the wheelchairs and walkers so that they can continue to live with purpose and dignity.

■ **What if I don't have a grandchild living close to me?**

Ask a little friend from your neighborhood or church to be your special partner. If he or she doesn't have grandparents, then the visit will be all the more meaningful because of the grandma or grandpa they are bound to "adopt."

■ **How is Florence getting the word out about this meaningful experience between grandparent and grandchild?**

Florence has been speaking out at church and women's retreats, describing how little grandchildren have touched the hearts and lives of seniors. But Florence is quick to add that it's not easy to coordinate visits with busy families or spend the time participating in this type of ministry.

"It takes work and sacrifice to spend time with older people you don't even know," says Florence. "If Christians who have been sitting at home for years only knew the blessing they would receive by taking grandchildren to a rest home, they would have started much sooner."

Think about it, and next time, let a little grandchild lead you. When you see the tired, aging faces light up with a look of new happiness, you'll choke up like Florence has on many occasions.

This chapter is adapted from writings by Mark Cutshall, a freelance writer and president of Mark Cutshall Creative Services in Seattle, Washington.

9

My Grandchildren Won't Listen!

....

■ I asked my four-year-old grandson, Timmy, to sit quietly for five minutes while I talked to a friend. My simple request fell on deaf ears. Not only did Timmy not "sit quietly," his distracting mischief made conversation with my neighbor all but impossible.

Later, I asked Timmy what he was supposed to have been doing during our conversation. "I don't know," came the contrite reply. I persisted. "Didn't you hear me say to sit quietly?" When the little boy shrugged, I felt my blood pressure rising. What can I do to get my grandkids to really *listen?*

Was something wrong with Timmy's hearing? Probably not. Though most guardians and parents of preschoolers invariably suspect their children have hearing problems, the vast majority of children can hear just fine. For them, hearing is not the problem. *Listening* is.

It is true that small children are bombarded with much information from television, computers, day care, siblings, and parents, which tends to distract them. These days many kids "tune out" what doesn't fit into their current program.

■ **I've always felt that all children can—and should—be required to respond to our direction. But the last time I had Timmy spend the night with us, I called out, "Timmy, time to brush your teeth!" Fifteen minutes later he walked up to me and showed me his teeth still caked with cookie crumbs! Wasn't I justified in getting upset?**

Yes, but was the TV on when you made the request? The CD player? Was Timmy absorbed in a book, a game, some toys? Some kids get so focused that they actually do tune out. Sometimes you need to physically remove distractions to get their attention.

Did you know that many preschool teachers rely on external signals before giving directions? Flashing lights, ringing bells, or clapping hands help alert children to stop what they're doing and pay attention.

You can use similar approaches with grandchildren in your home. You may have to literally get in front of Timmy and in his face. Make eye contact. If he's looking you in the eyes, he can't pretend he didn't hear you.

A gentle touch on the shoulder before speaking, getting down on the grandchild's level, using specific commands such as, "Please look at me" before speaking—all of these methods serve the purpose of getting children to tune in before grandparents address them.

■ **When I stroll along and announce, "Time to stop playing and put everything back where it belongs," they look at me like I just asked them to recite the Second Law of Thermodynamics. Have kids really changed that much since I was raising them?**

Maybe you've forgotten that you need to make your requests more specific and age-appropriate. Are you too wordy? With small children, less is better. For instance, maybe you want your grandchild to go upstairs, get her pajamas, put them on, brush her teeth, and climb into bed. Such a multi-faceted request may be fine for an eight-year-old, but for a preschooler, it's too complex. Why not simply say, "Pajama time"? Inherent in those two words is all that's involved in getting ready for bed.

It's easy too to forget that children perceive things differently than adults. Remember Timmy, who was asked to sit still quietly for five minutes while his grandmother finished her conversation with her friend? Complicated? Not for us. But for Timmy? You bet.

Let's get into his little mind for a minute and try to imagine how

WHEN KIDS ASK COMPLEX QUESTIONS

"Why doesn't God just zap bad people?"
"If God is so strong, why did He let those children die in the plane crash?"
"Is my kitten in heaven?"

Grandparents often have to field thought-provoking questions. Beneath the surface of your grandchild's mind lies a hotbed of complex questions, profound enough for any theologian. Unfortunately most of us aren't seminary graduates, yet it's up to us to furnish answers when our inquisitive grandchildren ask them.

Rather than cringing when those little ones approach you with difficult questions, remember that one of your privileges as a believer is to nurture their budding faith. How do we answer difficult questions—questions that we may struggle with—from a preschooler?

You begin by doing your part to cultivate faith in the Bible. In a society that's openly hostile to God's Word, challenges to a child's faith are everywhere. Let your grandchildren know that God loves them, and that everything we need to know about Him can be found in the Bible.

In his classic book, *How to Raise Your Child for Christ,* Andrew Murray wrote, "A child is naturally trustful; guide his young trust to that Word which never fails." This trust will enable you to answer your child's difficult questions later on.

Also, be sure to respond appropriately. Too often we have a tendency to dismiss a child's profound questions with a curt, "I have no idea," or "Go ask Grandma." Such dismissal, though, will likely stifle his curiosity. Henry Clay Trumbull wrote, "The beginning of all knowledge is a question. If a child were ever caused to stay his questionings, there would be at once an end to his progress in knowledge."

Jesus said, "Let the children come to me, and do not hinder them" (Matt. 19:14). We hinder little children when we dismiss as unimportant or irrelevant their sincere questions about God. We "let them come to Him" when we respond simply, honestly, and prudently, while simultaneously cultivating a simple faith in God and His Word.

he perceived this "simple" request: *Five minutes? How long is that? What's quietly? That doesn't mean no talking, does it? Sit? Who me? Are you crazy? What's in it for me?*

If you expect a four-year-old to sit quietly, you could say, "Timmy, sit on this chair here and read these books. I'll tell you when it's time to go home." Now Timmy's marching orders are clear. His mission, whether he realizes it or not, is to sit quietly while Grandma talks to her friend. His task is specific and age-appropriate—to look at the books.

■ How do I avoid repeating myself all the time?

Consistency and follow-up is the key. If you say something and don't mean it the first time, you're training them not to listen. In order to ensure that grandchildren are tuned in, many experienced grandparents like to obtain verbal responses from their grandchildren. Some require a "Yes, Grandpa" or "No thank you, Grandma," and then hold the child accountable for what he or she heard. Others expect the children to repeat or restate what was said. Some children don't connect until they've actually repeated what you said.

Another thing: You have to be a good listener too. If your three-year-old granddaughter, Elisa, comes running up to you, out of breath, eyes aglow with excitement, and tells you about the yellow butterfly she just saw in the backyard, she will wait expectantly for a response. What will it be?

Give her more than a "That's nice, dear," and a pat on the head—or a quick grunt of recognition before turning your attention elsewhere. Say something like, "How lovely! Shall we go outside and see if the butterfly is still there?"

This chapter is adapted from writings by Elaine Minamide of Escondido, California.

10

Have Grandchildren, Will Travel

· ·

■ My grandchildren are getting to an age where we can do fun things together, and I'm thinking that my husband and I would be up to taking a short trip with them. If we really are going to travel and make holidays with the grandkids, what do we need to know?

Virginia Smith Spurlock was in a similar situation. Shortly before her husband's death, Stephanie, their seven-year-old grand-daughter, expressed a fervent desire to see the White House. They promised to take her there during her summer vacation. When Virginia was suddenly widowed, she asked myself if she were brave enough to undertake such a venture alone.

She discussed it with her son and his ex-wife. Without hesitation, each gave Virginia a go-ahead. That boosted her self-confidence. Then she sat down with Stephanie to pour over maps and tour books.

Their week in Washington was fantastic. Since then, Virginia has become totally addicted to traveling with her grandchildren, and they are equally enthusiastic. They have toured, cruised, shared experiences unique to them and in so doing, established close, long-term relationships.

■ **Vacationing with our grandchildren sounds like fun. Where do we start?**

Begin by seeking approval from the parents. This must be done before even mentioning the possibility of a trip to your grandchild. In case the parents give a thumbs-down to the idea, don't cast them in the role of a Dr. Killjoy.

■ **What should I do if there isn't a definite no, but I sense some reluctance from the parents to allow their child to be carried away on a trip over which they have little control?**

What to do? Go easy. No hurt feelings, no pouting. Keep a smile on your face and let it drop—at least for the time being. Then it will be time to put Plan B into action.

■ **What is Plan B?**

Plan B is to invite the reticent parents and your grandchild on a day's outing. Do something you think both parent and child—especially the parent—will particularly enjoy. You plan it, you execute it, and you pay for it. If all works out and everyone enjoys a grand time at a museum and nearby merry-go-round, then some time later you'll be able to broach the subject of taking the grandchildren on a weekend trip.

If you're still receiving negative vibes, you'll have to wait until the grandchildren are older. Meanwhile, satisfy that "grandparent hunger" with one-day excursions, at least for the time being.

Assuming the scenario doesn't happen or your Plan B does the trick, you now have the sanction of Mom and Dad. Great. But you may have to have some tough decisions. The first one is probably the most important.

■ **What would that be? Oh, I bet I can guess. How old is old enough?**

You're right, and of course, everything depends on the maturity of the individual child. But you'll probably find, as Virginia did, that a minimum age of four is a good rule of thumb. Along with that rule comes a promise to the younger ones that their time will come.

A situation may arise where the grandchild will not want to go or isn't ready to leave Mom and Dad at home. Fine. Chances are the child will be ready next year. On the other hand, there may be a child who you *know* isn't ready, even if he and his parents think he is. In that case an overnight trial run would be appropriate.

Try to be as objective as possible when assessing your chances of success on a longer vacation. Miracles happen, and a child who seems hopelessly unready for a long trip away may turn out to be the best traveling companion ever. But if homesickness is potent, he probably won't be able to handle the trip for now. It's kinder to promise another trip next year and a lovely gift when you return from your trip to ease the disappointment.

■ **Should I take just one grandchild, or should I get really brave and take along two or three?**

If you have more than one grandchild, you must decide ahead of time how many you want to take because when a trip is mentioned, all your grandchildren will line up to go. Obviously you'll want to give them all a turn in a way that's fair and appropriate because you love them all. But the following guidelines that Virginia has come up with over the years will help you decide how many to take on each vacation.

- ▶ **Taking one grandchild at a time is unquestionably the easiest and most desirable option.** Nothing can replace that one-on-one relationship, especially during a child's early years.
- ▶ **If you have several grandchildren, you can still enjoy traveling with them . . . it just takes a little more planning.** You can keep the peace among the children by dividing your vacation time into smaller segments (maybe keeping one vacation just for you) and taking one child on each trip. That way, you'll be able to give and receive that all-important love and attention every person longs for.

■ **What should I do if my grandchild becomes homesick? We'll be a long way from home.**

No matter how well you plan or how close you are with a grand-child, problems can appear without warning. Darkness falls. The day is over. Tucked down in her hotel bed, Susie has visions of her home and little terrier dog. Did Mom remember to feed him? There is a big lump in her throat. It gets bigger and bigger. She can hardly breathe, and then the tears start.

What can Grandma do? Just what comes naturally. Put your arms around her, cuddle her closely, talk soothingly. Try to tell her that you know what she feels. Validate those feelings. Talking it out or getting involved in a new activity goes a long way to alleviate even the worst homesick attack. You might suggest that she draw a picture of her family and her pets. A telephone call home usually helps a lot as well.

This chapter is adapted from Have Grandchildren, Will Travel *by Virginia Smith Spurlock. To order a copy, call Pilot Books at its toll-free number: (800) 79 PILOT.*

Greater Love
Hath No Man

Editor's note: Here's an inspirational story that gives you a window into how grandchildren can view their world.

The Miracle

The violent grinding of brakes suddenly applied, and the harsh creaking of skidding wheels died as the big car came to a sudden stop. Little Eddie quickly picked himself up from the dusty pavement, where he had been thrown, and looked around wildly.

Susie! Where was his little sister that he had been holding by the hand when they started across the street? The next moment, he saw her under the big car that had run them down, her eyes closed, a dark stain slowly spreading under her white sweater.

It seemed like forever before the sirens announced the arrival of help. Susie was quickly examined, delicately put on a stretcher, then loaded into the ambulance. Little Eddie was allowed to ride in the back with her, and he held her hand all the way to the hospital. Something about the sturdy, shabbily dressed boy, who could not be more than ten years old, and his devotion to his little sister strangely touched the hearts of the hardened EMTs.

"We must operate at once," said the surgeon after a preliminary examination. "She has been injured internally and has lost a great deal of blood."

Eddie sat in the waiting room while the surgeons worked on Susie. After what seemed like an eternity, a nurse came looking for him.

"Eddie," she said kindly, "your sister is very badly hurt, and the doctor wants to make a transfusion. Do you know what that is?"

Eddie shook his head.

"She has lost so much blood that she cannot live unless someone gives her blood," she explained. "Will you do that for her?"

Eddie's wan face grew paler, and he gripped the arms of the chair so hard that his knuckles became white. For a moment he hesitated; then gulping back his tears, he nodded his head and stood up.

"That's a good boy," said the nurse, as she whisked him away to the elevator and the operating room. No one spoke to Eddie except the nurse who directed him in a low voice how to prepare for the ordeal. The boy bit his quivering lip and silently obeyed.

"Are you ready?" asked a man swathed in white from head to foot, turning from the table over which he had been bending. For the first time Eddie noticed who it was lying there so still. Little Susie! And he was going to make her well.

Two hours later, the surgeon looked up with a weary smile. "I think she's going to pull through," he said.

"That's wonderful news, Doctor," exclaimed one of the young interns. "A miracle!" Nothing, he thought, could be greater than the miracles of science.

After the transfusion, Eddie had been told to lie quietly on a cot in the corner of the room. In the excitement of the delicate operation, he had been entirely forgotten. As the doctor turned to explain the good news, he was caught off-guard when Eddie quietly asked, "When do I die?"

"Die, what do you mean, Son?" the doctor asked.

"I thought . . . when they took someone's blood . . . he died," whispered Eddie.

The smiles faded from the lips of the doctor and the nurses, and the young intern who had thought there was nothing greater than the miracle of modern science caught his breath as well.

This little soft-spoken lad had climbed to the very heights of devotion and sacrifice, and he had showed them a glimpse of the greatest miracle of all—selfless love!

**Greater love hath no man than this
That he lay down his life!**

This story comes courtesy of Rolf Benirschke of San Diego.

6

Your and
Your World

1

Calling All
Volunteers

. . . .

■ When I hear the words "Can you do me a favor?" my guard
goes up. I mentally calculate my own commitments: work, shopping, weeding, car repairs, and lunch with friends. Who has time
for favors? The lady next door, maybe. Who me? Volunteer? I
wish I wasn't too busy to run PTAs and help the elderly.

Maybe people are too busy, but we shouldn't be. Programmed
excuses roll off our tongues so swiftly that sometimes it seems volunteerism has reached the endangered-species list, and in some suburbs, volunteers are as rare as stay-at-home moms. But a Gallup poll
revealed that nearly 50 percent of all Americans said they were
involved in volunteer or charity work, nor is volunteering a province
of the idle rich: Nearly a quarter of all volunteers come from households with incomes of $20,000 or less. The average volunteer offers
nearly five hours a week—a staggering amount considering all the
time pressures families face these days.

Volunteers can be found in every walk of life: some are in international organizations, others are tucked away in unknown niches
of society. For many, volunteerism is a lifetime commitment, for
others a brief, spontaneous gesture. Some volunteer as teachers'
aides or pink ladies, others pitch in at soup kitchens. You'll see soccer

moms coaching their sons' teams, Red Cross volunteers at disaster areas, Marines collecting Toys for Tots, and strangers administering CPR to accident victims. Think of where our small towns and rural areas would be without volunteer firefighters.

■ **Now that the kids have left the nest, I'm ready to donate my time and energy where needed. Where are some good places to look?**

Anywhere around you. Churches have a huge need for extra help. Hands are needed to stuff envelopes, fold church bulletins, stuff inserts, vacuum the fellowship hall, set up chairs, drive seasoned citizens to church, staff the information booth, teach in Sunday School, serve on the deacon and elder boards—the list could fill this chapter!

When you volunteer at church, look at it like it's your own ministry. *You're in the Lord's service.* Let Him use you and your talents to show the love of Christ in your life. Let Him use your energy in the service of His church. After all if it's not you volunteering, then who will it be?

This is not to discount the needs outside the church. Helen is an outgoing Christian widow in her early sixties who leads Bible study groups and women's retreats. She's also aware of the social needs beyond the church's perimeter. A few years ago, a friend told her about the Court-Appointed Special Advocate (CASA) program that works on behalf of abused and neglected children. A CASA volunteer acts as the child's advocate during the long court process.

"I felt it would be a good place to make a difference in lives," Helen says. "It was a chance to witness without ever mentioning Christ's name because I was free to pray and love these families." Helen spends quality time with each child (sometimes at the park or out for a sandwich); monitors visits with siblings and parents; and reviews the social files as well as school, medical, and judicial records of the child. She also meets with the parents. "Although they know I may have to advocate against them, they see me as a friend—an independent person hearing their side."

Sometimes she recommends parenting classes to help them become adequate parents—not perfect but adequate. Helen's court reports and recommendations, made with the best interests of the child in mind, often help the judge determine the child's permanent placement, whether back in the home or with a foster or adoptive family.

■ **My mother is in her eighties and has volunteered all her life. She's been slowed down in recent years, but what could she do to help out?**

Some volunteers can accomplish incredible things without leaving home. Consider the story of eighty-nine-year-old Mildred, a robust great-grandmother who prays daily for missionaries.

Widowed early in her marriage, Mildred worked as a secretary in the Wheaton College business office for twenty years. When she retired, she headed west. With time to indulge her interest in missions, she became an enthusiastic correspondent and prayer warrior for missionaries. To keep good records, Mildred began a prayer portfolio. On one side were letters and information on missionaries in America; on the other side were missionaries in other lands.

"I alternate between the two," she explained. "Praying one day for home missions, the next for foreign." The pages

GETTING A START

Here are some addresses and phone numbers of national volunteer organizations:

American Cancer Society
1599 Clifton Rd NE
Atlanta, GA 30329
(404) 320-3333

National Braille Association
3 Town Line Circle
Rochester, NY 14623-2513
(716) 427-8260

International Union of Gospel Missions
1045 Swift
Kansas City, MO 64116
(800) 624-5156

Literacy Volunteers of America
635 James St.
Syracuse, NY 13203
(315) 472-0001

Mothers Against Drunk Drivers (MADD)
P.O. Box 541688
Dallas, TX 75354-1688
(214) 744-MADD

Prison Fellowship Ministries
P.O. Box 17500
Washington, DC 20041-0500
(703) 478-0100

Salvation Army
(800) SAL-ARMY

were filled with dates and prayer answers in Mildred's unsteady handwriting. "I date them so I can remember which group I'm praying for," she says.

Then there are people like Barbara Sulzbach, the founding president of a local adult day-care center. Barbara, active in countless community voluntary activities, may be short in stature, but she's large of heart. Married to a podiatrist and the mother of three grown children, she's volunteered for years at the center.

When she worked one-on-one with the elderly, she leaned forward—close, personal—as she talked with them. She helped them in their arts and crafts, assisted at mealtimes, relieved their apprehensions, and simply stood by as their friend. The response of the participants, many in wheelchairs and walkers, was payment enough.

"Volunteering at the adult day-care center," says Barbara, "is so much a part of my life that I wouldn't feel complete if I didn't come here."

The staff wouldn't feel complete either. Mallory Vega, the center's director, says, "Our volunteers are like little holiday sparklers. They provide us with their burst of energy and lighten the load. With their help, we're able to offer more activities for our participants and make this a happy, positive environment."

■ **I'm ready to turn my attention toward giving something back to the community. What are some good ideas?**

Volunteers are needed everywhere. Have you thought about helping with a Red Cross blood drive? You don't have to worry about being squeamish because volunteers are needed to help donors fill out medical forms.

Volunteer professionals are needed to produce materials in Braille, large print, and on tapes for the visually impaired. Have you thought about working as a docent at your local museum? Leading schoolchildren on tours can be rewarding.

Volunteers are also needed behind the scenes, helping file historical materials and books. If you have the gift for ministry, consider assisting families who have lost a loved one to a drunk driver. Or if you're a business professional, share your expertise in tax preparation and budgeting.

Crisis pregnancy centers desperately need volunteers. Your participation here can save a life—and there's no greater feeling! Other ministries counsel those who are going through post-abortion syndrome. For volunteer church and missionary opportunities, contact your home church, denominational headquarters, or an independent mission.

Finally, check under "Volunteer Centers" or "Volunteer Bureaus" in your phone directory or under "Social Service Organizations" in the Yellow Pages. An adventure is just a phone call away.

This chapter is adapted from writings by Doris Elaine Fall and Gloria Dvorak.

DON'T FORGET SENIOR CITIZENS

by Gloria Dvorak

Did you know that the number of people sixty-five and older climbed 100 percent between the years 1960 and 1994? This burgeoning population means more senior care will be required on the part of families and churches, and this can be an area of ministry for volunteers.

In fact, many older men and women are self-sufficient and want to help the aged. "It's not how many years we live, but what we do with them," said Evangeline Booth, former general and international leader of The Salvation Army. Besides, who wants to sit at home in a rocking chair? That's why we're seeing seniors volunteer their time at church, school, clubs, hospitals, and child-care centers.

I know many retired people who say they wish they had more time in the day to fit everything in. There are some seniors, however, whose bodies do not allow them to lead very active lives. They are confined to their homes, wheelchairs, or nursing homes. Although their flesh is weak, their minds are still active. Since the church can be a big help in offering activities for these seniors, here are some ideas:

1. Organize periodic "shut-in-days" in which church members visit seniors who are unable to attend a church service. You can share a short Bible study, sing, read, or show them a video.

2. Organize a senior lunch day once a month and bring in speakers to talk about interesting subjects such as health, travel, exercise, and investments.

3. Organize a foster grandparent program. Some younger families, without grandparents nearby, would love to "adopt" a foster grandparent.

4. Organize tours. Can the church bus take a seniors group to a play, concert, or dinner theater? How about a trip to Branson, Missouri?

2

Champs for Children

. . . .

When it comes to raising the next generation, most parents and grandparents understand that we get what we put into it. We usually don't see the fruit of our labors for ten, twenty, even thirty years later.

But what about children who didn't receive love, or parental guidance, at home? The following five men—John Croyle, Ron Evans, Bob Muzikowski, Bill Wilson, and Larry Jones—have poured their lives into young people without expecting anything in return. If you ever spend time with them, you'd see they wouldn't have it any other way.

Sure they'll tell you they've received much joy knowing they've made a difference. But think about it: As the children they ministered to grew older, much of their interaction ended. Those young people went off to college, started careers, fell in love, married, and began raising families of their own. Meanwhile contact dwindled to a few scattered phone calls or a Christmas card.

None of that matters to this group, who have heroically given of themselves to the next generation. As you ponder your retirement years and if the Lord could be calling you into some type of ministry, let their stories inspire you:

John Croyle
Age: forty-seven
Family: married to Teresa for twenty-three years; father of Reagan, twenty, and Brodie, sixteen
Residence: Gadsden, AL
Ministry: founder of the Big Oak Ranch, a Christian home for children needing a chance

Back in 1974, John Croyle was a quick-off-the-snap defensive end at the University of Alabama during the glory years of Coach Paul "Bear" Bryant. In John's final game, the Crimson Tide lost a squeaker—and its national championship hopes—to Notre Dame, 24–23, in the Sugar Bowl.

The next step was an all-expenses-paid-trip to the NFL. John was *that* good, but he saw professional football as a means to an end. When John was nineteen, he spent a summer as a counselor at King's Arrow Ranch, a Christian summer camp in Mississippi. He met a twelve-year-old boy from New Orleans whose mom was a prostitute. Talking about helping out at home: the boy was the banker and time-keeper while his mom "serviced" the clientele.

John sensed the boy's deep hunger to be loved, and when he befriended him, the boy blossomed and accepted Christ after hearing John present the Gospel. "I realized I had been given a gift—a gift that helped a boy who felt worthless to feel loved," John remembers. At that moment, he knew his calling in life was to help kids like that boy from New Orleans.

Upon John's graduation from Alabama, he discussed his plans to play pro ball and start a boy's home with Bear Bryant, figuring he would plow his NFL paycheck into his ministry. The revered 'Bama coach made an observation that changed John's life: "Don't play professional football unless you're willing to marry it," said Bryant.

John Croyle wasn't willing to eat, breathe, and you-know-what NFL football.

When a friend, John Hannah (an All-Pro center for the New England Patriots) heard about John's desire to start a boy's home, he made the down payment on an 120-acre ranch in Gadsden, Alabama. John and five boys lived in a dilapidated farmhouse, and the journey began. He loved, disciplined, fed, clothed, hugged, bathed, and stayed up late with kids who had been literally abandoned by their parents. It wasn't unusual, he recounts, for a parent to pull into the driveway and announce that he or she was leaving the child with John—just like that and without any prior arrangements.

Despite his selfless attitude, John doesn't want to be painted as God's gift to unwanted children. "I've made every mistake you can make as a man, a husband, and a father," he says. "But there came a time in my life when I drew a line in the sand and said 'no more.' And that's what I tell anyone I meet: It's never too late to be a good man, a good husband, and a good father, no matter what your past is like."

Last year, John hired Keith Denton, a strapping twenty-five-year-old, to be his director of development. When Keith speaks before groups, he often tells the story of a ten-year-old boy who was dropped off at Big Oak Ranch by a mama who said she could no longer raise him. The boy's world was shattered, but John and his Big Oak Ranch houseparents took the boy in and loved him. He blossomed as a student and graduated from a Christian high school as valedictorian, entertaining scholarship offers from Harvard, Princeton, and West Point.

"He chose the latter school, and later transferred to Birmingham Southern, where he graduated summa cum laude despite working thirty hours a week to put himself through school," says Keith. "He's been happily married for two years to a beautiful wife, and life has never looked better.

"The reason I can tell you this story is because that ten-year-old boy was me! I felt worthless when my mother gave me away and didn't want me, but the Lord used the Big Oak Ranch to dramatically change my life. The Lord has really blessed me and enabled me to be a success."

Yes, the Lord has blessed your life, Keith, and it's due to folks like John Croyle.

For more information, contact the Big Oak Ranch at 250 Jake Mintz Rd., Gadsden, AL 35905, or call (256) 892-0773.

Bob Muzikowski

Age: forty-one

Family: married to Tina for eleven years; father of six ranging in age from ten to two

Residence: Chicago, IL

Outreach: organizes Little League baseball leagues in the inner city

Growing up, Bob Muzikowski loved to run through the streets of Newark (yes, Newark), so when he moved to Chicago about 10 years ago, he continued to jog throughout the Windy City.

His route often took him through the West Side, home of massive public housing projects such as Cabrini Green and Rockwell Gardens. From the sidewalk, he saw a world without hope: decaying high-rise apartments with addicts huddled in the alcoves, coming down off a high, and kids who always looked over their shoulders, lest they be caught in the crossfire of another gang shoot-out.

"I did a lot of thinking when I was jogging, and to me, this was just like the story of the Good Samaritan," said Bob. "I could either continue running by, or I could stop and help out."

But what could he—an insurance salesman with a young family—do for fatherless, inner-city kids? During one afternoon jog, Bob noticed an abandoned ballfield in Cabrini. *If I build it, will they come?* Bob thought, having seen *Field of Dreams* a couple of years earlier.

So he built it. Bob Muzikowski started a Little League program in the inner city from the infield up, and he volunteered himself as the first coach. Others joined in the effort, but from the first practice, there was something different about this Little League. Normally when coaches show up before the game, they rake the infield and pitch batting practice. Muzikowski and the other coaches had extra duties, such as picking up the broken glass, used needles, and condom wrappers in the dugouts.

When the umpire yelled, "Play ball!" games were interrupted by gunfire. "One time gang members drove by the park going fifty miles per hour and sprayed the field," remembers Bob. "We all hit the deck." Fortunately, no one was hurt, but when the inaugural season was over, his first basemen took a bullet to the head. The grandmother called Bob for a ride to the coroner's office so she could ID the boy. "Mom was in prison and Dad was missing in action," said Bob.

This all happened eight years ago. As people heard about the changed lives and offered to help, Bob started a second Little League program in Chicago and one in New York City's East Harlem. The three leagues, which last from April to Labor Day, provide 1,000 boys with a chance to play ball—and be loved. Many of the coaches are Christians, and the games open and close with prayer. "We may be politically incorrect, but that's what we do," says Bob.

Muzikowski, whose small insurance brokerage business pays the bills, says several of his clients are coaches. This is how it works: When Bob approaches a downtown company like Merrill Lynch or Morgan Guaranty Trust and asks them to sponsor a team, he won't accept their check unless two employees volunteer to coach the team.

"I don't know who gets more out of it, the coaches or the kids," said Bob. "The coaches—yuppies, for the most part—would never have relationships with kids from the inner city, but when we put them together, it's something to see how lives are changed on both sides of the equation. The corporate sponsors pay $1,500, and for that amount, the kids get uniforms, equipment, and a week at a Christian summer camp."

One coach, Bennett Wong, didn't know a catcher's mitt from a catcher's cup when he began coaching, but he took a shine to one of his twelve-year-old players, Awvee Storey. When Bennett saw how the fatherless boy was left to fend for himself after the games, he began inviting him to spend the night. He and his wife later adopted the boy, who turned out to be a very good basketball player. Awvee is playing basketball at the University of Illinois, and his future is bright, thanks to a full-ride scholarship at a Big 10 school. "But he'd be dead if Bennett hadn't taken him in," said Bob.

There's one more amazing story about Bob Muzikowski you should know. Seven years ago, he and his family moved into a brownstone in the West Side, not far from the Rockwell diamonds. In other words, they live in the 'hood. During the summer months, it's not unusual for a half-dozen kids to knock on the door after dinnertime.

"They always say, 'Coach Bob, we're locked out.' So what am I supposed to say to that?" asked Muzikowski.

Bob always shrugs his shoulders. "Come on in, guys," he says. "I think Tina still has some chili on the stove. . . ."

Bob Muzikowski's latest goal is to open a Christian junior high and high school in Chicago's West Side. Contact him at (312) 781-2739 for more information or to help out.

Ron Evans
Age: fifty-three
Family: married to Pearl for twenty-eight years; father of
William Jr., twenty-seven, and Devon, eighteen
Residence: Camden, NJ
Outreach: counseling boys and young men in the inner city

In the spring of 1991, Ron Evans was invited by his pastor, the
Rev. John O. Parker of Antioch Baptist Church, to discuss the
start-up of Project Manhood, a community-church effort to mentor street-savvy and often fatherless boys. The pair met with the
Rev. Sheldon Nix, the program's founder and executive director.

Ron and Pastor Parker learned that six Camden churches would
begin Project Manhood at the same time. Ron, who had served
some jail time for drug use, felt led to get involved but he also felt
inadequate because he had been raised without a father.

As he readied himself to minister to young boys, Ron hung on to
the verse, "Not by My power, nor by My might, but by My spirit,
says the Lord." After studying Dr. Nix's curriculum, attending sem-
inars, and talking to anyone he could about ministering to boys,
Ron felt that God had prepared him for an important mission.

When Project Manhood started, Ron found himself in the basement of Antioch Baptist Church with twenty boys, ages six to
twenty, many of whom had never seen the inside of a church.
Although he and Gene Alford would show up on Thursday nights
at 6 P.M. to talk—and listen—to these youngsters off the street,
Project Manhood failed to get off the ground in the other five
churches for various reasons. No matter. These godly men would
wrap their arms around a troubled teen's shoulders and counsel
him, saying he could and would do better, that a man takes responsibility for his life, and Christ is the answer.

After several months of helping out kids on Thursday nights,
Ron's friend dropped out, however, and suddenly Ron was Project
Manhood. If he didn't show up, more than a dozen kids would be
taught that night by the streets. That didn't cut it for Ron Evans.

These kids needed godly direction, and Ron was going to provide
it, whether he had anyone helping him or not. He drove a church
van, crisscrossing Camden, to bring boys to Project Manhood, then

he would drive them home. Since he didn't own a car, Ron depended on a friend to come by the church at 11 P.M. for a ride home.

Then there were the once-a-month Saturday outings to a baseball game or a skating rink—wherever Ron could scrounge up some free tickets. He helped hundreds of kids like James, who was having all kinds of problems at home and at school. "James was eleven or twelve when we first got him," remembers Ron. "I went to his school and worked to resolve situations, then Brother Ed became a surrogate father to James. Today, he is one of the most consistently well-mannered boys who's active in the church choir, singing praises to the Lord."

"Brother Ed" is Ed Hemmings, who, along with William Ward, Jr., and Brian Tomlinson, came alongside Ron when he needed it most. That's good because Ron suffered a stroke a couple of years ago that left him partially paralyzed on his left side. There was a time when he was not expected to walk unaided.

But that hasn't slowed him down. Today Ron is also the Prison Fellowship coordinator in his area, ministering to families of incarcerated men and women, visiting teens and adults in jail and leading Bible studies behind bars, all in his "spare time."

So why does he do it?

"My heart is with young people," Ron says. "I have a sensitivity to what they are going through. I think about my own childhood, and I can feel what they are feeling."

Ron says he persevered when he was all alone because "Camden is a real devastated city, and we were finding that children were being destroyed before they even left elementary school. They were learning manhood in the streets. After the time we spent with them, they came to realize the true meaning of manhood, which is synonymous with Jesus Christ."

Ron shakes his head. "Kids are pretty much left to raise themselves these days, and that's a tough thing to do in the inner city with all the pressures and violence and drugs. We have to fight for our children!"

As you can see, Ron Evans fights for kids—all week long. He is no weekend warrior.

Ron Evans has received calls from all over the country asking how to begin Project Manhood ministries in their community. Call him at (609) 541-5871 for more information.

Bill Wilson
Age: forty-nine
Residence: Brooklyn, NY
Ministry: founder of Metro Ministries, an outreach to New York's inner city

Another warrior in inner-city ministry is the Rev. Bill Wilson, who blew out his voice years ago after "street preaching" for four and five hours a pop when he was in his twenties.

His raspy voice may be as gritty as the New York streets that are home to Metro Ministries, but that hasn't dimmed Bill's effectiveness. After nearly two decades in the trenches, Bill has reached tens of thousands of kids for Christ, and with the help of staffers and volunteers, Metro Ministries has become *the* model for inner-city ministry. Today, there are more than 400 "Metro Ministries" in the U.S. alone, as well as a hundred more in England, Ireland, the Netherlands, Italy, Asia, Australia . . . well, you get the idea.

In case you haven't heard of it, Metro has two distinctives in reaching young people:

1. Buses. Metro Ministries' bus ministry sends out fifty buses and ten "Sidewalk Sunday School" trucks six days a week to "gather the harvest." Their storehouses are overflowing because more than 20,000 kids attend various "Sunday Schools" held during the week.

2. Visitations. Each of those 20,000 children is visited every week by either Bill, 100 staff members, or 300 volunteers. "The key is consistency," said Bill. "We're not commuting in from the suburbs. We live here in Brooklyn. You have to earn the right to be heard; otherwise, you have nothing to say. We're all paying the price."

Personally, Bill has paid a hefty bill. He's been physically threatened, stabbed twice, had his jaw and ribs broken, shot at, and witnessed twenty-one murders. Nonetheless, he lives inside one of the church buildings—nothing more than reconditioned warehouse—and is America's answer to Mother Teresa.

Bill still drives Bus 12, cramming 100 kids on his sixty-six-seat bus as he delivers them to "Saturday Sunday School." Each child's hand is marked with his bus number so he or she won't get lost. Metro Ministries' fleet of ramshackle buses drive through four of New York's five boroughs. "If we are invading soldiers in enemy territory, the buses are the tanks," says Bill. "Besides, our whole premise of ministry is prevention versus intervention. I often say that I'm not so concerned about what our kids become as I'm concerned about what they do not become. The coming of age in the inner city is eleven, and if you haven't gotten to them by that age, it's not going to happen. That's why we go for the kids as young as we can."

Need proof? Then watch Bill's video called "Streets of Pain." One segment showed a couple of female druggies—with filthy hands, dirty clothes, and chipped teeth—shooting themselves up with heroin. The camera lingered for a minute or two as one woman worked the needle into a vein just below the right elbow. "I wish I didn't have to do this, but I do," said the woman as she grimaced.

In another segment, Bill interviewed a prostitute in her basement hovel—you wouldn't want your dog to live there—where she plied her trade. She told Bill that she wished she could get off drugs so she wouldn't have to give men oral sex for $10. Then there was the segment in which Bill visited a homeless guy in his cardboard lean-to right off the Hudson River. The man broke down as he recounted the time diarrhea soiled his only pair of pants. "Do you know how sickening that is?" cried the man.

Bill does, because he was there to reach out and remind him that Jesus loved him and was his only hope.

That's why Bill spends so much investing in the lives of young people; he doesn't want them to grow up sticking heroin-filled needles in their veins or selling their bodies or messing in their only pair of pants. He wants to win them to the Lord.

For more information, write Metro Ministries, P.O. Box 695, Brooklyn, NY 11237, or call (718) 453-3352.

Larry Jones
Age: fifty-seven
Residence: Oklahoma City
Family: married to Frances for thirty-six years, two adult children
Ministry: Feed the Children, which distributes food, medicine, clothes, and goods to the poor and hungry

Growing up in Kentucky in the 1950s, when Adolph Rupp's Wildcats at the University of Kentucky were huge, Larry Jones wanted to be a basketball player. Like Pete Maravich, he dribbled a basketball everywhere he went.

Larry was raised in a Christian home with parents who took him to church three times a week. At the age of twelve, he accepted Christ at Vacation Bible School and filled out a pledge card, noting that he felt the Lord was calling him to become a minister.

"I said yes to Him on Friday night, but the next morning, I didn't want to be a preacher, so I went to my pastor and asked him to take my name off that card," said Larry. "I wanted to do what I wanted to do, and that was to become a basketball player."

Just before his senior year, Larry was a shoe-in for a full ride to Vanderbilt, Air Force Academy, or basketball's mecca—the University of Kentucky. But in an early season game, Larry came down hard on a dribble-drive and suffered a terrible compound fracture. His college basketball dreams were as shattered as the bones in his right wrist.

"I literally got on my knees and put that broken wrist on my bed and prayed to God," recalls Larry. "I said, 'Lord, I've basically done what I've wanted to do for seventeen years. Now I give my broken wrist and broken life to You.'"

Life changed in many ways since Larry uttered that prayer on December 3, 1957. After high school, he enrolled at Oklahoma City University, where he could take pre-ministerial courses. A coach named Abe Lemons was looking for players, and Larry got back into the game.

"Isn't it amazing?" he says. "After I gave my life to Him, God gave me back basketball. Following college, I played on Venture for Victory, a forerunner of Athletes in Action. We played basketball overseas and shared our testimonies at halftime. Little did I know that God was preparing me for what I do now."

What Larry does now is oversee the efforts of Feed the Children, a hunger relief organization based in Oklahoma City. It all began about twenty years ago when Larry was attending an evangelistic meeting in Haiti. Outside his hotel, a young Haitian boy asked him for a nickel so he could buy a slice of bread. The boy said he hadn't eaten that day, and Larry believed him.

Larry handed the lad a nickel, but as he kept walking to the hotel, he thought about the surplus wheat stored in dozens of Oklahoma silos. When he returned to Oklahoma City, he began asking around for extra wheat, and farmers said they would give it away if someone could haul if off. Then truck drivers who heard his story offered to drive the wheat to Miami, where it could be shipped to Haiti. More and more surplus wheat was donated, and suddenly Larry was acting as a middleman between food producers and government and charitable organizations. Today Larry oversees a nonprofit organization that accepts donations of leftover food, medical supplies, clothes, and toys. Feed the Children's trucks—they have forty-three semis crisscrossing the country—pick up and deliver everything from canned vegetables, hams, water purification tablets, coats, powdered milk, Christmas candy, and even new food products that flopped in the marketplace. The foodstuffs and goods are delivered to Red Cross chapters, Salvation Army offices, Federal Emergency Management (FEMA) shelters, and international hunger relief organizations. Eighty percent of the food is distributed in the United States, the rest internationally.

Because of its high impact, Feed the Children has attracted the support of numerous pro athletes, country singers, and celebrities. Perhaps the most notable is country artist Garth Brooks, who asks concertgoers to bring enough canned food to fill up one of Feed the Children eighteen-wheelers. Other notables who pitch in are Reba McEntire, Willie Nelson, and Dallas Cowboys Troy Aikman and Emmitt Smith.

Could the next person to help out be you?

For more information, call the Feed the Children offices at (800) 627-4566.

This chapter is adapted from writings by Mike Yorkey.

3

Foster Parenting: With Love to Spare

. . . .

■ **We married in our early twenties, had two kids right away, raised them well, ushered them into adulthood, and all my husband and I can say to each other is, "Wow, that went fast!" Our child-raising days are over, and we don't want them to be over. When we were talking about this at our couple's Bible study, a friend suggested foster parenting, and my husband and I looked at each other and said, "This could work." We are now in the investigation phase. What should we know about foster parenting?**

Foster parenting is all about investing patience and tenderness that pays big dividends in a child's life.

Ask Don and Helen Gibbons, both in their fifties, about foster parenting. They have cared for ten youngsters in their Southern California home for several years. At the moment, they have four foster children: three sisters and two-year-old Michael.

Michael stretches out his arms. He wants to be held. Never mind that the Sunday morning visitor is a complete stranger—up, up, up go the arms, accompanied by a humming *p-l-e-a-s-e* sound. "He'll con anyone who'll give him attention," says Don. Indeed, foster babies have a certain tenacity—they quickly learn to get what they want.

Nearby, beguiling Janie, age four, wants her patronizing foster mom to "kiss lips." She has her own con game—a legitimate way of getting lipstick smeared on her face. Meanwhile, Don patiently buckles her three-year-old sister's shiny black patent leather shoes with a warning: "Leave them on this time!" Undaunted, the wily foster daughter affectionately strokes Don's thin, white beard as he leans toward her.

"Ready, set, out the door!" Don barks gently. Dressed in a checkered blue shirt, sporting an oversized silver belt buckle and a cache of keys dangling high above his gray boots, Don quickly hustles a carload of kids into infant seats and safety belts. "It's off to church we go!" he announces.

■ How did the Gibbons get involved in foster parenting?

A program at their neighborhood church enticed the Gibbons, parents of three grown children and three grandchildren, to try foster parenting. "We wanted to do what we could for children who are often abused, nearly starved, molested, and hungry for love," says Helen.

The need is great. More foster parents, like the Gibbons, are needed as court-ordered care increases throughout the United States. Illinois had a 32 percent rise in the demand for foster homes during one recent year. At the same time, the number of licensed homes fell in Illinois.

On a single day in New York City, several hundred children wait for placement, but beds for them can be found only one night at a time. Meanwhile, another 300 "boarder babies" born to drug-addicted mothers are kept in hospital care. Nationwide, an estimated 300,000 children under age eighteen are in substitute care; more than half were teenagers.

"Little people without a support system," Mary Rotzien calls them. Several years ago, while still an intern in clinical psychology at Fuller Theological Seminary in Pasadena, California—and also pregnant with her first child—Mary sensed God's call to do something about the escalating number of institutionalized children.

Mary and her husband, Brian, launched a foster family recruitment and support system specifically for the Christian community. They sketched the plan for Child SHARE (Shelter Homes: A Rescue Effort) on a paper napkin. Today, this innovative organization draws together foster parent "shareholders," volunteers, consultants, and financial partners.

Networking with about fifty Los Angeles churches, SHARE recruits 40 percent of the foster homes certified by the city's Children's Bureau.

"Families provide a healing ministry," says Mary. "It's traumatic for a child not to develop trusting relationships. When they have no concept of God's love during the early years, it's harder to accept a loving Savior later in life. I have a strong conviction that Christians must be responsible for these children."

■ **What do foster parents get paid by the state? Is it enough to even pay for the cereal?**

Although foster-parenting compensation varies widely throughout the United States, most agencies agree it's little more than token pay. Often children arrive directly from a police station with the clothes on their backs, or just wrapped in diapers and a blanket. The first family outing may be a shopping trip not only for clothes, but for baby furniture, toys, and basic medical supplies.

Some costs are not so obvious. To qualify for foster care, a family might be required to add additional bedrooms, enclose their yard, or fence a backyard pool. But, as Don Gibbons points out, those who expect to "make money, quick-fix the custody system, or straighten

BASIC REQUIREMENTS FOR LICENSED FOSTER PARENTING

In order to be considered for foster parenting, you should:

► be in good health (negative TB tests for all family members)
► meet your state's home safety requirements
► have sufficient financial income for present family needs
► have emotional stability and good character references
► have no criminal record (fingerprints required)
► have sufficient bedrooms
► be willing to work with social workers
► agree to discipline without physical punishment
► agree to attend foster-parenting workshops

out kids in short order are going to be disappointed." He recommends potential foster parents just concentrate on giving patience, time, and love—lots of each.

Health officials estimate that one-fourth to one-third of infants born with AIDS will not be cared for by their biological parents. In addition, children who are difficult to place in adoption—the handicapped, the high-risk (including drug babies), those who come from minority backgrounds, and those older than the more-in-demand infants—are relegated to institutional care unless a foster family takes them in.

Children abruptly removed from their birth parents bring hefty challenges to foster parents. Drug babies, who are usually "preemies," show little response to stimulation, suck poorly, cry a lot, and need a body-bonding papoose.

Preschool children may have nightmares or be susceptible to contagious diseases. School-age children are apt to be slow learners. Nearly all have sustained abuse or neglect. Older youngsters often rebel, threaten authority, and use foul language.

■ **Why do nonrelated adults voluntarily take on the gargantuan task of helping these children learn more constructive social patterns? Why do foster parents invite estranged kids into their intimate family circle?**

Some see this personalized ministry as a statement about the universal sanctity of human life. While right-to-life rallies focus on preventing abortion, foster care affirms that God's grace is intended from conception to death. Preventing abortion preserves life until birth, but Christian concern for an infant's growth and development dramatically affects the quality of ongoing life.

Seniors who have an empty nest may prefer a short-term responsibility with occasional breaks in parenting demands. For various reasons, Christian foster parents usually come back for more! In the Los Angeles area, Child SHARE finds that over half take another child, and most of the other 50 percent volunteer in a support capacity.

Perhaps so many repeat foster parenting through Child SHARE because the program draws on the resources of the whole church community. Legally certified backup parents offer respite weekends.

"Investors" baby-sit while parents attend choir practice—or just have a night out.

Other volunteers provide transportation, maintain an equipment co-op, and agree to pray for parents and their temporary offspring. And consultants offer professional services to SHARE parents—medical, legal, or counseling aid.

Christians are most apt to see beyond the physical care to the spiritual nurturing foster parenting can provide. Don and Helen Gibbons pray to instill a love for God in their ever-changing family.

One pastor who helped launch the fledgling interdenominational SHARE ministry gave thanks as he looked down from his pulpit on a white woman nuzzling a black infant. After he dedicated that foster baby to the Lord, he prayed for the parents, quoting from the Gospel of Luke: "Jesus said, 'Anyone who takes care of a little child like this is caring for me!' "

The Gibbons became godparents to a former foster son after he was reunited with his natural family. Although the birth mother felt threatened by the Gibbons at first, the two families bonded when they accepted each other's present ability to give.

■ **Can foster parents spank?**

Foster parents may resent that they cannot, by law, spank children who desperately need discipline. They will have to be "creative" in their punishments (no ice cream for dessert, loss of TV privileges, early to bed, etc.).

■ **What happens when the birth parents show up?**

Holiday fun and milestone events are relinquished to birth parents who may take almost no responsibility during other times of the year, and that can be emotionally difficult to handle.

Children indulged with toys, tasty treats, and unrestricted TV during weekend visits with birth parents may appear ungrateful for stricter, less exciting routine. Most foster parents agree that visits with natural parents—or even letters—seem to upset a foster child's emotional progress.

But kids cling to hope. Often children believe—or at least

fantasize—that their "own" mom or dad will make their dreams come true. Although foster parents understand that the goal is to reunite children with their natural parents, it's still the hardest thing they do. Don is close to tears when he talks about their foster godson. "Separation is the time when the healing of the church community means the most," he declares.

■ How long do children generally stay with foster parents?

Eighteen months is the median length of time a child remains in continuous substitute care. Foster parents have the opportunity to give 100 percent during this time in a needy child's life. Christians see this hands-on service as a way to share God's love. Such personalized ministry is catching! One of the Gibbons' married daughters and her husband—with two preschoolers of their own—are now licensed foster parents.

Meanwhile, at the Gibbons, little Michael has learned to raise his arms for another reason—not just to be picked up. Now, when asked, "Who do you love?" he's apt to exuberantly throw his arms high in the air and shout, "Jesus!"

■ So bottom line, how do we know that foster parenting is for us?

Go through this checklist of questions:
- ▶ Ask God for His wisdom and guidance.
- ▶ Counsel with your pastor to determine the support of your church community.
- ▶ Seek affirmation from your extended family and close friends. Ask them to give you an objective analysis of your strengths and weaknesses for a fostering ministry.
- ▶ Be honest with yourself. Consider your other commitments, time, energy, and your emotional stability in hard-to-handle situations. Do you get angry easily? Do you already feel overloaded with responsibilities?
- ▶ Do you picture having only a child of a certain age or sex?
- ▶ How long would you be willing to foster parent the same child? (Consistency is important to children.) Would you be

willing to care for a fragile or handicapped child?

► Before you enter into fostering, remember that the goal is to help restore the child to his natural family, if possible. You must be willing to graciously let go when that time comes.

► Be teachable. Foster parents often have much to learn.

This chapter is adapted from writings by Marjorie Lee Chandler of Solvang, California.

RESOURCES

► Department of Social Services: Foster Home Licensing; look under County Government offices in your local telephone directory

► Child SHARE, Joanne Feldmeth, Executive Director; 3536 Ocean View Blvd., Suite 250, Glendale, CA 91208. Phone: (818) 957-4452. Videos for churches, community, and family groups and print materials available.

If you're not able to take a foster child, you can participate in Child SHARE's work in other ways. Here are some ideas:

► **Create blankets and afghans.** Do you knit, crochet, or make quilts, or do you know of groups that would enjoy working together on this as a project?

► **Donate new items.** Infant items: clothes, stuffed animals, toys. Teenage gifts: sports equipment, beauty products, hygiene items, jewelry, journals, head sets, alarm clocks. Any age gifts: books, games, toys, music.

► **Gently used items:** Clothes: infant to seven years. Equipment: cribs, strollers, high chairs, car seats, and toys.

4

Unplugging Internet Porn

. . . .

■ You know that old saw about "You can't teach an old dog new tricks"? Well, my husband has discovered the computer, or, to be more precise, he has discovered the Internet. He's purchased one of those fancy mega-megahertz jobbies and plunked it down in his home office, and he's on that thing all day long and half the night, it seems.

One time, I walked in to peer over his shoulder—just being friendly—but before I could come around his desk, he hit some command and the screen went blank. It was like he didn't want me to see something. Was he on one of those Internet porn sites I read so much about?

He very well could have been. The Internet has exploded in the last couple of years, and as we enter a new millennium, the Internet just keeps getting *bigger.*

With the number of people using the Web approaching 100 million, some businesses are still fumbling with how to capitalize on this brand-new market, although most have figured it out quite nicely. Internet commerce is erupting before our very eyes. In 1996, Web merchandising was around $500 million, but in 2000, Internet analysts expect growth to $5 *billion* in sales. That's a *lot* of money.

Unfortunately, the Internet was built on the back of the porn industry. The most profitable areas of the Net are porn sites—places where men (and women) can see things they shouldn't, if you catch our drift. Lots of naked bodies performing sexual acts. Most Web-based pornography tends to lean toward the hard-core XXX brand: depictions of live sex—sometimes between men and women, sometimes between gays and lesbians, sometimes with animals.

Sexy centerfold pinups wearing skimpy bikinis while leaning over souped-up hot rods are long gone. And it's all there for your credit card and "the low, low price of $19.95!" Even worse, most of these sites post a lot of dirty pictures where users don't have to pay a cent, just to entice them to spend their money for the "privilege" of seeing more.

The lamentable thing is that finding these sites is easy. An innocent word search in one of the many Internet "search engines" for *Little Women,* the Louise Mary Alcott classic, will land you in a porn site dedicated to pictures of, well, *naked* little women.

If you suspect your husband is dabbling in these Internet porn areas, you will have to:

1. Ask him point blank about it, but make sure you do it in a *loving* confrontation.

2. Check "Favorite Places" or "Bookmarks" on the computer's browser to see if shortcuts are there to some of those Web porn sites. You can even look for downloaded pictures by searching for graphics files that end with .jpg or .gif. Most browsers also keep a history list of what sites have been visited. Checking that list may provide clues.

3. Look through your credit card statements for suspicious charges. Keep in mind that the entries for such activities usually look pretty innocent (you won't see a listing for "Joe's Sex Palace"), so look for unusual items or for things you don't remember buying.

Once a tool for doing the family finances or looking up information, the computer has become a tool for darkness in too many households, and all because of "cyberporn." With each click of your husband's mouse, he may be getting pulled deeper into an evil "web."

■ **Wait a minute. How worried should I be? Is there anything good about the Internet?**

Sure there is. Take bulletin boards. Photo galleries. Video viewing rooms. News. Reference material. There are plenty of good reasons to cruise cyberspace. You can log on to the Web, click the mouse, and "walk" through the Louvre Museum in Paris. Click again and view the Mona Lisa. Click again and read everything you ever wanted to know about America's Revolutionary War. The list of positive, wholesome material on the Web is endless.

Plus, our technologically driven society now *demands* a working knowledge of "virtual" interaction. The academic and business worlds use the Web for almost everything now. Research. Information. Communication. Public libraries are launching their own Web sites. And Christian ministries all over the world now use the Internet to spread the Gospel. The unique combination of mass communication and intimate contact provided by the Net has proven to be especially useful when sharing the Good News of Christ.

You can surf for months without running into anything evil or unwholesome. The problems come when you choose to venture into those dusky back alleys. And always remember that the Web is inherently unpredictable. You may be suddenly faced with a temptation to go somewhere you shouldn't, but rarely are you forced into it. You can still make your own choices.

How worried should you be? Here's the bottom line. The thing that makes Internet porn such a doozy of a problem is that it's so easy to get to. In "the old days" you had to go *way* out of your way to obtain pornography. A trip to the red light district. A walk to the adult bookstore. A secret meeting with a "dealer." And, as you might suspect, all of those types of activities were wrought with the possibility of exposure. The fear of "getting caught" kept many men far away from the evils of porn. Now, with cyberporn at everyone's finger tips in the privacy of home, that fear of getting caught is evaporating.

But your husband's character still determines what kind of choices he makes. Just because a temptation has suddenly become "accessible," doesn't mean that he will always give in to it. He may need some help (and we'll talk about that in a minute), but he may be diligently striving to do the right thing.

■ **I'm not convinced. I still think I ought to pull the plug on my husband. But I realize that just isn't going to happen in the real world. So how can I help him?**

Your husband needs to hear a pretty simple, time-honored concept—watch where you wander. Or in his case, watch where he clicks his mouse.

You can compare the Internet to a big city. When you're in a metropolitan area, you notice that there's always a juxtaposition between wide boulevards and narrow alleys, churches and night clubs, bookstores and smut shops. Where you walk becomes the important thing, not what else is out there. Sure, the evil exists, but that doesn't mean you have to walk right into its arms. And there's always help, when those temptations rear their attractive little heads. Remember, when Jesus promised His assistance and companionship, "even until the end of the age" (Matt. 28:20), He *already* knew all about the Internet. His power and friendship stretch into cyberspace too!

There are also one or two very concrete things you can do. The first is to purchase "blocking" software for the computer. Blocking software, such as Cyber Patrol, Cybersitter, SurfWatch, and Net Nanny, will keep most of the porn sites out of your husband's reach. It's not foolproof, but it is a big step in the right direction. Another option is to switch your service provider to one that promises "safe" browsing.

Many new service providers (many of them founded by Christians) block "the bad stuff" before it ever even gets to your home. Blocking software stops it *on* your computer, this stops it *before* it reaches your home. An added benefit of service provider blocking is that there is no way to force your way through their shield. You can do that with the blocking software if you're computer savvy enough.

■ **Is my husband in any real physical danger from his Web ramblings, or is he okay since he's here at home?**

He can be in danger physically if he interacts with other people on the Web. He may be putting himself—and you—at risk by sharing personal information with strangers who misrepresent themselves online. Even if all of the safety protocols are followed to the letter, the technology is available to track his location.

Marlene Maheu, a San Diego psychologist, told *USA Today* she has "clients who were stalked after being in chat rooms." She adds, "E-mail isn't even secure. Sometimes they can find your address." She's right. In fact, a man on the East Coast was beaten with a baseball bat after some of his online "friends" became angry at him, tracked down his home address, and showed up on his front porch. Imagine what an awful scene that was!

Of course, a little bit of logic and common sense will go a long way toward preventing these kinds of things from happening, but the truth is, there *are* dangers out there. Still, the most vivid danger the Internet proffers is to his mind and heart from ingesting sordid material that he would not have access to without the aid of the World Wide Web.

■ **Okay. My husband finally admitted he's been traveling through porn sites and is having other troubles online. How can we work together to help him get out—and stay out—of all that digitized danger?**

Cruising safely down the information superhighway is possible. But he'll have to use biblical standards and old-fashioned common sense. And here's the common sense part. Go over these seven ways to survive in cyberspace together, then . . . follow the advice:

1. Don't keep the computer in his home office or unused bedroom. If he places the computer in the family room or some open nook, secrecy is hard to come by. Remember: secrecy is his enemy. He should avoid it at all costs. It will be very difficult for him to view pornography with you in the same room.

2. Have him surf the Web with you. If you share this experience and become familiar with what he likes to do online, you will find out that there's a lot of good stuff out there, and he will benefit from knowing you are interested in his world. In the end, everyone's comfort level will rise.

3. Have him turn off the computer at night. Just like city streets, the Internet (especially chat rooms) is more hazardous the later you go into the night.

4. Tell him to be street smart. This means never giving out his name, address, phone number, credit card number, or any other personal information on the Web. Online purchases are becoming safer and safer as new technology arrives, but if he has been using the credit card to purchase porn, a good rule of thumb would be not to use it at all online.

5. Make sure he's very careful in those chat rooms. There are too many people who are making sexually suggestive and explicit remarks, and that can lead to sin. Too often, seemingly innocent chats turn into illicit relationships that can have lifelong consequences.

6. Obviously, don't do something stupid. "Something stupid" would be arranging a meeting with someone (usually for sexual purposes) he has "met" on the Internet.

7. Don't forget the biblical call to flee immorality. Jesus has promised that with every temptation, there is a way of escape. Fleeing immorality in this area can be as easy as purchasing some blocking software or switching to a safe service provider like we talked about earlier. If he doesn't trust himself to stay pure on his own, help him by installing the software or switching the provider yourself.

The Internet isn't something that's really so different from everything else in our lives. If we use the same rules and morality that we exercise in our "real world" lives in cyberspace, there won't be any problems. Together, you can beat the porn monster and, in the process, discover the true benefits of cyberspace.

This chapter is adapted from writings by Steven Isaac, associate editor of Plugged In, *a Focus on the Family publication that evaluates popular media, including the Internet.*

5

Room for Dessert, Pastor?

■ **Pies. Cakes. Potlucks. Picnics. As someone who could stand to lose fifteen pounds, how can we even consider staying healthy? It seems like every church get-together is just another excuse to eat, plus we lead an active social life. Any ideas?**

Andrea Stephens, a pastor's wife, has been where you are. Before we go much further, you should know that Andrea has never been one of those health nuts who sprinkles fiber on her cereal or straps a three-quart water bottle to her hip. But three years ago she and her husband, Bill (a church pastor), faced up to a crisis in their health that had started with six words: "Pastor, don't you want some dessert?"

The Stephens had been in ministry for twelve years when they had their revelation, and no one ever challenged them as did the ladies of Covington Presbyterian Church in Lafayette, Louisiana, where they served at the time. Whenever the congregation gathered, these women would show up with pecan pies, double-fudge brownies, cherry tarts—you name it.

Besides those church gatherings, Bill and Andrea had made McDonald's and Sonic Burger their daily hangouts, and every Friday night meant pepperoni stuffed-crust pizza and a couple of sugary

JUST SAY MAYBE

Not sure how to say no to Mrs. Oldenwald's homemade apple-raisin pie? Just say maybe. (Husbands: Don't try these tricks at home):

► "My wife would just love this recipe. Can I wrap up the rest to take home for her to taste?"

► "Yes, I'll have some pie, but I'll catch the ice cream on the next round."

► "That dessert was simply wonderful. Can I have the rest to go? I'll finish it at my office tomorrow."

► "That meal was so delicious that I can handle only a small slice of pie."

Cokes. The result? Bill and Andrea couldn't even get their jeans zipped comfortably.

It didn't take the couple long to see that they were wearing those calories, but a few months passed before they realized the other effects—they felt awful. In the years before the light came on, they'd had more bouts with the flu and colds than they could count, and they were always tired. To compound their problem, they hadn't exercised for months. All those things threw Bill and Andrea into a slump.

After waking up exhausted one Monday morning, the Stephens decided to make a change. Bill couldn't give his all to the ministry if he continued on his path. Andrea, a writer, was tired of falling asleep at her keyboard during the daylight hours.

Well, they're four years into their change now, and even a fiber-sprinkling health freak would give them kudos for the modifications they've made.

■ **What a minute. What did the Stephens do to break out of their nutritional rut?**

Andrea sat down and wrote out what they did. Here's their account:

► **They put health on their agenda.** For years, Bill and Andrea had used the ministry as an excuse to eat poorly and not exercise. But they realized that a person has time only for things he or she makes time for. When one of them is lying on a stretcher after a heart attack at age fifty-five, will one say, "But I didn't have time to exercise"?

► **They cut the fat.** It didn't take a diet expert to tell them that the 26 fat grams and 500 calories in McDonald's Big Macs were slowly killing them. Now, instead of heading for fast food, they cook low-fat food: grilled chicken, steamed broccoli, vegetable pizza at home. So can you.

When Bill and Andrea eat out, they choose such foods as Wendy's plain baked potato or a bowl of water-based soup. (In case they're tempted to cheat, they carry a *Fat Counter* book with them, which tells them how many fat grams are in most fast foods. Purchase one at your book or grocery store. The fat content of fried-chicken sandwiches with "secret sauce" will astound you.)

▶ **They eat more fruits and vegetables.** A hefty dose (six per day is the recommendation of the U.S. Food and Drug Administration) of foods such as raw carrots, bananas, tomatoes, and oranges provides enzymes to boost our bodies' immune system. Even a glass of fresh apple juice counts as a fruit.

WORK IT OUT FOR YOURSELF

No time to exercise? Combine your family and church time into your workout time:

▶ Bring your health club home. You can talk to your wife and kids, watch the news, and even do some paperwork—all while on a treadmill or stationary bike.

▶ Walk or jog with your spouse every day. That will give you time away from your whirlwind pace and a chance to connect with him or her.

▶ Take the steps. The next time you visit an office building, climb those two, four, eight flights of stairs instead of taking the elevator. The extra work will strengthen your muscles and burn calories.

▶ Play hide-and-seek with your grandkids. That'll get the heart beating!

▶ If you have older teens or young adults, shoot hoops with them. They'll love it, and it'll keep you on your toes.

▶ Make an exercise appointment. Whenever you decide to work out, write it on your calendar and treat it as you would any important meeting.

▶ Include exercise in church activities. Join a church basketball or volleyball program. That will encourage both fitness and fellowship every week.

▶ **They choose smart snacks.** Bill and Andrea substitute energy bars for Snickers and air-popped popcorn (sorry, no butter, just a sprinkle of fat-free parmesan) for Twinkies. It's amazing what you'll eat—and even enjoy—when nothing else is available in the cupboards.

▶ **They exercise.** Andrea speed-walks at least three times a week, and Bill jogs at the end of a long day at the church office. Who would've ever thought that exercising when you're pooped could actually give you energy?

▶ **They drink more water.** No, Andrea's still not a water junkie who lugs around containers with her. But she has managed to down the FDA-recommended eight glasses of water per day, which initially sent her to the restroom every five minutes but now cleans out her insides regularly. For a boost of vitamin C, she squeezes fresh lemon, lime, or orange in her water.

▶ **They get picky.** It can seem impossible to eat healthy when a spread of fattening foods at potlucks and picnics lies before you. But instead of trying everything in huge portions, they major on the "best of the worst"—the lowest-fat foods available. Also, the Stephens make their contribution to the potluck a fresh fruit salad or some other low-fat item so they'll know they'll have at least one low-fat, low-cal item to eat.

To avoid hurting friends' feelings, they take at least a "taste" of everything else. It's okay to give in every now and then—just do so in moderation.

■ **None of these ideas is earth-shattering: We heard them all from our fourth-grade teachers, who told us to eat three healthy meals a day and to exercise. But what happened when Bill and Andrea put these tips to the test?**

You'd be amazed. Bill's energy boost has made him a less grouchy husband and a more attentive counselor. Andrea can make it through a full day without feeling as if she'll collapse to the couch in exhaustion. They've managed to stay out of the doctor's office. Neither of them was obese, but they each shed some pounds.

The way Bill and Andrea see it, they can't be the kind of servants God wants them to be unless they take care of themselves. He has given us our bodies for a time, and He wants us to care for them.

This chapter is adapted from writings by Andrea Stephens, who lives in Bakersfield, California.

6

The Anatomy of Death

. . . .

■ *It never should have happened,* I thought, as I watched the hearse drive away from church, taking my wife to the cemetery. Why did Mariah have to die?

Just last week we were making plans to winter in Arizona. Now, Mariah was dead—killed in a tragic car accident. She knew the Lord, which provides great comfort. But I can't help but think: *Where's God amidst all this sadness?*

Death touches us all. And, like it or not, one day you will answer its call. Physical death is our inevitable destiny. But when we examine death, we find the reason for living.

In the meantime, we each view death a little differently. According to New Orleans Baptist Theological Seminary professor Macklyn W. Hubbell, how we look at death depends, for the most part, on our age: children feel death as an absence—someone is not here. Young people see death in a more spiritual way, not as an absence but as an abstraction. And as we grow older, there's a growing recognition that we will soon be with God and loved ones who've gone on before us. No matter what our age, however, death for a Christian is part of the process of moving into eternity.

While the Bible tells us heaven is a wonderful place where we'll no longer suffer or sorrow, where God will wipe away our tears (Rev. 7:17), we still have to deal with our emotions on earth when loved ones die. We also have to complete the practical tasks of arranging for funerals and burials and saying final good-byes.

■ What can help me cope during this painful time?

To a large extent, the rituals surrounding death (funeral services, wakes or visitation, meals at the family's home, and even the casket) bring us comfort, providing a tangible way to acknowledge the death of our loved one, affirm the life he or she lived, express our grief, and witness a final disposition. For Christians, rituals of death provide opportunities to affirm our beliefs about eternal life and the resurrection of the body.

■ How did our present system of dealing with death evolve?

Since the beginning of time, people have used rituals to honor those who've died. The Bible is filled with instances of funerals and burial instructions, from Sarah's burial by Abraham at the cave of Machpelah (Gen. 23) to Jesus' burial found in Matthew 27:57-60.

"Funerals are for the living, not the dead," explains Robert Don Hughes, associate vice president for academic programs at Southern Baptist Theological Seminary. A former pastor and missionary, Hughes believes rituals play an important role in our lives. "Wakes or visitation at funeral homes, with people standing by the casket, give us more time to feel that this one is truly gone. They provide a social and community process for dealing with one's passing and for expressing comfort and concern to the family for their loss."

Funerals, also known as memorial services, provide an opportunity for closure and celebration, both for individuals and for the greater community of friends and family. A memorial service should celebrate someone's life and involve the participants, providing the bereaved an opportunity to feel as many emotions as possible relating to the deceased says author and psychologist Neil Clark Warren.

"When I'm at a funeral, I want it to be personal," says Dr. Warren. "I want to tap into the sense of loss, fun, laughter, anger, abandonment, specialness, and irreplaceability of this person. I also want to consider how I'll deal with letting him or her go."

Additionally, funerals provide the opportunity to express grief and reestablish our identities apart from the one who died. "We in the United States miss lots of opportunities to take advantage of everything involved in death," says Dr. Warren. "Out of the loss, we can gain the motivation and energy to reconfigure our own identities."

Most of all, says Robert Don Hughes, funerals remind us there's a promise in the Resurrection to which we can cling. "I mostly use Scripture in funerals," he explains, "because at this time people particularly find comfort and meaning in them."

After all, Jesus comforted Martha in the same way when her brother Lazarus died. "I am the resurrection and the life," He said. "He who believes in me will live, even though he dies; and whoever lives and believes in me will never die. Do you believe this?" (John 11:25) Martha believed and was comforted because she understood she served a God of hope, and that hope will not disappoint.

■ **We have a will, but I've heard about living trusts. What do I need to know?**

Part of stewardship is planning ahead and drawing up the legal documents your family will need to take care of your estate when you die. Here are the basics:

▶ **A will.** This is the most important document since it provides for distribution of your assets. At death, any documents you hold jointly or with a beneficiary, such as bank accounts or IRAs, will go to the beneficiary named on them. Items you hold title to yourself will have to go through probate—a costly and time-consuming court procedure. If you have children, you can designate a guardian in your will. (If you don't designate a guardian, and you're a single parent or you and your spouse die at the same time, the court will appoint a guardian, usually the closest blood relative.)

While you don't have to have an attorney draw up a will, an attorney can provide valuable advice in addition to creating documents that make it easy for your heirs to distribute your estate.

▶ **A trust** (or "living will"). You can avoid probate by setting up a trust into which you put assets including mutual funds, real property, cash accounts, automobile titles, and so on. You maintain control over the property during your life, and at death the items in the trust are distributed to the beneficiaries without going through probate.

▶ **Basic information.** Make sure you let someone know where your legal documents are kept. Write a letter of instruction for your family listing your bank accounts, credit cards, insurance policies, company benefits, safe deposit box location, tax returns, stock certificates, will, and the name of your lawyer. If you want your organs donated to enable others to live, let your family and physician know now. Remember, planning now for your death and funeral will be a source of strength and comfort to your family as they act on your wishes in the future.

"We never think we're going to die," says attorney David Paul Gromis, of Gromis & Aguirre, Fresno, California. "We all think, *I'm in control.* Well, we're not. And because of that, we need to be good stewards of all God has given us."

■ **This is really hard to talk about, but should I be buried or cremated?**

"Earth to earth, ashes to ashes, dust to dust; in sure and certain hope of the Resurrection unto eternal life" *(The Book of Common Prayer: Burial of the Dead).* "For you are dust, and to dust you shall return" (Gen. 3:19).

After years of disfavor, cremation, a common practice in the ancient world, is becoming a popular alternative to burial. According to the Cremation Association of North America, in the late 1950s, less than 4 percent of people chose cremation. In 1995, more than 21 percent did. In California, that figure tops 38 percent.

Cost is a factor for many. The average in-ground burial costs around $8,000; direct cremation can cost as little as $350 in some places.

■ **But what do Christians believe about the practice?**

While many Christians see it as perfectly acceptable, others oppose it. Some cremation opponents believe that since a believer's body is a temple for the Holy Spirit, there's a certain sanctity about burial. Others believe cremation hinders the grieving process while actual burial brings proper closure to the physical relationship with the departed and enables grieving loved ones to accept the reality of the death. There's also the philosophy that cremation fails to give appropriate honor to the body since it was made "in the image of God."

While not addressing all of the concerns about cremation, evangelist Billy Graham, in his nationally syndicated column, "My Answer," shed light on one of the primary concerns—the relationship between cremation and resurrection.

"The aspect of cremation that worries some Christians is the thought of the total annihilation of the body. We need to get our thinking in a right perspective here. The body is annihilated as completely in the grave as it is in cremation. . . . Our bodies are our temporary tents. Our resurrected bodies will be our permanent homes. They are similar in appearance but different in substance. Cremation is therefore no hindrance to the resurrection."

Running out of cemetery ground space is an issue across the country, but the lack of "dead space" hasn't reached crisis proportions, due to the rising trend in cremation as an alternative to traditional in-ground burial. The states of Oregon, Washington, and California are seeing sharp increases in cremation, as is Canada.

One practice becoming more common in cemeteries—with a potential for abuse—is that of stacking caskets on top of each other, instead of placing them side by side, for people who wish to be buried together. Without the consent of the family, "layering" caskets is illegal.

■ **It sounds crass to "shop" for a better price when it comes to funerals, but I've heard there are mortuaries out there that take advantage of families at a time when they are most vulnerable. Is that true?**

While basic burial needs exist, shopping around for services and products, preferably ahead of time, can mean considerable savings. Most prices are negotiable, and you can offer alternatives, such as bringing your own flowers or even making your own casket, if you're so inclined. Don't worry; very few are.

You can also buy a casket from a discount manufacturer such as Consumer Casket USA (800-611-8778) or Direct Casket (800-732-2753). Prices are often considerably less than those of funeral homes. In some places, you can rent a casket for a viewing (the liner the body rests in is removable) and then bury the body in a cloth-covered casket.

Costs can be roughly broken into three areas: service, caskets, and other products:

- ▶ Direct burial ($995–$1,500) includes no-frills "alternative casket" but not a cemetery charge.
- ▶ Nondeclinable fee ($600–$1,200) is the funeral home's cover charge; you can't get around paying this.
- ▶ Opening/closing grave ($500–$800) is the weekday rate; costs are 30–50 percent more on weekends.
- ▶ Direct cremation ($350–$1,000) should include a no-frills cremation casket.
- ▶ Funeral service ($200–$400) if held at a funeral home. Most churches open their facilities for a funeral, although you may consider giving a love offering.
- ▶ Viewing ($200–$400) is another add-on; watch out for extra fees for the "drawing room."
- ▶ Embalming ($150–$300) is not required by the state, but you need it if there is a viewing or the body is transported by common carrier across state lines.
- ▶ Hearse and driver ($155–$250) costs this amount for a twenty-five-mile radius; there is a per-mile charge for longer distances.
- ▶ Other body preparation ($150–$200) is little more than washing and transferring the body to a casket and makeup.
- ▶ Services of staff ($125–$175) covers the viewing, funeral, or memorial service.
- ▶ Removal of body from place of death ($100) covers a twenty-five-mile radius.

Caskets come in all prices. For instance, the price for the same top-of-the-line casket can range from $15,000 at a discount casket manufacturer to $70,000 at a funeral home. While the cost of the average casket is approximately $2,000, the following is a list of the best-selling casket models from Batesville Casket.

- ▶ Bronze (The Promethean) $16,000–$17,000
- ▶ Hardwood (Mahogany) $7,800–$8,800
- ▶ Bronze (The Persian) $5,200
- ▶ Copper (Y-33) $3,220
- ▶ Hardwood (Brittany Oak) $2,000
- ▶ Gasketed steel (Primrose) $1,700
- ▶ Non-gasketed steel (Greystone) $695
- ▶ Cloth-covered ($395)

Don't forget these other items:

- ▶ Cemetery plot ($750-$1,500). Veterans and families may qualify for free burial in national cemeteries.
- ▶ Grave marker ($650-$1,000 for a bronze plaque). You may want to put your money here; it's the only visible part.
- ▶ Grave liner or concrete vault ($350 for liner; $625 for vault). You should only buy a liner or vault if the cemetery requires one.
- ▶ Flower van ($65-$85). If there are only a few bouquets, friends can take them to the cemetery in their cars.

■ What do the experts recommend when talking about death with children and grandchildren?

The best way to tell children about death, say psychologists, is honestly, clearly, and truthfully. "If parents explain death well and from a Christian position," says psychologist Neil Clark Warren, "I think it's exciting, not frightening. The truth is always friendlier than anything less than the truth."

But how do you do that? You use words that say just what happened: "Grandpa died. His life is over on earth. But we'll see him again in heaven."

"If it's in Scripture, it's right and is wonderfully positive," says Dr.

Warren. When questions come, answer then as briefly and factually as possible.

But here's what you don't say:

▶ "Grandma's sleeping."

This will create fear in a child, causing him to be afraid to go to sleep.

▶ "Grandma's gone on a long trip."

For a young child, something as simple as a parent going on a "trip" to the grocery store can cause anxiety.

▶ "She was so good, Jesus took her to heaven."

Another fear-inducer, causing the child to wonder, "If I'm good, will Jesus take me away too?" Don't be afraid, however, to let your child know you miss your loved one too. It's all right to say, "It's hard for me to understand, and I miss her too."

This chapter is adapted from writings by Sue Schumann of Rancho Palos Verdes, California.

7

. . . .

You and Your Retirement Finances

Don't Retire, Refire!

· ·

Editor's note: Thinking about retirement? Thinking about if you'll be able to afford retirement? Bernie Minton, a financial and management consultant, is in his mid-fifties. In this chapter, he shares some interesting views on the subject.

■ **What should families be doing about investments and retirement?**

Bernie: I have little confidence that I will ever see the money I have put into the Social Security system. Although the economy chugged along pretty well in the 1990s, the long term remains uncertain. Indeed, we are seeing many companies cutting back on retirement plans. I think our parents' generation was the last one to have broad-based retirement plans.

■ **Gee, you're a lot of help.**

Bernie: Fortunately, we serve a mighty God. I try to put into practice Matthew 6:33-34, which says you should "seek first His kingdom and His righteousness, and all these things will be given to you as well. Therefore, do not worry about tomorrow, for tomorrow will worry about itself. Each day has enough trouble of its own."

From the time when my wife, Elaine, and I got married, even when we didn't have much, we always tithed to the Lord and lived on what was left over. We wanted her to be at home and raise our children. This meant that many times I carried an extra part-time job, and Elaine did her best to stretch our funds. But I am convinced that it was not just our hard work and budgeting but our faithfulness in tithing that made our budget balance. Not only did God bring money into the front door, but, more importantly, He arranged opportunities to keep that money from flowing out the back door.

For example, we did not have to buy our kids new clothes until they were eight and ten years old. A neighbor with a son just a little older than ours sold us her son's top-quality, outgrown clothing for a fraction of the cost. Our two boys dressed in styles and brands that I could have never afforded. I keep this example in Matthew 6 in mind when I look at retirement.

■ How has that affected your view of retirement?

Bernie: Although I'm able to earn more now, I still live conservatively. I have saved a little, but my biggest investment is in the Lord's work. I used to think retirement meant kicking back in a rocking chair and puttering around the house. But that view has changed. I don't think there will come a time in my life when I will quit work and live entirely off of what I have saved.

My goal is to get my expenses down. I hope to do this by paying off my home mortgage and getting my two boys through college. When these financial obligations are behind me, I want to cut back on the hours I spend earning a living and spend more and more hours involved in ministry.

My father, who is in his mid-eighties, is still a practicing attorney. He works only five hours a day, but he loves it. It keeps him young. My father-in-law is eighty-two, and although he has retired from the corporate world, he stays busy building dollhouses for his grandchildren, painting the church, and doing carpentry projects around my house that I just don't have the time to get to.

I tell my boys that a better retirement security than the amount of money you have in the bank is the skills you acquire to support yourself. I believe that if they can develop the talents God has given them, they will be able to provide a service that someone needs. We know a retired man in our community who likes to tinker. He comes to our house to fix our washer and dryer when they break down. He doesn't charge much. He's friendly, skilled, and prompt, and lots of people use his services. He has a real ministry. He meets our needs, and the Lord is meeting his.

Of course, this assumes that you still have your health. I believe that if I am wise in serving the Lord and meeting my obligations while I'm able, then He will take care of me when I'm not able. It is also my impression that wisdom is not building up a huge retirement account. I am not saying that couples shouldn't save for the future, because I am doing that. It's just that my motivation for retirement has changed. I'm not saving to provide for myself a life of ease. Rather, as the man who "built bigger and better barns" in the Gospel of Matthew, my absolutely secure retirement investment is what I invest of my money and my time into the Lord's work. And that is an investment I will enjoy for eternity.

That's why I don't ever plan to "retire." I plan to refire. I want to use my job skills to be a self-supporting missionary. Paul made tents. My "tents" are different, but I want my focus to be the same as his.

■ How does your wife feel about this?

Bernie: With money beyond our tithe, I tend to be more of a giver, while Elaine tends to be more of a saver. However, my wife trusts me to provide. She tells me that the thing that gives her the most security is seeing me consistently in fellowship with the Lord and seeking His direction.

This chapter is adapted from writings by Mike Yorkey.

2

Exploring Your Financial Future

. . . .

■ **I'm not sure where we're going on the path to wise investing. The word *investment* gives me an automatic headache.
My heart freezes when someone says "portfolio," "stock market," or "mutual fund." I feel like I'm learning from scratch
about investing, which is a sad thing to say at fifty-five years
of age, but we poured our lives into our kids. We think we
made the right decision. Anyway, now that we have the empty
nest, we know it's time to turn our attention to our upcoming
golden years. Where do we start?**

Do you have an investment plan yet? If not, you can start by following these three steps:

1. Define your needs. What is your target? Is it paying for your
children's college, buying a new car, or adding to your retirement
account? You need to define the time in which to achieve your
goal, and what tolerance you're willing to endure to attain your
goal.

Let's use a man called Jack Smart, fifty-two years old, as an example. He realizes that though he and his wife have no money socked
away, retirement is on the horizon. The Smarts decide that their
target should be retirement. The total cost? They estimate they'll

need $250,000, which they have about fifteen years to accumulate. To do so, the Smarts have to be willing to accept a moderate level of risk (tolerance) in their investments.

2. Identify the best strategy to meet those needs. There are three investment strategies:

A. Accumulating wealth using moderate- to high-risk investments.

B. Preserving wealth using a combination of low- and limited-risk investments.

C. Using a combination of growth and preservation.

Your goals, time frame, and comfort with risk will determine which strategy is most appropriate for you.

3. Select investments based on your strategy. Ask yourself several questions when evaluating an investment:

A. Does this investment meet my needs? Will it grow at the appropriate rate for me to reach my financial goals?

B. How is this investment expected to perform? To determine this, review the investment's performance for at least the past five years. Has it performed well enough to meet your goals?

C. Next look at the period during which the investment performed the worst. Ask yourself, *Would I be comfortable holding the investment during such a time?*

■ **I'm afraid we don't have a plan. For seventeen years, my wife and I (we're both in our early fifties) served at the Christian Embassy in Washington, D.C., a ministry affiliated with Campus Crusade for Christ. We have two grown children, Michael and Patrick.**

Here's our financial picture. Through years of frugal living and investment choices such as mutual funds, we have accumulated a retirement nest egg of $120,000. These investments, however, were not chosen in line with an investment plan, so what do we need to do?

Since your money is invested primarily in similar large-company growth mutual funds, the risks are not spread out enough. You need to fine-tune your portfolio.

Step 1: Your needs. You want to accumulate at least $250,000 by the time your husband is sixty-five (target), with a moderate-to high-risk tolerance.

Step 2: Your strategy. Though your tolerance for risk is high, the ten years remaining until retirement isn't sufficient for a high-growth strategy. That's why a moderate-growth strategy with high diversification is most appropriate.

Step 3: Your best investment. A moderate-growth strategy that is 65 percent moderate-risk investments and 35 percent limited-risk investments will give you the potential of reaching the $250,000 mark in the next ten years.

■ What is risk?

Risk is the likelihood that you will lose money on your investment. The greater the risk, the greater your potential loss—and potential reward. All investments have some risk. Good investors understand their risks before investing.

A. Low risk: savings accounts, money market funds, certificate of deposit (CDs), and savings bonds.

B. Limited risk: treasury bonds and high-dividend stocks (e.g., utilities).

C. Moderate risk: blue chip stocks, mutual funds, corporate bonds, and real estate.

D. High risk: (also called "speculative risk") junk bonds, speculative stocks, options, futures, and land.

■ What is an investment strategy and how can I get one?

Choose between these strategies when creating an investment portfolio:

A. Accumulating wealth using moderate- to high-risk investments

B. Preserving wealth using a combination of low- and limited-risk investment

C. Using a combination of growth and preservation to grow wealth with minimal risk

Your goals, time frame, and comfort with risk will determine which strategy is most appropriate for you. Let's take a closer look at them:

▶ **High Growth (an investment portfolio containing 100 percent stocks).** This strategy offers the greatest opportunity for growing your investments, but is appropriate only for investors who have more than ten years and are comfortable with huge swings in the value of their investments.

▶ **Moderate Growth (60 to 70 percent stocks, 30 to 40 percent long-term fixed income).** This is the strategy for those who want to grow their wealth for at least seven years. The potential returns are less than those of the high-risk strategy, but so are the risks.

▶ **Combination Growth (40 percent stocks, 40 percent long-term fixed income, 20 percent short-term fixed income).** For investors who have between three and ten years to meet their goal, this is often the best strategy. Investors who use this strategy will not experience large swings in their investment's value.

▶ **Capital Preservation (20 percent stocks. 30 percent long-term fixed income, 50 percent short-term fixed income).** This is a wise strategy for investors whose target is less than five years away and who want minimal risk of decline. The small component of stocks adds some growth to keep up with inflation.

■ **What's so scary about the stock market?**

Nothing, if you have time.

■ **Why do people fear the stock market?**

Because it fluctuates so often. It feels unstable to have one's money in such a vulnerable position. Yet the wise investor knows that the longer you can give your money to grow, the less likely you will lose it.

In any one-year period since 1926, the stock market was down less than 30 percent of the time. During any five-year period, it was down only 10 percent of the time. For ten-year periods, the stock market dropped less than 3 percent of the time. And it has yet to show a decline for any twenty-year period.

An example is the 1987 "Black Monday" crash. On October 19, 1987, the stock market plummeted by 23 percent. The total value of all stocks on the New York Stock Exchange fell from $2.5 trillion to $1.9 trillion. Ten years later, the stock market had not merely recovered, but had quadrupled! The value of New York Stock Exchange stocks had risen from $1.9 trillion to more than $9.4 trillion. Many long-term investors would have recouped their losses within three years had they stayed invested.

There have been fifteen declines averaging 26 percent in the last fifty years. But if an investor had stayed invested through all of them, he or she would not have experienced a loss. The message is clear: The more time you have to invest in stocks, the less risky it is. Long-term equals low risk!

■ **All this stock market stuff sounds so worldly. What's the spiritual perspective on this?**

For a Christian, the first question is not, "How do I invest?" but "Should I invest?" After all, Jesus did say, "Do not store up for yourselves treasures on earth. . . . For where your treasure is, there your heart will be also" (Matt. 6:19-21). Does investing contradict that teaching? Is setting aside money a sign of small faith?

Each Christian must answer these questions for himself and his family. As you decide, consider:

A. Jesus knew enough of the seductive power of money to single it out as a rival to the true God: "You cannot serve both God and Money" (Matt. 6:24). Whatever we do as money managers, we must keep our hearts on guard.

B. Jesus used financial dealings to illustrate several of His parables. At least one of them, the Parable of the Talents (Matt. 25:14-29), referred directly to investing. Jesus apparently did not condemn the practice; in fact, the master in the story rewarded wise management above fearful hoarding.

C. The Bible does not condemn planning for the future. It is equally clear, however, that the future—including investments—is in God's hands (James 4:13-15).

D. Jesus assured His followers that we don't need to worry about the future. God cares for us and will provide for our needs

(Matt. 6:25). It is possible He may do so through wise invest-ments. But Christians should trust Him, not their portfolios.

This material is adapted from writings by Ray Linder, author of Making the Most of Your Money *(Victor). He is a registered investment adviser who lives with his family in Herndon, Virginia.*

RATES AND MEASURES

Here are some quick definitions of financial instruments:

- ▶ **Checking and savings accounts.** Federally insured cash hold-ings; no tax advantages. **Average annual rate of return:** Zero to 3 percent.
- ▶ **Money market account.** Investment instrument similar to bank savings accounts, but not federally insured; no tax advantages. **Average annual rate of return:** 2 to 3 percent.
- ▶ **CD** (Certificate of Deposit). Federally insured debt instrument; guaranteed rates of return over time; no tax benefits. **Average annual rate of return:** 3.5 to 7 percent.
- ▶ **Bond.** Debt a company, municipality, or government owes the holder. Fixed rate of return over a set period of time; some tax benefits. **Average annual rate of return:** 5 to 6 percent for corporate or municipal bonds; 4 percent for government bonds.
- ▶ **Stock.** Part ownership of a company. Variable rates of return over time; no tax benefits. **Average annual rate of return:** 12.5 percent.
- ▶ **Mutual fund.** Professionally managed financial vehicle that groups different investments, such as stocks and bonds, into one pool. Variable rates of return over time; more diversified than individual stocks/bonds; no tax benefits. **Average annual rate of return:** 12 percent.
- ▶ **IRA** (Individual Retirement Account). Retirement vehicle that can use everything from money market accounts to mutual funds. Federally con-trolled; tight restrictions on payout; annual contribution limit; tax benefits. **Average annual rate of return:** 3 to 18 percent.
- ▶ **401(k)** (section number of the Internal Revenue Code). Retirement vehi-cle that can employ a number of investment options. Usually an employee benefit; higher annual contribution limit than IRAs; tax benefits. Nonprofits and public institutions offer the same vehicle under a different name, a 403(b). **Average annual rate of return:** 7 percent. (Note: This figure is artificially low because many savers choose not to invest their 401(k)s in stocks or stock mutual funds. Based on historical data, stocks or stock mutual fund invested in a 401(k) would yield an average annual rate of return of 12 percent or more.)

Source: Chris Jones, WMA Securities, Inc. Average annual rates of return are subject to change.

3

How Do I Give Money to My Grandkids?

■ **I'm nearly afraid to ask, but what rules does the U.S. government have about how much can I give to our grandchildren? Does the tax man take a big bite? If so, how much? My husband left me a sizable inheritance, and I want to help fund the grandkids' college education.**

Here's how it works. You may give up to $10,000 per year to each of your grandchildren (or children). If your husband was alive, he could also give $10,000 to each grandchild.

■ **What if I want to give more than $10,000?**

The answer is that you will have to start cutting into your lifetime exemption from estate taxes. Currently, the exemption is $625,000 and will go up every year for the next ten years to $1,000,000. Of course, most of the increase is in the last few years and the only guarantee we have that the exemption will ever reach the $1,000,000 is the word of our President and Speaker of the House. (In fact, Congress may have changed those limits by the time you read this.) You can decide if you believe it or not. If you use up your entire exemption, you have to start paying a gift tax on the money you give your kids!

Now, if your grandchildren are minors, under eighteen years of age, you can give them money and open an account for them under the "Uniform Gifts to Minors Act." Your banker will be pleased to help you do this.

■ What happens when my grandchildren reach the age of eighteen, or I decide to give that money to one of my children?

Such an account may not be a good idea. Once your grandchildren (or children) reach the ripe old age of eighteen, they get the dough! Did you have a lick of sense when you were eighteen? Of course not, and neither should you expect your grandchildren to have the wisdom you possess today.

In fact, if you could overhear your grandkids talking over lunch at school, they would be calling this kind of money gift the "Corvette Fund" because the money is more likely to be spent on a shiny red two-seater than a college education.

■ But can't I involve my children to make sure that the money is used for college?

Of course you can, although legally the child can do what he or she wants with the money. But as long as everyone understands what the money is to be used for, the chances are good that your grandchild will do the right thing.

There is also an alternative. You can set up a special kind of irrevocable trust for your grandchildren. It is called a "Crummy Trust." It is not called this because the trust is not well-prepared, but because there is a case, called the Crummy case, which forces the IRS to allow this kind of gift.

You'll have to consult with a financial expert or a lawyer to get more details on how this kind of trust works, but the good thing about this kind of trust is that you can have your attorney place provisions in the trust that say when the grandchildren get the money and what purposes it can be used for.

A popular provision is to give the grandchildren the money when they reach an "age of reason"; you know, forty-five or fifty!

Seriously, you can require the trustee to use the money for the grand-children's education, benefit, or comfort, or any combination of these. In the new year, you may want to give a gift of money to your grandchildren. In making the gift, remember these rules and think about that shiny new 'vette they'll be getting if you don't do it right. If you really love your grandchildren, make a gift that will make their lives better in the long run and will protect them from their worst enemies—themselves.

After all, you were once young. As Ben Franklin said, "Experience keeps an expensive school, and a fool will learn in no other."

■ Since we're talking about inheritances, it is better to have a will or a trust?

The answers are "It depends" and "Probably both."

If the gross value of your estate is more than $100,000 and you have a will—or even if you don't have a will—your estate will go through probate.

■ I need to get a handle on terms. I know what a will is, but what is a trust? And what is probate?

A trust, which is usually called a revocable living trust, is a way for your family to inherit your property and possessions without going through long and costly court proceedings.

Probate is a court proceeding that legally establishes the validity of wills. This comes at a price, however. If the gross value of your estate were $300,000, for example, the attorney's fees for the probate would be a minimum of $14,000, and the administrator's fees would tack on another $14,000, for a total of $28,000!

Probate takes time, usually a year. Sometimes it takes years, which ties up the estate. This can be a real problem for families. A trust, on the other hand, avoids the very substantial cost of probate, saves your family time, and allows someone you trust to administer your affairs if you are seriously ill or die. If you have a will and become disabled or seriously ill, the usual solution is a conservator-ship proceeding in Superior Court. This is expensive, and again, takes lots and lots of time.

While the court is figuring out who should be your conservator, the lights are being turned off, the house is going into foreclosure, and no one can pay the medical bills! If you have a trust, your Successor Trustee can immediately take over and handle the house payments, utility payments, and other bills.

It is recommended to have a trust and a will. People, after all, are human, and your trust can only protect from probate those assets that you put in the trust. There is always the chance that you will forget to put something in the trust, or take something out of the trust and not put it back in.

■ What are the downsides of trusts?

The biggest problem with a trust is that you have to "trust" someone. With a will that goes through probate, the court is "looking over the shoulder" of your administrator to be sure things are distributed as you directed in your will. With a trust, you have to trust your Successor Trustee to do what you have instructed him or her to do.

■ Can you make out a living trust and then change your mind?

Yes, if it is a revocable living trust, which most people do when executing a living trust. You can add properties, change the beneficiaries, name a different successor trustee, or even revoke the trust completely.

As usual, it's best to consult an attorney, but for do-it-yourselfers, you can purchase computer software such as Living Trust Maker by Nolo Press and make your own legally binding revocable living trust by answering seven questions prompted to you on the computer screen. Such software often costs less than $50, a fraction of the cost to use an attorney to fill in the blanks with you.

This chapter is adapted from writings by R. Michael Walters, an attorney and writer living in Rancho Bernardo, California.

4

Meet the
Freedom Account

. . . .

■ **With two kids in college and our budget hemorrhaging red ink every month, it's a race to the finish line to see if we will have any money left in the checking account at the end of the month. Will we have to dip into our meager savings account?**

Anytime we do get a bit ahead of the curve, an unexpected bill or car breakdown has us scrambling. Short of telling us to spend less, what's an effective strategy that will keep our necks above the waterline?

First of all, somehow you manage to pay your mortgage every month because past experience has taught you that failure to do so brings swift and painful consequences. Imagine you are notified that effective immediately you will no longer pay your mortgage payment (or rent) each month but rather in one lump sum for the entire year. Your first yearly payment will be due one year from today.

Even though you aren't required to pay the mortgage each month, would you continue to see 1/12th of that annual payment as being critical to put away each month? Probably not. Some of us may actually experience a feeling of exhilaration calculating how this new arrangement will free up an "extra" $1,000 each month.

Knowing yourself, what do you think of your chances of coming up with the, oh, $12,000 annual payment one year from now? About as good as your having cash put away for most of your other intermittent expenses!

Wise people, however, know the only right way to respond is to act as if 1/12th of the mortgage is still "due" every month and put that amount under the mattress or in a coffee can religiously on the first day of each month, come heaven or high water.

Lest any of you get too used to such an insane idea, let's go back to reality. Your mortgage payment is due every month just as it always has been. But 1/12th of your automobile maintenance is due every month, along with 1/12th of your property taxes and 1/12th of quite a few other things that you fail to consider on a monthly basis.

Expenses that are not paid monthly are called irregular expenses. This is where selective amnesia becomes a virtual epidemic. Folks forget over the course of a year that cars break down and college tuition must be paid every September and life insurance premiums become due. That's why you need to start planning ahead for your irregular expenses.

■ How can I do that?

Mary Hunt, publisher of the *Cheapskate Monthly* newsletter, has devised a method that is so exciting, so effective, so easy to handle, it borders on being miraculous. It's called (drum roll, please) the Freedom Account, and it is truly at the heart of turning your financial life around forever.

Opening a Freedom Account will bring you a new sense of dignity, control, and personal worth. You start by determining your irregular expenses, which can be everything from auto repair to college bills. We're talking about things like property taxes, life insurance, clothing, and summer vacations.

Once you've figured all those annual expenses, divide by 12, and voilà, there's the amount you need to be putting aside in a special Freedom Account you open at your bank. Let that account build up, and you'll have money saved for the proverbial rainy day.

■ **But you don't know that we're drowning in debt. A Freedom Account could never work for us.**

Are flimsy contrivances keeping you stuck in that big-debt, small-savings situation? Excuses may let you off the hook for now, but it's only a temporary reprieve. Typically one excuse just leads to another and another. Isn't it time to explode your weak "explanations" once and for all?

Excuse: I've never been good with money.

That's probably because you've never been exposed to very simple financial principles. Think about the things you are good with. Did that level of competency happen overnight or did you start at the beginning and progress just one step at a time? Take the first step to understanding finances today.

Excuse: I don't have time to study personal finance.

You have time to do the things that matter to you. It's unwise to work as hard as you do only to end up with no solid assets to show for it.

Excuse: I can't stick to a budget.

Perhaps that's because you've been trying to cram yourself into a spending plan that doesn't fit your style. Why not create a spending plan that fits you perfectly? To do this, you'll need to make a record of every dime you spend for the next month, then total each category. You'll see immediately where you need to make adjustments. For most, it's eating out in restaurants or buying a Starbucks coffee each day. Can you do with less in these areas?

Excuse: I can't cancel my credit card account because the entire balance will become due immediately.

When you cancel the account, you cancel your ability to add new purchases. The balance may still be paid in monthly payments. As long as that account is open you will find reasons to add new purchases, which is probably the real reason you don't want to cancel it.

Excuse: I don't have enough to make my entire credit card payment on time, so I'll just skip this month and catch up later.

You can send any amount at any time during the month toward your credit card account, and you should because interest is calculated on a daily basis. Paying any amount sooner than later will be to your advantage.

Excuse: It's only a $50 purchase on my credit card. I owe so much now anyway, this small amount won't matter.

That $50 purchase added to a typical credit card balance of $1,000 immediately turns into a $106 purchase and adds a full three months to the time it will take to repay. Keep this up and you'll never get out of debt.

Excuse: I work hard and commute a long way, so I deserve a luxury car.

Of course you work hard, but luxury items like leased automobiles may not be worth what they cost. Driving a less flamboyant car while saving the equivalent of those lease payments will allow you to pay cash for a better car in a few years. Never underestimate the luxury of driving a fully paid-for car.

Excuse: I'm using all the credit I can get so I can enjoy life while I can.

Statistics indicate you will live to be a very old person. The short-lived "joy" of your credit purchases will surely become the enduring bane of your mature years. Old age and poverty shouldn't show up in the same sentence.

Mary Hunt says there's plenty more to know about setting up Freedom Accounts, so call her at Cheapskate Monthly (562-630-6474, write P.O. Box 2135, Paramount, CA 90723-8135 or e-mail at www.cheapskatemonthly.com). Mary will be happy to send along a step-by-step program if you ask for the special Freedom Account offer.

5

Flying the Friendly Skies . . . for Less

. . . .

■ **Like many grandparents, we have children and grandchildren spread out across the country. We've determined that the driving time is too great, so our vacation dollars pay for flights to see the family—and little else. We're okay with that because we know that's the only way we can see those little munchkins grow up. How can we fly for fewer bucks?**

The airline business is a turbulent industry that sends 20,000 flights into the air each day. If you're looking to save bucks on air travel, consider these tips:

1. Plan ahead. No, make that: plan *way* ahead. If you're going to see family—especially during a holiday period—you better firm up plans three to six months out. Granted, it's difficult to commit on a trip way in the future and some people don't like to be tied down, but the fact remains that often the best Christmas fares are available in July and August.

If you're just not able to book months in advance, the best fares require a fourteen-, twenty-one-, or thirty-day advance purchase, and nearly all discount seats require a Saturday night stayover. And you know that discount seats are nonrefundable, although for a $75 fee they can often be used toward the purchase of a new ticket with that airline.

2. Be flexible. Generally speaking, airlines follow the normal school calendar. If you want to fly when grandkids are out of school, it will cost more. Fares are highest over Thanksgiving, Christmas, spring break, and summer.

Let your travel agent know you can be flexible on flight times, dates, and destination cities. If you request two tickets with a departure of Friday, December 19 and a return date of Friday, January 2, you're not leaving him or her much room to maneuver. Instead, you should ask, "What is the lowest possible price for Christmas travel, and what do I have to do to get it?"

Because of the stage of life you're in, you should be fairly flexible when it comes to traveling during the holiday periods. For instance, flying on the Monday or Tuesday before Thanksgiving is much cheaper than leaving Wednesday evening—"the busiest flight day of the year." At the same time, you could return on Saturday morning or roll your departure into the following week, when low fares are possible.

3. Become best buddies with an on-the-ball travel agent. Since the airlines post over 100,000 rate changes a day (incredible!), you can't expect an agent to call you if the price of a flight from Phoenix to Pittsburgh suddenly drops from $448 to $249.

When airlines slash prices, they are practicing "seat management," in which computers set the prices based on anticipated demand. If sales are slow for a particular flight, the computer stimulates bookings by tweaking the rates. Realize, however, that travel agents don't have the time to watch out for fare-specific flights for you. That's why good travel agents won't mind if you call in every day to see where the rates are. They know the game!

4. Fly "off-peak" times. Be aware of "peak" and "off-peak" flying times. Flights that are convenient for business travelers—who pay the freight for the airlines—are early in the morning and late in the afternoon. Naturally, the computers are going to keep the fares on those flights higher. But traveling before 7 A.M., late morning, early afternoon, or "red-eye" flights can result in significant savings. Not only are "red-eyes" the least expensive, but you can gain an extra vacation day.

5. Ask for the senior discount. Don't be bashful; hey, you earned it. Some airlines will offer 10 percent off its cheapest seats to seniors age 62 and over. Some of the major airlines also offer senior coupon paks, which can be real money savers. Each coupon allows a one-way trip to either a certain destination or any city within the continental U.S. that the airline flies. If you have grandchildren hither and yon, this might be a great way to get around the country.

6. Consider driving to a different airport. Major metropolitan areas often have two or three airports (i.e., New York's Kennedy, La Guardia, and Newark). You'll find different pricing on all three. Decide first if it's worth your time to drive out of your way to another airport. If a two-hour journey saves you and your spouse $500 on cross-country fares, make the drive.

7. Watch for "companion" fares. Sometimes, the airlines offer special companion fares: fly with a spouse or friend and get a discount. Be careful, however, since the fine print says you have to buy one seat at the "regular coach price," which can sometimes be more than two deeply discounted fares!

8. Check out the vacation department of major airlines. Believe it or not, it's sometimes cheaper to book the airfare through the airline's vacation department, or at least you can get a rental car thrown into the deal.

9. Don't forget charter flights. Charters typically service vacation hot spots—Orlando, Cancun, Los Angeles, and San Francisco—but many travelers are unaware that charters fly to many other cities as well.

Keep in mind that while major airlines play by the rules and match each other on fares, charters (and the smaller airlines like Southwest) have to do things differently to remain competitive.

10. Think through your frequent-flier mileage. Whether you accumulate frequent-flier miles through your business travel or credit-card charges, most forget that many airlines are expiring miles after three years. Generally speaking, frequent-flier miles are worth two cents a mile, so you don't want to blow 25,000 miles on a flight from Dallas to Atlanta. Your miles should be used on cross-country flights or to small cities serviced by the big airlines.

11. Finally, don't forget the consolidators. Look in the travel section of your Sunday newspaper for advertisements from "consolidators." They are usually found in the one-square ads filled with tiny type. Consolidators purchase tickets in bulk from the airlines and resell them on the open market at deep discounts. If they can't sell them, they're stuck.

Some consolidators sell nothing but TWA tickets; others specialize in European destinations. How good are the prices? Very good, although they probably won't be better than the "fare war" prices that pop up every few months.

The big advantage to consolidators is that they don't have any advance purchase requirements. Thus, if you have a daughter who's about to give birth or want to visit a sick grandchild immediately, consolidators are the way to go.

Remember this advice in case a family member dies and you need to attend the memorial service. Although many airlines offer "bereavement" fares, a consolidator's price is often cheaper. Be careful, though: some consolidators may not be able to get you the ticket in time on short notice, unless you're dealing with a local company.

Some of the more reputable consolidators include Cheap Seats (800-451-7200), TFI Tours International (800-745-8000) and 1-800-FLY-CHEAP.

■ Is there a downside to using consolidators?

Some consolidators are literally fly-by-night operations that have disappeared and absconded with people's money. If it sounds too good to be true, it probably is. Some travelers prefer to use travel agents as go-betweens in booking with consolidators because they know more about how legit the wholesale company is.

■ My husband is computer savvy. Can airline tickets be purchased on the Internet?

Yes, and this is a growing area of commerce. Good deals can be found if you're plugged into the World Wide Web. A new service, found at www.priceline.com, lets you "set the price" for flying. Here's the catch: You can only order these tickets on the Internet, although you can call toll-free 800-PRICELINE and pay an operator $4 to use the Internet for you.

Once on the Net, you type in your routing (say, Dallas to San

Francisco), how much you'd pay (you have to be reasonable; let's say $225 roundtrip) and then type in your credit card. Within an hour (one day for international tickets), you have an answer. If the airline says they'll take you up on your offer, you've purchased the tickets. In other words, you can't "test the system" to see if an airline will accept $100 roundtrip; once your credit card is typed in, the tickets are nonrefundable if the airline agrees to your price. Interesting concept.

There's more than one way to skin an Internet ticket, however. Travelocity (www.travelocity.com) is worth a look, as is Preview Travel (www.previewtravel.com). Best Fares (www.bestfares.com), which also publishes *Best Fares* magazine (for a hefty $59.50 per year) has a "free" area and a "subscriber" area. It seems like you will have to use this service a lot to justify the extra price.

Some international airlines, such as Cathay Pacific, have been experimenting with auctioning off tickets by e-mail to the highest bidders.

In the fast-changing world of the Internet, however, ideas come and ideas go—rapidly. If you're serious about pursuing e-mail tickets, you'll have to "noodle" around the Net to get the lay of cyberspace.

This chapter is adapted from 21 Days to a Thrifty Lifestyle *by Mike Yorkey and published by Zondervan Publishing House.*

LET'S CRUISE

Have you ever taken a cruise? Once just for seasoned citizens, cruises are attracting a younger crowd, and that includes you!

Are cruises expensive? Well, they're not cheap, but they are a good value for the money. One price includes your meals (sumptuous, and you can eat six times a day), evening's entertainment, shipboard recreation, and transportation to the next port of call—all while you're relaxing and sleeping. In the Caribbean, for instance, you wake up at a new island each morning.

"Shoulder" seasons—early fall and late spring—are the best times to find cabins discounted. You also might consider "repositioning" cruises—special deals offered when a cruise line is moving a ship to a different part of the world (for instance, from Alaska to the Caribbean in the fall).

If you want to pursue this option, attend a cruise show offered by travel agencies. It's a great way to learn about cruise lines, and sometimes they offer "show specials" only to those attending the presentation. You can also ask your travel agent or AAA office for free cruise videos, which explain all the amenities of cruising.

Cruise specials, discounts, and free-air add-ons abound. If you can travel on short notice, a knowledgeable travel agent can find you 50 percent discounts. If you're willing to take an inside cabin (no porthole) at the bottom of the ship, you'll pay a lot less. How much time do you spend in your cabin anyway?

Another way to pick up last-minute cruise deals is to watch the Travel Channel on cable TV or search the Internet. If you're not able to cruise on the spur of the moment, you can receive an early-booking discount by making reservations six months to a year in advance. The cruise line may offer a cabin upgrade at no additional cost because you paid for the cruise so far ahead. Caution: you'll be shipwrecked if you change your mind. You might consider purchasing trip cancellation insurance.

6

Trash or Treasure?

. . . .

■ **Ever since my husband took early retirement, we've been enjoying ourselves—but watching very closely the way we spend money. Thus we try to buy used. I've always liked to check out garage sales, but what else should I know about buying second-hand?**

There's no denying that buying stuff used saves bucketloads of money, so let's talk about garage sales first. So much depends on the city you live in, the climate, your neighborhood, and the state of the local economy. But there's no denying that garage sales contain some great deals, and they are a nice diversion.

In addition, when you reach the senior years, garage sales can become a great Saturday morning tradition for your adult children and grandchildren. Imagine three generations of the family sifting through other people's gems and junk. It's inexpensive family fun, and your grandchildren will learn some valuable lessons: the value of a buck; how to bargain, and humility. We shouldn't be too proud to wear or use someone else's used stuff if it's in good shape.

Garage sales make sense, especially for those young families with toddlers and preschoolers who leapfrog from one size to the next every fortnight. They can also be a superb place to pick up used sports equipment, an unexpected budget-breaker for families. Better yet, you don't pay sales tax.

■ **It's been awhile since I hit the garage sale circuit. Anything I need to know besides the obvious—bring small bills?**

Yes, having exact change—a lot of fives, ones, and quarters—is one bargaining ploy, but better yet, if you or the grandkids have a special need, ask God to open the door. Because garage-saleing is like shopping for a needle in the haystack of boxed clothes, we usually need a miracle to find those cute OshKosh overalls for the new grandbaby or used roller blades for the grandkids. Praying with your grandchildren can build everyone's faith, especially when you find items on your prayer list.

■ **I'm a Sunday School volunteer, and we have a great need for toy furniture and bookcases. Besides prayer, how do I find those items?**

By literally asking. Even if you don't see those items set out, inform the woman behind the card table, "I'm looking for a toy stove and refrigerator and twelve bookcases. Would you have any of those items available?"

Maybe what you're looking for is in the basement and they were too rushed to bring the stuff to the street. You never know.

■ **My husband likes to get in the car Saturday morning and "see what's out there." I like a more prepared approach. How can I get him on board?**

On Friday night or early Saturday morning, look through the newspaper's garage sale listings and circle the ones that seem promising. Then locate those streets on a city map before you leave home so you don't waste time driving around and asking for directions. If you don't, you'll both get frustrated. If you happen to get lost looking for that garage sale advertising the antique armoire, call a cab company. They can set you straight every time.

■ **I think it's rude to show up too early for a garage sale. What time should we start out in the morning?**

A significant part of the shopping strategy is when you arrive at a garage sale. Sometimes when a sale lists the start as 9 o'clock, they really mean 8. People do this knowing that if they advertise an earlier opening, dealers will show up on their doorstep at 7! Other families say 9 o'clock and mean it.

Let's say you arrive a tad early for a garage sale, but the family is still setting up. If you spot some furniture or items that look promising, you could say something like, "If I help you get ready, can I have first dibs?"

Being an early-bird shopper can work for you and against you. If your arrive early, you have first crack at the bargains. If the prices are right, you're a winner. However, if the prices are high, the sellers may not be in a mood to bargain since they're expecting more customers. On the other hand, if you arrive late in the morning or in the early afternoon, you can pick up some incredible bargains on unsold items. The last thing the family wants is to cart their junk back into the garage or basement.

■ **Where are the best deals found?**

It depends on what your needs are. If you're garage-saleing with grandkids and looking for nice children's clothing, the latest toys, or classic books, you're going to want to go to garage sales in "yuppie neighborhoods." You can sweep up special deals where young urban professionals and their families live. Their kids have outgrown their clothes, toys, and shoes, and they often have much to choose from.

Every city features great, good, and mediocre areas for garage sales. The most affluent neighborhoods won't have Tonka toys or children's clothes (wealthy people tend to be older), but you might find a nice dining room table or china hutch in their neighborhood.

■ **I've never been a good bargainer. Without being a cheapskate, how can I get my most bang for my buck?**

Unless items cost only a quarter, most sellers expect to be chiseled down. If you're buying several small items that add up to $5, offer four. A buck saved is a buck earned.

■ If I'm trying to buy clothes for the grandkids, what should I look out for?

Sometimes people don't do a good job displaying clothing. They may set out several cardboard boxes filled with children's shirts and pants, but after several people have rummaged through them, everything is a mess. Don't be deterred. Look at each item carefully and imagine what the shirt or pants will look like after being washed and ironed. Are there any holes? Any buttons missing? Permanent stains?

If the clothes are in good shape, you should pay a quarter or fifty cents for T-shirts, fifty to seventy-five cents for dress shirts, $1 for sweatshirts and ties, $1 to $3 for sweaters and OshKosh overalls, and a couple of bucks for skirts and out-of-fashion dresses. Department store dresses worn only a couple of times usually sell for $5 to $10.

Look for brand names: Healthtex, Benetton, Maui & Sons, Levis, Guess?, Cavarrichi, and Esprit. Nike and Reebok sneakers are excellent buys for infants and toddlers because the shoes aren't worn out. Actually, until your grandchild is six years old, you can do a lot of shopping at garage sales since the clothes haven't faded and usually don't have holes. They're just outgrown.

Little girls' dresses are another good buy. Polly Flinders dresses, which retail in stores for $30 to $100, can be found at garage sales for between $1 and $5. You shouldn't pay more than a quarter or fifty cents for children's books and tapes.

■ Do garage sale items come with any guarantee?

Are you kidding? Shopping garage sales requires serious consideration of the saying, *caveat emptor*, "Let the buyer beware." Always check out electric appliances—irons, blenders, televisions, cassette players—by plugging them in to see if they work. Remember, it won't be worth paying someone to repair an appliance or piece of electronic equipment.

You're on surer ground with furniture, which is among the most sought-after merchandise. It's a big seller because most people can't afford to pay retail. Sellers have the upper hand here. Buyers will have to make a snap judgment on whether the price is fair and fits their need.

Be on the lookout for "moving sales." Families relocating to another city or state are typically willing to bargain on chests of drawers and dressers. You know people are serious about getting rid of stuff if a moving sale is held during the winter or in the nippy fall or chilly spring months.

■ What's an estate sale? I sometimes see them advertised?

Estate sales are a whole different breed from garage sales. By definition, estate sales occur after a death in the family. The surviving family members—or a third party—often sell off the effects. Thus estate sales are more organized. Since they are often held in private homes, those holding the estate sale limit the number of buyers who can enter. They naturally want to prevent light-fingered customers from shoplifting Grandma's silver and jewelry.

Prices are generally nonnegotiable in the morning. If you want to negotiate, ask, "Are your prices firm?"

The person behind the table may reply, "We are firm until 1 P.M."

"Are you going to half-price then?" If he or she says yes, come back at noontime, make your selections, and carry them around until 1 o'clock.

Final thought regarding estate sales: If you are getting up there in years, have you made your wishes known regarding your personal belongings? That's something to think about.

■ I'm seeing more and more consignment stores opening in my part of town. What's the story behind them?

Like a Mercedes Benz dealer who sells "pre-owned" cars, consignments stores view themselves as a cut above thrift shops and second-hand stores. Many consignment stores are middlemen who sell name-brand clothes and dresses in superb shape. A good-sized city may have a dozen consignment stores, which you can find listed in the Yellow Pages under "Clothing—Used."

Consignment stores sell a broad spectrum of high-end merchandise. You can buy everything from an expensive ladies' teddy to a full-length mink stole. You're going to pay considerably more than garage sale prices, but you're also going to pay considerably less than retail. Consignment stores like Rags Fifth Avenue and Second Hand Rose sell single-owner dresses, ladies' wool suits, cocktail dresses, expensive furs, fashionable blazers, jewelry, leather belts, hats, alligator purses, and Bally shoes—all at tremendous discounts.

■ How much of a discount are we talking about?

You can figure 60 to 80 percent off retail. In a retail store, a woman's Pendleton wool suit might run almost $200 for the jacket and $100 for the pants. At a consignment store, you can buy both pieces for $60 to $90, and the Pendleton suit—perhaps worn only a few times—will look like it has never been worn. If you're shopping for an Easter hat, it will run from $2 to $10, a considerable discount from $10 to $50 new.

■ We have active teenagers into every kind of sport. How can we save in this expensive area?

Stores that deal with second-hand sports equipment—such as Play It Again Sports and Recycled Sports—have become popular in recent years, although the prices aren't dirt cheap. You can purchase baseball gloves, golf clubs, and ice skates very easily.

If you don't want to pay the higher prices at these recycled sporting goods stores, then keep an eye out for seasonal "swaps" for items such as bikes, skis, soccer shoes, and ice hockey equipment. Bike and ski swaps are often advertised in the newspaper.

Mail-order is a great way to purchase tennis rackets and golf clubs—if you know what you want. Specialty stores are fighting the mail-order companies by being service-oriented, so don't take advantage of the local retailer. It's not fair to try out a Great Big Bertha at the local discount golf shop and then order it from the mail-order company. Instead, borrow a friend's Great Big Bertha if you're going the mail-order route.

■ **It's not Big Berthas and Odyssey putters that are big in our homes, but sneakers for our teens. What can we do about the peer pressure to buy the latest $150 Air Jordan or $125 Shaq Attaq shoes?**

This one is easy. Tell your youngster that $50 (or whatever amount) is your limit, and if he wants MJ's shoes that badly, then he will have to cough up the difference. Occasionally, you can find close-outs or end lots of Nikes and Reeboks at Marshalls, TJ Maxx, and Ross Dress for Less.

Keep in mind that some stores sell "blems" or blemished shoes that really aren't all that damaged. Somebody may have worn them for a morning and returned them, or perhaps the sole wasn't glued perfectly. Deep discounts can be gained here.

This chapter is adapted from writings by Mike Yorkey.

8

You and Your
Older Parents

1

Grandma's Great Adventure

· ·

■ **My mother-in-law is in her mid-eighties and in failing health. I can tell that she doesn't want to talk about what will happen to her when she dies, and her son—my husband— would be the first one to admit that he doesn't have a way with words. She's a Christian, but what can I say to encourage her?**

It's great that you are so concerned about your mother-in-law. Her pending death is an important time for you, your husband, and your children.

That's what Gertrude Slabach, a mother of five from Alton, Virginia, would tell you if she could sit down and have coffee with you. Gertrude, you see, walked through the same valley you're walking through with her mother-in-law, except that Mom Slabach was a pistol. Whenever this eighty-five-old grandmother of thirteen was around one of her grandchildren, she would say "Aren't we having fun?" or "Didn't we have a good time today?"

■ **What did Mom Slabach do to have fun with her grandkids? She was pretty old.**

Mom Slabach could have fun doing anything, whether it was

accompanying the kids to Wal-Mart, sipping a Pepsi, or eating at Hardee's, she lived life to the fullest.

Gertrude says she never had mother-in-law conflicts, like some people, because Mom Slabach was her friend and mentor. That is why it was so difficult to believe that she was going to die.

■ What was her diagnosis?

Metastatic liver cancer. Typically, Mom Slabach tackled the situation head-on. "Don't call it my death; call it my arrival," she announced one evening shortly after learning the news. Then she cleaned out her lingerie drawer because "I'm not having you kids going through my dresser when I'm gone."

She took the lead in planning her memorial service. "And when I have arrived," she said as she worked furiously on a baby afghan that she wouldn't finish in time, "don't be a pile of mush. I want you to remember that life goes on."

■ We're getting ahead of ourselves here. Can you back up and tell me the whole story?

It all started after Labor Day. As autumn passed and winter arrived, Mom Slabach seemed to realize that it would probably be her last holiday season. Late in November, she asked Gertrude, "Do you think I'll be here for Christmas?"

"Sure, you'll be here for Christmas," she replied.

"You reckon I'll make it till Easter? Will I see Paul and Regina's baby?" she probed.

"Sure, you'll be here for Easter," Gertrude answered, secretly hoping she was right. "We'll just keep on having babies so you'll have to live a little longer to see the next grandchild."

Gertrude caught a faint sparkle in her eyes. "I don't know, Gert. Sometimes I think there ain't no way this cancer's gonna kill me, and then other days, I believe it just might."

A few weeks later Mom Slabach told Gertrude that she had a heart-to-heart talk with a friend who was having marital difficulties. Mom Slabach didn't hold anything back when it came to giving toe-to-the-line advice.

"Goodness, Mom," Gertrude exclaimed, "you didn't waste any words, did you?"

"I've got to make fast tracks, Gert, because I don't have much time left. People listen to me now because they know I'm dying."

■ When did Mom Slabach start to go downhill?

It was after the holidays. In late January, Mom Slabach was hospitalized and put on morphine to control her pain. She told her doctor that her wish was to go home and die. He agreed to the request, but on the stipulation that she receive twenty-four-hour care.

The entire family made plans to care for the woman they all loved. Mom's eight children all lived within a three-hour driving radius, which helped them schedule around-the-clock shifts.

"How gracious," she smiled when she heard about our plans. "Now I know why I had all those babies—so they could take care of me when I die."

They borrowed a hospital bed and put it in Mom's bedroom. A footstool helped her get in and out of the high bed. One night, she had to go to the bathroom, so she rang her dinner bell and waited. Dave, her son, was sleeping in the family room just down the hall. He didn't hear the bell, so Mom climbed down herself.

Hanging on to her IV pole, she walked to the family room and clanged her bell in her son's face. Dave awoke to see Mom's grinning expression that said it all: *Got you that time!*

Another Friday afternoon a neighbor brought Kentucky Fried Chicken to the house. At the end of a long week, everyone was tired and hungry.

"You kids know Aunt Babe is bringing supper tonight," Mom reminded us. "You better put that chicken away for another time."

"But I'm hungry," Dave said, as he stared at the bucket of extra crispy thighs and drumsticks. "I skipped lunch to get a job done early so I could take care of you."

"Then go ahead and eat," she said, spurring him and the rest of the family on.

Everyone dug into the Colonel's bucket as though it was their last meal.

"Now don't you kids tell Aunt Babe what you've done," she

admonished. "That would be an insult for her to bring supper and then you not be hungry."

Two hours later, when her sister delivered the promised meal, Mom asked Aunt Babe to bring some Jell-O to her room. Gertrude followed her down the hallway.

"Babe, you won't believe what these kids did," Mom said, as her sister spooned raspberry gelatin into her mouth.

"What's that, Orph?"

"Somebody brought Kentucky Fried Chicken, and they pigged out on it at 4 o'clock. The whole bunch of them. Didn't you notice that no one was in a hurry to eat your supper?"

"Mom!" Gertrude exclaimed. "You told us not to tell, and now you're telling!"

"I told you not to tell," she gloated, "because I wanted to."

■ **But back to my original question. How did Mom Slabach handle being on the edge of eternity?**

She took it well in the sense that her illness debilitated her strength slowly over time. Grandma Slabach's loss of weight and strength confined her more and more to bed. Even though she was pale and tired, she always had time for her baker's dozen grand-kids—especially for goodnight kisses. The children were too short to reach over the rails of her hospital bed, so they stood on a stool and tiptoed to reach her through the "kissing window." Their puckered lips met hers between the rails.

One bright Saturday morning, Gertrude gave her mother-in-law a bath. "Now you know you can't die today, Mom. It's the 29th day of February, and we would have to wait every four years to cele-brate your arrival."

"No, we wouldn't want that to happen," she replied. "But we're sure having fun dying, aren't we?"

Gertrude nodded yes, but inside she felt a catch in her throat.

As her condition deteriorated, Grandma began to ask questions that caught everyone off guard.

■ **What kind of questions did Grandma Slabach ask? Can I expect to hear these same questions?**

Maybe, maybe not. It depends on whether your family member wants to talk about his or her impending death. Grandma Slabach did. She wanted to know answers to questions such as these: "What will it be like—this departure, this arrival? Will there be a tunnel? I know Jesus will be on the other side, but will there be darkness first? Will I be alone? When do you think I will first see Jesus?"

■ **Those are heavy questions. What should I say if I hear them?**

Bring out a Bible and turn to that familiar passage of Scripture, Psalm 23. Read it as if you are reading it for the first time, especially verses 4-6:

> Even though I walk through the valley of the shadow
> of death, I will fear no evil, for You are with me; Your
> rod and your staff, they comfort me.
> You prepare a table before me in the presence of my
> enemies. You anoint my head with oil; my cup overflows.
> Surely goodness and love will follow me all the days of
> my life, and I will dwell in the house of the Lord forever.

Comfort your loved one with the knowledge that Jesus is preparing a place for him or her, a place where he or she will be able to dwell forever!

When Mom Slabach heard Psalm 23 presented this way, it answered many of her questions. "I won't just see Jesus on the other side," she said. "He's going with me through the valley. I won't be alone."

■ **How did her grandchildren take her impending death?**

One evening, after a day of intense pain, Mom Slabach announced, "When I am gone from here, don't think about what I've been through—think about where I've gone."

That prompted a question from her five-year-old grandson, Benjamin. "Grandma, are you going to die soon?"

"Yes, I probably will, Benji. But you be good and love Jesus, so when you get old and die you can come and be with me. Grandma will be waiting for you."

To the adults, she said, "After I'm gone, let your children cry. And don't be afraid to let them see you cry too."

■ Her final passing must have been special. What happened at the end?

One evening, Gertrude slipped into Mom's room alone. Though weak, she could still communicate. Several questions burned inside her. Gertrude knew she wouldn't have many more opportunities to talk with her mother-in-law.

"How does it feel to know you're going to die soon?" she asked. "How does it feel knowing you're going to heaven although you've never been there? How does it feel to know you can't come back to tell us what it's like?"

Gertrude reached for her hand as she leaned over to catch her words. Mom Slabach pondered those questions for a long moment.

"I do feel a lot of uncertainty, Gert, because I've never gone this road before. But there is also peace because I know Jesus is going with me."

She felt the end was very near. "Please don't pray for me to stay anymore," she whispered. "Don't hold me back."

"We won't, Mom," Gertrude answered. "When those angels come, you just go with them."

On March 16, 1992, the entire family knew the angels would be arriving any moment. No amount of Demerol could ease her pain, even momentarily. She thrashed and moaned, and her wish of going peacefully in her sleep was not happening. Everyone felt helpless as she struggled.

At 5:25 P.M., they saw her body suddenly relax. Her color changed to a pale gray. She stopped breathing. Then her face broke into a beautiful smile. That is when they knew Mom Slabach had arrived.

In the morning, the family hung a red banner (her favorite color) on the side of the house. It said:

Mom Has Arrived!

At the funeral home, Benjamin told his four-year-old brother, "That isn't really Grandma there, Timmy. It's just like an old turtle shell you'd find in the woods somewhere."

The parents all laughed at the story. "Wouldn't Mom have enjoyed that?" said one of her daughters-in-law.

Yes, she would have. And Mom Slabach? Well, she's having fun—for eternity!

This chapter is adapted from writings by Gertrude Slabach of Alton, Virginia.

2

When Alzheimer's Strikes

■ "I think everything that's coming ahead is bad for me now." That's what my mother said during my visit with her last week. I had to turn my head as I cried, knowing neither I nor the doctors can change that dismal future for her.

After a series of tests, doctors suggested Mama had symptoms of the early stages of Alzheimer's disease. This is a progressivly demeaning illness. Symptoms, which are gradual, include severe memory loss, impairments in language and reasoning, and visual spatial problems. A true diagnosis is only possible through autopsy.

Watching my mother decline socially, mentally, and physically over the last few years has been an overwhelming experience. Can you give me an understanding of how the disease works and how it affects both the affected person and the caregiver?

People who have had experience with this terrible disease offer these positive ways of dealing with Alzheimer's disease:

1. Separate the actions from the person. An Alzheimer's victim often uses profanity and may even become aggressive toward a caregiver. Accept that the frustration of not being able to accomplish ordinary tasks may cause the agitation and anger at the closest person.

Remember, for Alzheimer's victims, the world as they have known it is changing. They are slowly losing control of their life. Understanding that the anger is directed at the situation, not at you, helps you to control your response.

Your mother may even start cursing you, but don't judge her for it, even though you should still try to discourage it.

2. Don't say, "You already told me that!" Since she has no memory, she has no reason to refrain from telling you again. It is not to annoy you. Respond the first time and let the other words go in one ear and out the other.

3. Keep your language simple. Don't use detailed explanations because reasoning skills are weakening as well. Use simple words and short sentences to explain what you want done. When necessary, explain things one step at a time. You will have to repeat yourself over again. Do that with kindness in your voice.

4. Don't ask many questions. Questions turn off the brain. It is difficult enough for the Alzheimer's patient to recall information, much less understand what you want. Information is still there; it just can't be retrieved on demand. Make statements that don't require a response, or talk about things she brings up. Communicating this way reduces stress and the pressure of having to make a failing recall system perform.

5. Keep the quality of life as meaningful as possible. Always include the Alzheimer's victim in meaningful and fun experiences until it becomes too difficult. Continue to include her in activities and take her places, even if she is just a spectator. As the disease progresses, there may be complaints of never going anywhere or doing anything, but you can be satisfied personally knowing the daily quality of life is good.

6. Require the Alzheimer's patient to do as many daily living skills as possible for as long as possible. You may feel sorry and want to help her by doing things yourself. In reality, you will be helping the disease rob that particular skill sooner. Once a skill is stopped, no matter how simple, it cannot be relearned.

7. Know when to stop requiring certain skills. As it becomes more difficult to perform a skill, frustration and possibly anger will result if you require that it be done. There are many reactions, from becoming violent with you, to just hanging her head in shame and despair. Be discerning and know when to expect her to continue on and when to provide assistance.

This is not always a cut-and-dried decision. One day a task can be performed, and the next day completely forgotten. There will be times when right in the middle of a confusing conversation something sensible or even witty will be said. When this happens, smile or laugh—enjoy a special moment together. You will want to just freeze it in time and make her stay that way. And then you will wonder if it could be done now, why not all the time?

That's just the way this degenerative disease works. Things will go back and forth between the person you know and this shell of a personality until your loved one is gone completely. Knowing it's not just stubbornness helps keep a lid on possible anger and frustration on your part.

8. When you know the struggle is too great to use a fork, allow the use of a spoon. Don't make it worse because it hurts or embarrasses you to see your parent use a spoon, or because you're convinced that together you will beat this disease. It's okay to feel the hurt and the anger, but the skill is going to fade away, and the struggle is senseless. You have to accept each stage and go on.

9. Keep the environment as simple as possible, and don't leave that safe haven unless it is necessary. Everyday surroundings provide security. When you take the person out of this security, anxiety increases. She may not want to go somewhere to do something previously enjoyed. It is because she no longer feels safe outside her home, the sanctuary. It is only there that things are familiar.

If your mother is still able to live in her home (with or without at-home caregiver help), she may feel lost when she leaves her house. If taken somewhere, she may frequently ask to go home. You may have to decide that all visiting will be done at her home. She needs that home-court advantage. When you must take her somewhere, it's not a bad idea to keep one familiar person in her sight, so she will not feel completely lost and abandoned.

10. Guard this person's dignity. Let's say your mother is eating with all of you around the table. She tries to sneak and use her hands to pick up the soft food. Instead of scolding her, accept that she needs help and place the food on the spoon and the spoon in her hand.

She may become despondent and feel like a fool—and your heart may break—but try not to "parade" her lack of skills when possible.

When she says, "I used to be able to do a lot, but I'm not worth a thing anymore," just continue to love her. God loves us all in whatever stage of life we are. We are all people of worth to Him. Always communicate His love and your love when statements like this are made.

11. If you are the primary caretaker, arrange some time away for yourself. Everyone needs time of their own. If we are only taking care of someone else's needs, we may develop emotional problems of our own because of the well-known situation of "burn out." If you expect to continue to take care of your loved one, take care of yourself.

12. Find a little humor during your time together. Sometimes when your loved one makes a mistake, you might feel like laughing, but you think it would be inappropriate. Laugh! Often the person will laugh right along with you and the moment suddenly becomes a regular, more bearable life experience. Laughter is a stress reliever and indeed, as Proverbs 17:22 says, "A cheerful heart is good medicine."

■ **What can I do to hold on to the memories of what Mother *was* instead of what she is now?**

Above all, it's imperative to hold on to memories of who your loved one was. As this disease has robbed your mother of her personality and dignity, it will attempt to rob you of all of your precious memories of times together. Let's face it: Alzheimer's produces a different person with some characteristics that are hard to accept. It is sometimes a battle to keep the current unpleasant happenings from overshadowing the old memories.

It's quite likely that your mother won't "do" anything anymore. She won't remember the steps for completing simple tasks. She will probably just sit there most of the time. Stand her up, when you can. Take her on walks around the neighborhood. Hold her hand and cuddle with her.

Tell her what a great cook she was and how she would sew up a new dress for you in a day for a special occasion. Tell her how you remember the times when you would lay in bed together and laugh and talk for hours.

■ **If Mother can't remember us, can she remember the Lord?**

Great question! During Alzheimer's early stages, your mother will still be able to pray and read her Bible. But if Alzheimer's grabs control, the disease will most likely make her forget the Lord also. But know that He remembers her and loves her. Jesus understands all the trauma and feelings of unworthiness she is suffering.

My seven-year-old grandson once asked, "Will Great-Grandma remember everything when she gets to heaven?" My heart slipped into my throat, and I didn't know what to say.

It's easy for a young child to wonder if a delusional great-grandmother will still remember him. We don't know a whole lot about heaven, but we do know that Revelation 21:4-5 says, "He will wipe every tear from their eyes. There will be no more death or mourning or crying or pain, for the older order of things has passed away. He who was seated on the throne said, 'I am making everything new!' "

Assure him that Great-Grandma will be all right when she gets her "new mind" in heaven. You should both experience a sense of peace as you ponder this promise, and cling to it daily with all your heart.

You'll need thoughtful moments like that in the coming days ahead.

This chapter is adapted from writings by Karen Greene of Tabor City, North Carolina.

3

Mom and the Talking Bears

. . . .

Editor's note: In God's great plan for our lives, generations come and generations go. On a personal level, however, that stark sentence means that our parents will one day die, just as we will one day become very old and leave this earth for our heavenly inheritance. In the following chapter, Doris Elaine Fell vividly captures the emotions she felt as her mother grew more frail and ill. Their roles seemed to reverse. Doris became the mother, she became the child.

If you are in this stage of life, or see it on the horizon, please read this chapter closely.

I never thought Mother would grow old.

To me, Mother stood for living and laughter. Vibrance and enthusiasm. A five-foot, one-inch retired school teacher with shiny brown hair and hazel eyes that sparkled with life.

She had her flaws, of course. Sometimes she was stubborn and shortsighted. Sometimes cranky or passively resistant. Yet she flourished on friends and parties, travel and new experiences—an ordinary woman who loved her church and her God. She was too busy to grow old and wrinkled.

I remember well the day in England when I noticed the first threat of her aging. We were on the last day of a three-week, ten-country whirlwind European tour. I couldn't budge—I had hit mileage exhaustion. But my then seventy-two-year-old mother hovered over me fully dressed, a list of the day's activities already mapped out.

As she prodded me to wakefulness, the sun pierced the London fog and stole through the window of our mediocre hotel—its filtered beams highlighting flecks of gray in Mother's hair.

"Mother," I stammered incredulously. "You've got gray hair."

She gave me a hand-to-hip stance, her amused expression ageless. "I'm old enough," she announced.

Even then, I laughed her old age away, deluded into thinking that she was invincible, eons away from frailty.

Sudden Downturn

Three weeks shy of her eighty-sixth birthday, Mother was still traveling, planning more trips, active in a hand bell choir, and contemplating her next birthday party. But then cerebral strokes hit her like an eighteen-wheeler splintering a wooden barricade, thrusting ill health and old age on her. Her illness hurled her back in time to other days, other memories. She fought back with everything within her—groping for recall, clutching at normalcy, refusing to quit.

In the days following that first mini-stroke, I cried all the way home, a thirty-mile round-trip of tears. I was blinded to the thousands of others bearing a similar pain and was haunted by my long-standing promise to the Lord to always take care of my mother.

As Mother became more dependent, my freedom dwindled. I went from full-time registered nurse at a hospital to full-time caregiver at home. Soon two of us were living Mother's life; no one was living mine. My frustration mounted. *Counting it all joy* never entered my thought process.

I was splintered from the same block. I had Mom's creativity and integrity, her stubbornness and tenacity. But I was explosive in my personality. We seemed always to be two iron wills locking, grating against each other. But we were fiercely loyal. Somehow, we'd survive.

For Mother, life's dignities dropped slowly, one by one. She described herself well, saying, "Here I come just scuffing along—sheer grit, dogged determination." Then she whispered, "It's so sad. Nine-tenths of it is nothing but old age. I'm growing old, and I can't do anything about it. It's happening so fast."

Even though she was failing, I determined that she would keep the dignity of looking nice—hair permed, clothes neat, and matching shoes shined. I focused on the outward appearance, forgetting her heart cries. Then one day as she shuffled into the kitchen, gripping her walker, she said, "Steer me over to the sink, Doris. I may not be much good anymore, but I can still dry dishes."

My throat tightened. Had I robbed her of the dignity of being needed? From then on, as long as she was able, she dried dishes—at times only one or two.

Somewhere along those early days of her illness, the reversal of roles slipped in unannounced. I became like the mother; she like the child. I tried to shield her from rejection when friends stopped visiting and the phone ceased ringing. I read Bible passages and sang hymns to her at bedtime. As the years slipped by, I cringed at the sight of blenderized vegetables, fumed at spilt juices, and scowled at missing buttons. But when she stumbled and fell, over and over, I lifted her to her feet and gently helped her take those first halting steps again.

Mom constantly resisted mother-sitters, but she found joy at the home of a friend—a home alive with five toddlers, two grandmothers, and two poodle dogs. And she always marched off proudly to the Garden Grove Day Care Center (*school*, as she called it). I framed her art work from the center, and tucked her loving, witty sayings in my heart and in my journal.

In these lonely, painful days of my single parenting, she pressed me with questions about dying, innocent and childlike in their intensity: *Will I be afraid? How long does it take to get to heaven? Will my Mom and Dad know me?*

Yes, her parents would know her. But I was still earthbound. I balked when she forgot my name, sometimes calling me Helen, Bella, or Marion. I felt like *my* identity was slipping until she said sadly, "All those names I've known for years. I keep forgetting them. One moment they're here. The next they're gone."

After that, I conceived ways to help her remember names. We took frequent hand-treks through the old-fashioned family album with pictures dating back one hundred years or more. We sorted through the snapshots of her seven siblings, her children, and grandchildren. And then, in the third year of her illness, we stumbled upon the most effective way of all to help her remember. A friend gave Mother a cuddly stuffed bear with a lavender ribbon around its neck. Mother laughed and hugged the bear. We named it Elmira for her mother. After that friends and family—even Mother's hairdresser—showered her with thirty bears of every shape and personality. We named each one for a family member.

The Talking Bears

The biggest bear of all—covered in plaid—was named Alonzo for the dad she so dearly loved. The one with the sailor suit for Harold, the Navy man in the family. And the smallest bear, Ryan, for her handsome, dark-eyed great-grandson.

It was easy for me to go from hugging the stuffed bears to frequently reaching out and bear-hugging Mother. One day when her spirits seemed low, I picked up the biggest bear and went to her. Pretending to speak for the bear, I said, "Hello, Edith. I'm Alonzo Cotton. Do you remember me?"

Her eyes misted. "Oh, yes. You're my pop."

"Do you remember walking down that dusty trail with me to meet Jesus?" the bear asked.

"Yes, she said clearly. "When I was seventeen."

I nudged the bear's face closer to her own. "Edith, you're my only child not in heaven."

"The only one?"

"The only one."

"My brothers? Harold . . . Ed . . . Alex?"

"They're all here with Mother and me. And someday Jesus is going to call you to heaven, too Edith. Then we'll all be together again."

She nodded, her face so full of understanding. "And I'll be ready to go," she answered softly. "I'm so very tired now."

I pressed the bear into her arms and she hugged it, a hug that must have reached clear to heaven.

The Long Road

Sometimes, however, heaven seemed distant to me as the days of Mother's painful journey toward eternity stretched on. I was angry with everyone, including God. From the beginning, it had been an almost insurmountable emotional journey. But even more, it was spiritual warfare: a battle to maintain *faith, hope, and love.*

Once in my frustration, I cried out, "Why am I taking care of you? What do you ever do for me?"

She looked so vulnerable when she answered, "I have always loved you, Doris."

I noted these things that Mother said and did in my journal. Her love and faith kept shining through. I began to see beyond her deteriorating body and began to catch glimmerings of that person tucked inside. Her body was dying, but her soul that would live forever was sparked with victory. God had not forgotten Mother or me. He was still holding our hands, walking with us, sheltering us in His love, carrying us over the rough spots, and bottling up our tears in eternity.

I gathered these truths like bouquets of flowers. Now I saw them as tiny delicate rosebuds of her love, His love. In her frailty, God allowed me to see her inner strengths. Through Mother, He awakened me to the nearness of heaven.

One such truth stands like a rose, taller than the rest. I was leaning against the kitchen sink one day, my hands thrust deep in the dishwater. Agonizing self-pity pricked my soul. I was arguing with God—putting limitations on my twelve-year-old impossible burden. I confessed that I was botching the job. I couldn't make it one more day.

The room was midnight-still, but inside I was half screaming, begging for a way out. I turned suddenly. Mother stood framed in the narrow hallway, gripping her walker for balance. Her hazel eyes held mine. For a fleeting moment, I wondered how long she had watched me. In a fragile whisper she said, "Someday, Doris, you'll be glad you took care of me."

Amazingly, she who bore me knew me better than I knew myself. I caught the fragrance of her love like a rose in bloom as I crossed the room to her and buried my chin in her salt-and-pepper waves. "I'm already glad I'm caring for you," I said sincerely.

I remember when we celebrated Mother's ninety-first birthday. As her thin, vein-rippled hands tugged at the birthday wrappings, I realized again that Mother had never intended to grow old or ill or helpless. Our gaze met; she smiled happily. Watching her joy, I was keenly aware of my godly heritage.

Mother will not leave me houses and lands, padded bank accounts or sparkling diamonds. But she is leaving me her strength of character as a living legacy. That tremendous capacity to love and forgive. Her amazing fairness. Her spiritual wisdom. Her humor. Her unquestionable integrity. Her ability to sometimes melt my impatience and cutting remarks with a trusting smile. And her confident, unswerving conviction that the *Lord is her Shepherd.*

Edith Fell lived one more year before dying at the age of ninety-two. Doris Elaine Fell is a writer living in Huntington Beach, California.

4

Facing Up to a Nursing Home

■ I have loved my independence as much as anyone, so the thought of whether to put Mother into a nursing home has been quite distressing for our household. We are not physically able to care for her; we live 1,000 miles away, and we still have two college-age children living at home while they commute to a local university to save money. Although I dread it, the time is drawing nigh when we will have to talk about putting Mother in a nursing home, or should we have her move in and live with us? This is such a complicated decision.

Scripture commands children to care for their parents. Sometimes this can best be provided in the children's home. Sometimes a nursing home is a better choice.

Both elderly parents and children should recognize that God's command does not exclude nursing homes. Adult children need to know that they are not necessarily abandoning their parents by helping them move to a retirement facility.

Caring for aged parents at home is a tremendous responsibility that presents many challenges for both parents and children. If the house is very small and bathrooms limited, it can be more difficult for an elderly person to live in a house with a family.

■ What advice do those who have gone ahead of me have?

Early planning is extremely important. Believe it or not, the most important preparation is not financial or emotional. Rather, it's taking your need to the Lord and asking Him for guidance as you prepare to talk about a nursing home with your elderly parent.

If at all possible, the discussion has to be face-to-face for such an important decision. Say something to the affect of: "Mother, Andrew and I have been concerned about your health and whether you will be well taken care of. Can we spend a few minutes talking about what we should do?"

She may be embarrassed to talk about it. Gently ask where money and important papers are located. Who does she want to be given power of attorney over her financial and personal matters?

If your talk proceeds smoothly, turn to her medical care. What medical steps does she want taken in the terminal stages of an illness? Does she want dramatic measures taken to prolong her life? Does she want CPR, life support, or tube feeding?

Finally, and this discussion may have to wait (although it's better to get it all done at once), what are her instructions about her funeral arrangements? What are her wishes for the type of memorial service she would like?

Instructions should be written and signed by her. Power of attorney should be notarized. Don't leave anything to chance.

■ At what age do aging parents move into a retirement facility?

Everyone ages differently. Everyone's health is different. As average life expectancy rises (seventy-three for males, seventy-eight for females) to ages unheard of a century ago, many seasoned citizens are not ready for a nursing home until their mid-eighties, even early nineties.

A move into a nursing home should be made when it will enhance the quality of life for your loved one. Are the everyday details of life—doctor's visits, shopping, upkeep of the house, transportation—becoming burdens? The caring environment of a home can free a person to enjoy friends, activities, and life once again.

Many people think life ends once they enter a nursing home.

But many seasoned citizens—who worried that they were too much of a burden to their families—have blossomed under a nursing home environment. The new lifestyle worked for them.

■ **What happens if Mother suffers a slight stroke and we have to suddenly contemplate a nursing home for her?**

All too often a hospital will tell a patient and his family on Thursday afternoon that Mother will be released on Monday morning. The family then has three frantic days to search for a nursing home. Not an ideal situation.

If your mother's sudden illness has caught you and the family flatfooted, you will have to scramble. Look at facilities affiliated with a Christian institution or church—even if it is some distance away and not entirely convenient for the family. A Christian home usually has an entirely different spirit of love and concern from one that is not church-related.

The facility doesn't have to be affiliated with your denomination, but it should have a philosophy of care based on biblical principles and an attitude of service and ministry to the residents.

Quickly, visit several homes.

FOR MORE INFORMATION

If you are caring for an aging parent, be sure you know your own limits. Otherwise, you run the risk of becoming exhausted, sick, depressed, and burned out. When you're in that condition, you're not going to be in shape to help aging parents.

If you need more information, here are some helpful resources:

▶ **American Association of Retired Persons** has various free publications on caregiving, long-term care, and nursing homes. Write: AARP, 601 E Street N.W., Washington, DC 20049. Phone: (800) 424-3410. If writing, include a self-addressed, stamped envelope.

▶ **American Association of Homes for the Aging** can help you locate a suitable nursing home. Contact them at 901 E Street, N.W., Suite 500, Washington, DC 20004. Phone: (800) 508-9442.

▶ **Family Caregiver Alliance** offers legal information, workshops, and referrals to local support groups for caregivers. Contact them at 425 Bush St., Suite 500, San Francisco, CA 94108. Phone: (800) 445-8106.

Take family members along. When you visit, ask about the home's philosophy of caring. Notice whether you sense genuine staff interest in the residents.

Ask about admissions procedures and criteria. Investigate extra charges not covered in the basic rate: laundry, disposable paper products, trips to the doctor, television, and telephone calls. Policies different from home to home.

■ How hard it will be for Mother to adjust?

It all depends on the person: adjustment can range from a "piece of cake" to a living hell. Talk to your mother about the change in lifestyle that will be happening in her life. She will be suddenly living in close quarters with other people. While this offers opportunities to make new friends and develop close relationships, it certainly requires adjustment.

Family members need to give as much support and encouragement as possible during the first day, week, and month in a retirement facility. Frequent visits, if you live close enough, emphasize that none of the importance or love in your relationship has changed because of the new circumstances.

■ Is there anything we can do to make the adjustments easier?

Bring as much of her furnishings and personal belongings as possible. Some nursing homes encourage bringing quilts, bedspreads, photographs, and other personal effects. If she has developed interests or hobbies in retirement, she doesn't have to give them up now. She can continue enjoying almost everything she did before, while finding new friends with whom to share them.

No doubt that your mother will have to make an attitude adjustment—more easily said than done at her age. Be kind and patient as you explain that life will be different but not worse.

■ Whenever I broach a subject like her age, Mom bristles and we don't get anywhere. Is there something else I can say?

Tell her that God understands aging. His people in the Bible grew old just as we do. Both David and Elisha were bedfast at the close of their lives—they weren't strong and mighty to the end. In later years, Isaac couldn't even distinguish his own sons.

The aging process is entirely natural. In fact, one of God's blessings is the gift of a long life. "Gray hair is a crown of splendor; it is attained by a righteous life," Proverbs 16:31 reminds us. Regardless of one's mental or physical condition, God promises His everlasting care and love.

Here is another portion of Scripture you can read to your mother from Isaiah 46:4: "Even to your old age and gray hairs I am he, I am he who will sustain you. I have made you and I carry you; I will sustain you and I will rescue you."

The chapter is adapted from writings by Bill Weir, the administrator of the one-hundred-bed Presbyterian Reformed Home in Pittsburgh, Pennsylvania, and Ann A. Gordon, a writer from New Castle, Pennsylvania.

5

Ten Tips for Trips with Older Travelers

▪ **As full-fledged members of the "Sandwich Generation," we have to look out for my mother.** Mom has always loved to travel, and when I told her about a big camping trip that we were planning for the summer, she wistfully said, "Oh, that's something I'd love to do."

I know my mother well enough that she would never ask to accompany us, but I know that it would thrill her to no end to sit in our minivan and watch the sights pass while we rack up the miles. If we're really going to do this—invite Grandma on our summer vacation—what do I need to know?

You need to know two things:

1. You'll never regret taking your parent on a family vacation and the memories that trip will create for you and the children.

2. It's not going to be easy.

We're talking about one parent here. If both your parents are alive, the logistics of organizing two different families and their advanced age could be too much. In that case, you're probably better off planning some "long weekend" trips with Granddad and Grandma instead of a two-week, gotta-see-the-Grand Canyon-and-the-entire-West Coast-trip.

Colleen Reece of Auburn, Washington, did take one of those big touring events, but it was just with her mother. They traveled 3,742 miles (yes, she kept track) on a route that ranged from Idaho's Sawtooth Mountains to the canyonlands of Utah. They also traveled through southern Colorado, northern New Mexico, and Albuquerque. Their fortnight on the road took them to national parks and relatives, and they experienced just about every summer meteorological phenomenon known to man: stifling heat, claps of thunder, sheets of lightning, sudden cloudbursts, and gale-force winds.

But what was unusual about the excursion? Colleen's mom turned ninety-five a few weeks after they returned home.

■ **How did Colleen manage to accomplish that? Didn't she have reservations about starting a trip with, I dare say it, such an old mother?**

Yes, she certainly did, and Colleen thought long and hard while deciding to bring her mother along. But as long as your older traveler is in reasonably good health, you should forget your worries and go, she says. You'll have the time of your life, and so will your passenger, as long as you consider these tips:

1. Think ahead. Consider your itinerary with your parent in mind, but don't be afraid to include places you want to see that may be difficult for him or her. When Colleen and her mother visited Mesa Verde National Park in Colorado, Mom didn't feel like doing much walking in the 8,500-foot altitude.

Solution? They parked in a shady spot and unloaded a folding lawn chair. Mom could see the cliff dwellings across the canyon while Colleen hiked. When she returned, Mom was chatting with several friendly travelers. Several commented, "What a good idea to bring your own chair. I'm going to do that with my mom or dad."

2. Allow more time—maybe 50 percent more time. This is not going to be a trip where you walk from one end of the Las Vegas Strip in the morning, see Boulder Dam in the afternoon, and take in the Cirque du Soleil circus that evening at the Mirage Hotel. You should skip the taxing walk and instead start the day with the trip to the Boulder Dam, leaving you plenty of time to be rested and ready for an evening show.

Older parents move slower and don't like to be rushed. They may need to sleep longer in the morning. If that's the case, use that time to do something on your own, like taking a sightseeing walk or visiting a nearby tourist attraction.

3. Get your parent his or her own room. Everyone needs a break from each other. If you can afford it, reserve separate rooms, even if you have to scale down your accommodations. In other words, this might not be the year you stay in Hyatt's.

However, some chains, such as Embassy Suites, have two-bedroom suites, which can often be cheaper than renting two separate rooms. Look for off-the-highway motels to reduce traffic and freeway noise; it may take another five minutes of driving, but it will be worth it. Request a room on the back side and away from the street. You can also carry a small electric fan to drown out noise inside and outside the building. If other guests are noisy beyond reason, call the manager. You have a right to a good night's sleep, that's what you're paying for, and managers handle these situations all the time.

One last thought: Everyone in the family will be in a better mood if everyone sleeps well. Adding a snoring grandparent to the mix can make for a miserable vacation.

4. Keep a regular schedule. Most seniors prefer a set routine of on-time meals and a regular bedtime. Others just have to have their prunes for breakfast and tea at 4 P.M. Go with the flow.

If you're on the road, have a picnic lunch or easy snacks in the

---

QUICK TIPS

▶ Pack a night-light or two. Waking up in unfamiliar, ever-different rooms can lead to groping, stumbling, or even a fall on the way to the bathroom.

▶ Double-check necessary medicine, glasses, and sanitary needs prior to leaving.

▶ Lighten up by packing light. Most likely, you'll have to do the heavy lifting, so if you're schlepping heavy suitcases for two weeks, you'll end up grumpy.

▶ Take along a digital clock with large, red numerals.

▶ Don't bother with books. You probably won't have time to read them.

▶ Actually, you should bring one book—the Bible. Begin and end each day with prayer. This little act can speak volumes, especially if you're traveling with an unbelieving parent.

car. Crackers, chips, fresh fruit, dried fruit, and Nips candy are easy to pack and bring along. Carry plenty of drinking water, and if your parent needs to take certain medication at certain times of the day, *you* do the remembering. They might forget because they're out of their set routine.

5. Avoid the exotic. If you're traveling through Cajun country, this might not be the time you insist on ordering braised crawfish for the entire table. Or oysters on the half-shell. That's a recipe for some severe indigestion. If you enjoy spicy, hard-to-digest food, order it yourself, but don't insist on everyone at the table having to sample *l'escargot.*

6. Take plenty of bathroom breaks. Some seniors may dread auto trips because they require a "pit stop" every hour or 65 miles, whichever comes first. Highway rest stops may be a hundred miles apart, and once there, the "facilities" may be primitive at best or foul and dirty at the worst. You'll need to anticipate restroom stops and realize that you won't be able to cover as many miles as you're used to making.

Traveling by motor home can mitigate this concern, unless there isn't a toilet on board. In this case, you may want to pack a portable potty.

7. Stop to smell the flowers along the way. A trip with Mom or Dad will not be a trip in which you rack up 600 miles before the sun goes down. Back off the accelerator. Stop at points of interest. Realize the point of the trip is not getting from here to there but what you see between here and there.

Besides, everyone needs to stretch muscles and get some fresh air, especially senior travelers and small children. They'll both be glad you stopped.

8. Wear loose clothing. A long-sleeved, loosely woven shirt or blouse protects arms from the intense summer sun that pierces even an air-conditioned car.

9. Wear plenty of sunscreen. Some senior travelers may figure that they are beyond the need for sunscreen, but you want them to lather lotion on so they won't get sunburned and be miserable for the rest of the trip.

10. Take a soft pillow to use as a backrest. Car seats and couches on motor homes can get hard and uncomfortable after hours of driving. You can also use that soft pillow in motel beds if their pillow is unsatisfactory.

This chapter is adapted from writings by Colleen L. Reece of Auburn, Washington. She's glad she made that big trip with her mother because she died less than a year later.

6

How to Enjoy Your Elderly Parents

. . . .

■ **Deep in my heart, I want these to be the golden years for my parents, times full of laughter and love and sentiment. We want to be able to look back with no regrets. How can we do that?**

To do so requires some specific actions now. If you're going to be visiting your parents or in-laws in the near future—especially those past the "active senior" stage—remember to shift into a lower gear. Things move along at a slower pace, so be prepared to bring plenty of patience with you.

For those of us who've been addicted to the adrenal high of our fast-paced lives, to teenagers in the house, to young adults still living in your home, the slower pace of elderly parents can be difficult to adopt. An elderly parent in her eighties can be an exercise in patience when you're helping her spoon applesauce into her mouth. Just take your time and remember that doing even the most mundane tasks take longer.

■ **Yes, I have noticed that I lose my patience with Mom and Dad. But I'm telling myself that the elderly, if they are still** mentally alert, intuitively know that the sands of time are about to reach the other end of the hourglass. What are some practical ways I can reach out to them?

Keep touching your elderly parents. A touch of the hands means much more than the simple gesture that it is. If you walk over to your mother to talk to her, stand next to her and put your hand on her shoulder. The touch will warm her and say *I care about you. You're my only mom.* You can do other simple things that bring physical interaction between the two of your. For instance, you can brush her hair, trim her toenails, hold her arm as you assist her into the car, rub her feet with lotion, and even lock arms when you walk. At night, tuck your mother into bed and plant a kiss on her forehead. Look for opportunities to touch that precious person!

Another way to show you care is to call and ask if you can pick up anything at the supermarket for your elderly parents. Their refrigerators and cupboards are often bare, and seniors find it all too easy to open a can of soup or pop a frozen item into the microwave. Meanwhile, they stop eating fresh fruits and vegetables. You can also do some clothes shopping as well, offering to pick up new underwear or replace that worn-out coat. You can have the store gift-wrap each item so she has the joy of unwrapping each "present."

■ Can I still plan family reunions, or is that too much for an elderly parent?

By all means, get that family reunion on next summer's calendar now! This will often give your elderly mother or father something to look forward to. If possible, ask them to help in the planning. Perhaps they can address envelopes or help organize the activities. Having an important family event on the calendar offers hope for the future.

At the reunion, make sure the grandchildren and great-grandchildren spend at least ten to fifteen minutes with your elderly parents. This might be their only memories of them in future years.

■ It's frustrating when I ask my parents to talk about the past. Sometimes, Dad can better remember a cross-country move fifty years ago than what he had for dinner last night.

But Dad loves talking about his childhood, and I can still recall the evening he listed all the cars he ever owned, from the 1954 Chevrolet to the '94 Honda Accord he's still driving.

Keep Dad talking, which will keep him alert. Sometimes, if you have to prod things along, take your father to an antique store. Walking past television sets from the early 1950s might unleash a flood of memories for him. He'll enjoy remembering those early shows from Milton Berle and Jack Benny, and what a technological wonder it was to have "TV pictures" in the home. Maybe he even remembers "TV dinner trays" that were so popular in the 1950s.

If possible, drive your parents back to where they grew up. Take a spin through the old neighborhood, and don't be bashful about knocking on the door of your old house. You may even be invited in, which will delight everyone in the family.

■ **Since I'm the closest child to my parents—they live twenty miles away—it seems like my brothers and sisters expect *me* to drop everything and tend to Mom and Dad when they need something.**

Understand that you may have to carry the load since you live the closest. Don't let your attitude sour, although it's easy to grumble about what has happened. Just give the gift of love to the one who gave you so much in years gone by.

■ **What happens if I can't visit often since I live in another state?**

The next best thing is calling and writing regularly. When Barbara Crosley's mother was hospitalized, she felt badly about having to stay with her job 300 miles away. What could she do to let her know she still cared?

She decided to send a card or write a short letter every day for two-and-a-half weeks—eighteen notes in all. She didn't view it as a large effort on her part, but in phone conversations with her mother later on, she reminded her time after time how much those letters lifted her spirits.

There's almost no excuse for not keeping in steady phone contact these days. Many of the long-distance phone services charge around ten cents a minute for evening and weekend phone calls. Whether near or far, a phone call will lift an elderly parent's spirits.

■ **My husband is retired, and we have the flexibility to move. I feel like we should be closer to Mom, and my husband has given me the blessing to move. Can you encourage me to go through with it?**

Barbara Crosley can. After her mother's health worsened, she and her husband, Ron, moved back to Kansas, where they found it necessary to put her into a twenty-four-hour total care facility. Once a week Barbara makes the ninety-five mile trip. "It's a commitment we made when we decided to move back," says Barbara. "Last week I enjoyed lunch with her, and we journeyed through her photo album, and sang together. Mom is capable of remembering the old songs and enjoys singing with me. Then she let me read a book to her.

"One thing I've found is that Mother is very jealous of our time and attention. She really doesn't appreciate if we stop to chat with others. Mother truly appreciates when I fix her hair using a curling iron and applying cosmetics—anything to give her attention. She has always strived to look nice, and we lavish her with lotions and creams. We buy expensive ones, and as the nurses rub her, they can feel her soft skin and smell the pleasant fragrance. Consequently, we are doing her a favor."

■ **You mean that's one way that Barbara is keeping an eye on her mother's care by how much cream and lotion is used?**

In a way, yes. Whenever Barbara and Ron visit, they note if she has been bathed lately, had her hair combed, and served all the meals she wants. At the same time, Barbara asks the staff how her mother is eating and if she has been needing more assistance. Do any of her clothes need mending? Is she getting up and about and playing dominoes and other games? Has she been participating in crafts activities?

"When weather permits, I take Mother outside in her wheelchair, and we walk up and down the small town sidewalks," said Barbara. "The other day, she asked, 'Barbara, if you bought another car, would you buy this one?' as she pointed at a shiny new convertible.

"When I told my brother this story, he said, 'Perhaps she has wanted a convertible all these years and we never knew it!' We try hard to keep a sense of humor. We also try to keep Mother's room cheerful. I keep a floral arrangement on her bedroom wall and change it at different seasons. At Christmas, we have a small tree with bright lights and a few things such as a Christmas bear that we place in her room. Each week I usually take a bright carnation with a sprig of green to brighten the room. We have a large cork board completely covered with pictures of the family. We attend the special events such as Thanksgiving dinner, Christmas dinner, summer picnics, and homemade ice cream socials.

"I can tell you this: Mother notices how I look when I go to visit. She will compliment me several times, so this tells me it is important to her that I look nice. I want her to know that my visits are important to me also.

"One time I took Mother out for a ride, and she had so much pleasure driving into the Kansas farm fields, watching the combines harvest the wheat. She waves at folks and genuinely enjoys herself.

"My dog Muffin goes straight to Mother's room, and dogs lift an elderly person's spirits. I am there at mealtime, and many volunteers from the small town come to assist with feeding those who cannot feed themselves. We visit and laugh. Some come just to fold bibs and towels and put them away. Many hands make light work."

■ **What does Barbara find to talk about? That has to be difficult.**

Barbara says she shares what her family has been doing, who's been where, things like that. She tries to refrain from mentioning ones who have died, unless her mother asks for news about that particular person. "We try to be cheerful, and we cherish the time with her," said Barbara. "Every day with her is a blessing."

This chapter is adapted from writings by Barbara Crosley, who lives in Elkhart, Kansas.

7

The Perfect Gift

. . . .

■ What do you give a father who is terminally ill? Shopping for Dad had never been easy. What he wanted, he bought for himself. Never excited about gifts, he always thanked me politely but sometimes left the package unopened for days.

I always sent him something on special occasions: a soft blue shirt, studio pictures of my three sons, a box of homemade peanut brittle—something to let him know I cared. But with my father on his deathbed, the right gift seems impossible to find right now.

Does your father know the Lord? If not, that is the only gift that matters—a belief in Jesus Christ and eternity in heaven with Him.

Joanne Long wondered the same thing when her elderly father was admitted to the hospital, where he was slowly succumbing to the chronic leukemia he had battled for five years. When word came in November that he was critically ill, she flew out from Oklahoma to be with him. Joanne and her brothers spent several days at his bedside. Seeing the family gave him the desire to rally.

Those hours were sweet, quiet ones, for Dad's toughness had mellowed. For the first time since he had become an adult, he was able to show Joanne he loved her by touching her gently. Still, he could not believe in Jesus.

■ **Why was that? Was he never a Christian like my father?**

As a young medical student, Joanne's father had embraced Darwin's theory of evolution and forsaken his parents' Christian beliefs. He became increasingly scornful of religion until science itself became his source of faith, his guide, his god.

No wonder her father was dismayed when Jesus became the most important person in Joanne's life. He hadn't expected such a thing to happen. "I can't believe this," he would say. "You're supposed to be an educated woman."

In their frequent arguments, he insisted that even though she was a college graduate, her decision for Christ completely refuted her intelligence.

■ **Didn't she try to explain her faith?**

Repeatedly. But all her attempts for meaningful spiritual discussions with him appeared fruitless. Even when he learned of his serious illness, he refused to consider the possibility of eternal life and his need for the Savior.

As Joanne kept vigil beside his hospital bed, her father slept. Holding his frail, heavily veined hand, she prayed aloud softly. She thanked God for loving her earthly father. She thanked Him that Jesus had died so her dad might go to heaven. She trusted Him that by the working of the Holy Spirit her dad would come to know Jesus.

On the fifth day of her visit, Dad was much improved, but the time had come for her to return home to her family and her classroom. Holding back tears so her father wouldn't be embarrassed and turn from her, she kissed him good-bye as though they would be together soon.

Christmas neared. Once her father was able to talk briefly on the phone. When she told him she was praying for him, he responded weakly, "You keep doing that, Jo."

Joanne's spirit leaped with joy. It was the first time her father had *ever* made a positive response to a faith overture. After that talk, she continually repeated to herself the biblical promise from Acts 16:31, "Believe on the Lord Jesus Christ and you will be saved—you and your household."

Her Christmas shopping was nearly completed. But what could she send her dying father—a father who needed Jesus?

■ **Yes, I have wondered the same thing about my loved ones. It seems like a shirt, candy, or even pictures just doesn't fill the bill.**

You're right, because material things—even expensive and thoughtful ones—pale in importance when placed next to the importance of eternal salvation.

When Joanne stared at the pots of lush red poinsettias at the florist's, she turned away with burning eyes. Dad didn't need flowers. There would be plenty of them—later. The only thing he needed, the only thing that could make an eternal difference, was Jesus.

Sitting at the kitchen table where she wrote notes, paid bills, and graded student themes, Joanne tried to force herself to begin addressing the stack of Christmas cards. But the list of names was a blur before her. She could think of nothing except her helpless, hopeless father. Softly, she repeated the words, "You—and your household."

Suddenly a quiet, deep assurance came to her, as clearly as though an audible voice had spoken. *There is time. This is the time. Write a letter. This time the words will be right and he will hear.*

With confidence born of the Holy Spirit, she began to write. The words flowed into her mind more rapidly than she could ink them onto the paper. There was no pondering, no hesitancy, no doubt.

As you read Joanne's letter to her father, imagine incorporating the same words into a letter to your unsaved parent:

> Dear Dad,
> I love you. I miss you. I wish I could be there with you while you need me. Particularly, I'd like to sit beside you and read some beautiful thoughts from my Bible. God loves you so very much. It is His desire for you to understand that.

Jesus has gone into heaven to prepare a place for each of us (John 14:2). That place in heaven is very real to me, and I look forward eagerly to being with the Lord. We have all eternity to enjoy each other and to praise God for all His blessings. God has provided abundantly for us here. But these good things can't compare with the unending joy He planned for us in heaven, where there will be no tears, no sorrow!

I know, Dad, that Jesus is providing for you right now because that promise is in the Bible. Paul said in Philippians 4:19, "My God shall supply all your needs according to his riches in glory by Christ Jesus." And Jesus hasn't changed. He is "the same, yesterday, today, and forever." He is now what he proclaimed 2,000 years ago, which is "the way, and the truth, and the life." When we know the loving Jesus, we know the loving God.

Isn't that good news! How happy I am to be able to tell you that Jesus lives. That He loves us. That He plans for each of us who know Him to share His glory.

My prayer this moment is that you will take from God the gift of eternal life by receiving Jesus Himself into your heart. May the joy of Jesus be yours this Christmas and forever. I love you as my father and as a son of God.

Always your loving daughter,

Joanne

■ What happened after Joanne mailed the letter?

From the moment she began the letter, peace surrounded her. There was no more worry about her father, only a continuing calm assurance.

Shortly after sending the letter, Joanne talked with him—hearing only a few faded words—for the last time. Ten days later, the final news arrived.

The family buried Dad three days before Christmas. As the family was leaving the cemetery, a dear elderly woman who had helped care for him at the end called Joanne aside. Taking Joanne's hands in hers, she smiled confidently.

"I want you to know for sure," said the nurse. "Your father was all right with God before he died. I had the joy of being able to pray with him. While his mind was still clear, he gave his heart to Jesus."

Joanne cried then, but the tears were blessed. The Lord had provided Himself as the Perfect Gift.

All you have to do is present that Gift to your loved ones.

This chapter is adapted from writings by Joanne Long of Cordell, Oklahoma.

The
Last Enemy

Editor's note: For another perspective on talking to elderly family members about the Lord, Rebecca Price Janney captures her last emotive days with her grandmother.

"I'm never going to look in a mirror again," my feisty grandmother announced on her ninetieth birthday. Her raised chin defied the encroaching years.

"Why not?" I asked. "You look so good for your age."

"Because I look droopy and wrinkled, but inside I feel so young."

I knew the real reason, though. My grandmother was terrified of death. Whenever conversations turned toward things mortal, Grammy would remark, "Well, I'm never going to die!" This always got a laugh, but I sensed her turmoil.

Perhaps that's because Grammy didn't have much of a personal relationship with God. As much as I wanted Grammy—and myself—to be sure of her salvation and walk close to the Lord, I always hesitated to discuss it with her.

The two of us often butted heads like stubborn goats. For example, I liked fixing my meals from scratch and avoiding fat, but Grammy's idea of nourishment was frozen macaroni and cheese dinners warmed up in the microwave, followed by a Snickers bar

WHAT DO YOU SEE?

Editor's note: A woman who died at Ashludie Hospital hear Dunde, England, left behind this powerful poem that all of us need to ponder as we become older and older.

What do you see, Nurse, what do you see?
Are you thinking when you look at me—
A crabbed old woman, not very wise,
Uncertain of habit with faraway eyes,
Who dribbles her food and makes no reply
When you say in a loud voice, "I do wish you'd try."
Who seems not to notice the things that you do
And forever is losing a stocking or shoe,
Who resisting or not, lets you do as you will
With bathing and feeding, the long day to fill.
Is that what you're thinking, is that what you see?
Then open your eyes, Nurse. You're not looking at me.

I'll tell you who I am as I sit here so still.
As I move at your bidding, eat at your will.
I'm a small child of ten with a father and mother,
Brothers and sisters who love one another;
A young girl of sixteen with wings on her feet,
Dreaming that soon a love she'll meet;
A bride at twenty, my heart gives a leap,
Remembering the vows that I promised to keep;
At twenty-five now I have young of my own
Who need me to build a secure, happy home.

A woman of thirty, my young now grow fast,
Bound together with ties that should last.
At forty, my young sons have grown up and gone,
But my man's beside me to see I don't mourn.
At fifty once more babies play round my knee—
Again we know children, my loved one and me.
Dark days are upon me, my husband is dead.
I look to the future, I shudder with dread.
For my young are all rearing young of their own,
And I think of the years and the love that I've known.

continued next page

I'm an old woman now and nature is cruel.
'Tis her jest to make old age look like a fool.
The body it crumbles, grace and vigor depart.
There is a stone where I once had a heart.
But inside this old carcass a young girl still dwells,
And now again my bittered heart swells.
I remember the joys, I remember the pain
And I'm loving and living life all over again.
I think of the years, all too few, gone too fast,
And accept the stark fact that nothing can last.
So open your eyes, Nurse, open and see
Not a crabbed old woman
Look closer—see me!

and cookies. She didn't like the way I washed her clothes either, but *her* method excluded the rinse cycle.

I figured that with a track record like ours, I'd make a lousy witness for the Lord. "Please, Father," I would pray, "send someone to Grammy who can lead her to You."

Dark Clouds

I had recently married and was finishing graduate school when Grammy suffered a series of strokes. She took the changes hard, becoming irritable and demanding with my mother, her primary caregiver. I knew Grammy wouldn't last to her ninety-first birthday. If I was ever going to share the plan of salvation, I knew it had to be soon.

In the hospital a week before Easter, I went to Grammy's room determined to broach the subject she so hated. I trembled with fear. In her fragile condition, the last thing I wanted to do was upset her. She smiled weakly as I kissed her forehead.

"Are you okay, Grammy?" I asked, noticing how thin she had become.

She blinked her eyes in affirmation.

"You tell me if they're not nice to you here," I teased.

Again, the smile. She seemed so serene, but I gripped the cold bed railing tensely. "Well, I, uh, just wanted to know if you're still afraid, Grammy," I blurted. "If you're still afraid of death, I mean."

I expected her blazing green eyes to order me out of the room. Instead, Grammy took me completely by surprise. She shook her head "no" with great determination.

I didn't know what had happened, but I suddenly felt very sure that she had a relationship with Jesus and that she wasn't afraid. Before leaving, I briefly prayed with her.

A week later, I went to see Grammy after the Easter service. "Grammy keeps asking for something," said my mother, "and I don't know what it is. Can you figure it out?"

I leaned over Grammy's bed. "What is it? Can we get you something?" I asked softly.

She whispered very faintly, and then I finally understood. My eyes went all shiny as I said, "It's Jesus, right, Grammy? You want Jesus?"

She grinned and nodded like her old self.

"She wants Jesus," I said, turning to my puzzled relatives. Then a realization hit me. I ran upstairs and found a small plastic picture of Jesus. Triumphantly, I presented it to Grammy. "Is this what you wanted?"

"Je-sus," she whispered joyfully, grabbing the picture and clutching it to her breast. A smile lit her face. I think she would have been pleased with what she could see in a mirror at that moment.

At Peace

Grammy died the next day. After the funeral a few days later, my pastor told me that he had spent a long time with Grammy one afternoon. At that time, she confessed something that had kept her spirit in bondage for years. When my pastor assured her that Jesus would forgive all her sins, she accepted that gift. From then on, she was totally at peace with life—and death.

I think it's fitting that she died the day after Easter, that triumphant time when the last enemy of us all—death—was swallowed up in victory.

This material was adapted from writings by Rebecca Price Janney of Horsham, Pennsylvania.

9

You and Your
Tough Times

Losing a Parent, Losing a Child: When Life Has Let You Down

. . . .

■ My father suffered a heart attack in his late sixties, but by the time I flew to Reno to be by his side, he had already slipped into a coma. He lived only another week, and when he was gone, I never felt emptier in my life. Losing a parent wasn't an unbearable pain, but I still go through occasions when something reminds me of him and I tear up. I'm still working through the sorry fact of life that tragedies, illnesses, and setbacks happen to the best of families. What is the best perspective I can put on these situations?

Couples who have gone through the loss of an older parent or younger child say that the event helped them learn to support each other through pray for and with each other. They shudder to think what they would have done without having an Almighty God they could take their troubles to.

We live in an imperfect world. See if you can see yourself in any of the following true examples:

▶ **Years into her marriage, a Montana woman began grieving for the loss of two children she aborted during her teenage years.** She wasn't a Christian back then, but that didn't excuse her deeds, she thought. She went through post-abortion counseling, which culminated in a memorial service. The aborted children were given names, and prayers were offered. It was a traumatic time, but her husband never left her side.

▶ **A New Jersey couple's oldest son was in a car accident that killed his fiancée a week before their wedding.** While recovering, he rededicated himself to Christ. The parents? They learned that caring for an injured son didn't mean they could neglect their young child—or each other. "Fortunately, my husband and I were close friends," said the mother, "or this tragedy could have torn us apart."

▶ **A Texas woman suffered a debilitating illness that put her out of commission for two years.** On a good day she could get dressed; on a bad one she couldn't get out of bed. The marriage was put on hold, and their sexual relations came to a grinding halt. Her husband, however, weathered the storm faithfully. Since he had pledged his love to her in sickness and in health, he saw her illness as a two-year blip over a lifetime of commitment. When she was finally cured, he knew their relationship would be stronger than ever.

■ **Tell me more: How do couples face life's difficult situations? How do couples respond when life has let them down? Do marriages automatically move to a deeper level, or does the fissure cause a marital split? It seems to me that I've heard that the death of a child, especially, can be the springboard to many marriages ending in divorce.**

First, know that there is no right way to respond to a tragedy. Because few of us get much practice, we can't expect each person to react the same way. Some people need their "space," while others have to cling to their spouse. Some clam up, while others have to "get it out." Just as we all look different, God gives us different defense mechanisms to cope with tragedy.

The second thing is that tragedies test the mettle of a marriage like no other ordeal. Of course, we can't go through life thinking, *Well, today my daughter could get killed crossing the street to her college classes*, but we can take some halfway measures so any unexpected events won't catch us *completely off* guard.

For those marriages that have yet to be touched by family trials, let this chapter promote discussion about how you might respond if a tragedy does strike your family. Who would you call for support? Have you prepared a will? (You *have* to state in writing how you want your estate managed in the event of your simultaneous death with your spouse, or if your death precedes your spouse's.)

■ **When my husband died in his early fifties, I wanted to shake my fist at God. I wanted to say,** *How could You—the God I serve—do this to me? Why couldn't You have taken me instead? Don had his whole life ahead of him.*

If grief can be measured (and it can't), what lessons can we learn when a loved one or spouse dies unexpectantly? What can we learn about dealing with a crisis at any level?

Here are some ideas:

1. Don't neglect each other. If a family tragedy strikes, don't immerse yourselves with your marital or work-outside-the-home roles.

2. Know that life is tough. Very few people travel through life accident- or disease-free and then die in their sleep at the ripe old age of eighty-five. These things happen.

3. Try to uncover each other's feelings, no matter how painful. It's unhealthy to try to handle grief alone. Yes, you have to respect a spouse's desire for privacy, but you also have to talk.

▶ Know that your relationship will change forever. The temptation is to put the marriage on autopilot and to occasionally check the instruments to see where the relationship is headed. From the air, everything may look fine, but the marriage has to come to earth some time.

▶ Remember that your future doesn't have to be determined by your past. Extreme tragedies in a marriage can make for deep wedges in a marriage. Don't fill them by looking outside your spouse or your faith.

Though it's impossible to predict every potential tragedy that may befall a family, playing "What if . . ." isn't a bad idea. Before you get to the stage where older parents become ill, discuss how you'll react if certain things occur. Are there any circumstances under which you'd be willing and able to take in a feeble or terminally ill parent? What will you do if you have to make the choice between a nursing facility or in-home care? Planning ahead will help you avoid making snap decisions based on your emotions.

■ **The loss of a child, I've heard, is _the_ most difficult and terrifying prospect for any parent who naturally expects any children to outlive them. Our son experienced a serious traffic accident that caused us to think long and hard about this issue. What advice comes from those brave parents who have walked this road that no parent wants to travel?**

Phyllis Cochran, a grandmother from Winchendon, Massachusetts, lost her middle child, Susan, to a brain tumor. When her daughter died, she thought her world had come to an end. No support group existed in her area at the time. Alone on her knees for months on end, Phyllis looked to the Lord for comfort and strength.

Instinctively, Phyllis knew that every day, in hundreds of towns and cities across North America, parents lose a son or daughter without warning. Miscarriages, stillbirths, fatal accidents, suicides, murders, and various illnesses snuff out thousands of young lives.

It is not uncommon for a bereaved parent to verbalize thoughts of suicide to join the child in death. It's not uncommon for a grieving mother not to able to walk down the cereal aisle at the supermarket, lest she start crying at the sight of her son's favorite breakfast food.

Most suffering parents agree that their priorities are "now in order." No longer will they expend energy on small disturbances. No longer are material comforts of lasting importance.

■ **What should I say if a good friend loses a son or daughter unexpectantly?**

Unless you've experienced the loss of a child, try not to say, "I know how you feel." The magnitude of pain and suffering for the grieving parents is difficult for anyone to understand. "I'm sorry" is usually sufficient.

In a home where God has been greatly acknowledged, the family will either find solace in Him or turn their backs on religion and God. If the latter occurs in your home, don't ask you spouse, "What happened to your faith?" Instead, continue to pray for him or her. Listen attentively and respond with a great deal of patience.

■ **What if a good friend loses a child to leukemia or a terrible accident? How can I be a blessing and not a burden?**

Phyllis Cochran lists these seven ways:

1. Be honest with yourself. Take a moment and ask if you are genuinely concerned for the grieving parents. Are you able to empathize and sympathize?

2. Pray for direction. Ask God to provide you with wisdom and discernment as you minister to your friend's needs.

3. Listen attentively. Assist the mourning parent in "getting it all out" when he or she starts describing pent-up emotions. But never force anyone to talk who is not ready. If someone talks about the child's death over and over, listen prayerfully. Often, healing is taking place and the afflicted is beginning to accept the death.

> **MORE ON GRIEF FOR A CHILD**
>
> For more on dealing with grief following the loss of a child, please read the following chapter, which contains a roundtable discussion from parents who've traveled down that sad path.

4. Offer your services. Don't wait for the person who lost a child to call you first. It usually never happens. Take the initiative. Make a meal. Run an errand. Do things the parents are too weak to do.

5. Mention the child's name. Contrary to what some friends assume to be painful, the sound of the late offspring's name is sweet music to the parent's ear. It says, "I remember. I care."

6. Encourage the bereaved. Gently let them know that it's all right to cry. One mother, after learning her teen son had drowned, buried her feelings.

The ancient Wailing Wall in Jerusalem served as a place to scream, shout, and cry unashamedly. We would do well to have our "Wailing Wall" when grief strikes. At times, the bereaved appear to make great strides in redirecting their lives. Then boom!—the anniversary of the death, birthday, or major holiday hits. Severe pain returns. Help them realize this is not unusual. Setbacks become more infrequent as time passes.

7. Finally, share Scriptures and offer prayer when appropriate. The Bible is filled with comforting verses of support, strength, and hope. Many will hunger to hear of God's love during grief. Share your faith in love. When the person is receptive, offer to pray with him or her. Prayer is a powerful resource and reminds us that God is sovereign.

This chapter is adapted from writings by Mike Yorkey and Greg Johnson. Phyllis Cochran lives in Winchendon, Massachusetts.

2

The Circle of Grief

. . . .

■ **With the children grown and into their twenties, I still worry about them a great deal. I worry about reckless behavior, that anything from a traffic accident to a bungee-jumping episode could claim their lives prematurely. In case the unthinkable happens—the death of a child—what should I know at this stage of my parenting life?**

Ask any parent who has walked through this valley, and there will be universal agreement: There is no greater sadness than the death of a child.

Jon Walker, editor-in-chief of *HomeLife* magazine, heard about the following story. It seems early one Saturday morning, Bill Pendle was talking to God. He said, "Do anything in the lives of my three children that will bring honor, grace, and glory to You. Whatever You choose to do, You do."

Then the phone rang. When Bill answered, he was told his middle child, Bryan, had been killed in an automobile accident at 7:20 that morning. "Wasn't that interesting?" Bill says. "To pray that, then have the phone ring and, in essence hear God reply, "I've decided to take one of your children back."

Bill and his wife, Ramona, wrestled with God over the death of their son. Their testimony and the lessons God taught them through their grief were so compelling that Jon Walker asked them and another couple, Malcolm and Dee Privette, to join in the roundtable discussion. The Privettes daughter Katie died when she was sixty-eight days old.

In addition, Jon asked Steve Pettit, a counselor and pastor, to sit in. Steve's son Gabriel, after suffering a seizure as an infant, now lives with cerebral palsy. "Gabe is still alive," says Steve, "but, in effect, I have lost a child. The son who entered the hospital is different from the son who came home."

Finally, please keep in mind that Jon Walker, who facilitated this discussion, lost two children of his own. Here is their transcript:

■ **Jon: Bill, what did you and Ramona think when you first learned that Brian died in a car accident early that morning?**

Bill: I didn't understand the reason for it. Our son had been living for God. He'd been sharing his testimony at high school and had just shared it at our church the Sunday night before his accident. I frankly asked God, "Why didn't You take some reprobate on drugs?"

But then, and I can't explain how He did this, God told me, "Your son was ready, but many others aren't. Bryan lived seventeen years, and that was all he needed."

I started thinking that if God had initially said He was going to give me a choice—I could have Bryan for seventeen years and then lose him, or I could never have him at all—I would have said, "God, let me have him." I also knew that God didn't have to ask my permission. He's in charge, whether I like what happens or not. Nonetheless I was angry at God for letting it happen.

Ramona: We just had to ask, *"Why? Why was Bryan killed when his friend in the car didn't have a scratch?"* And we started asking: *What if? What if Bryan hadn't gone to the beach that day? What if the lady who hit him hadn't been coming down the road then? What if . . . what if?*

Then we'd say "If only." *If only the doctors had done that . . .* or *if only Bryan had been delayed five more minutes.* We were playing a mind game because we didn't like our circumstances. We thought if we could play this mind game, maybe things would change, but they didn't. Finally God said, "Stop! Stop asking the 'what ifs' and the 'if onlys.' "

It's like looking in the rearview mirror and trying to figure out what's back there. God told us to look ahead.

Steve: When you experience such a loss, there's a sense of being out of control. Your whole life centers around the circumstances, and you search for an explanation because that will help you regain control.

Then God comes along and says, "You're not going to figure this one out. You have two choices: Stay frustrated or trust Me." Eventually, I had to say, "God, I trust You."

Ramona: Bryan's death taught us how our lives were totally dependent on circumstances. When things were going well, we were happy. When things weren't going well, we weren't happy. It was like a roller coaster ride. Slowly we realized there's something better than happiness, and that something is joy. Joy is a state of or satisfaction with Jesus. I wasn't happy about Bryan's death, but God is still good.

Dee: Someone in our church was telling another person about Katie, who died at less than three months old. I overheard her say, "Bad things happen to good people." I wanted to respond, "But we're not good. We are all sinners!" And that made me wonder if Katie had died because of some sin of mine. When you look in the Bible, people were penalized for their sins, and yet, I rest in the fact that Jesus died for my sins.

Steve: It's almost automatic that the enemy will try to use an event that causes us pain to make us introspective about it. We think, "If we were living right, then this wouldn't have happened." And the enemy just piles judgment upon judgment on us. People actually told me after Gabe had his seizure, "This happened because of sin in your life, because you lack faith. Your lack of faith has allowed the enemy to steal this child; but if you'll have more faith, he can he healed."

Sometimes taking that blame makes us feel better because it brings some sort of balance out of the chaos; at least there's an answer to why this happened. But in reality, the only thing those feelings of judgment do is to get your eyes focused on you and off Jesus, who is the Healer.

Malcolm: Having children helped me to understand some of what we're talking about. Sometimes I have to tell them "no" and not offer an explanation. That's taught me to trust God that some good will come from his death even though the explanation may be too heavy for me to carry right now.

■ **Jon: Let's talk about how others expected you to handle your grief. I've found that Christians, in particular, placed a lot of expectations on how my wife and I should grieve about the death of our two children.**

Bill: About six months after Bryan's death, people from the church started coming to us, saying, "Come on, Bill. It's been six months. You're a deacon; you're a leader in the church; you ought to be able to handle this."

Malcolm: I felt this was a private moment between God and me, and I thought I'll feel whatever I want!

Ramona: We all have to deal with grief individually. For instance, I went out to the cemetery every single day for a long time after Bryan's funeral. That was against a lot of people's wishes. But I could get away from everything at the grave site. There were no phone calls, and nobody visited me at the cemetery; and it wasn't a morbid place. I needed time to be totally uninterrupted; that was important to me. I did that for several months, and then, one day, I noticed I hadn't gone the day before. That was okay.

Bill: People will tell you what you should and shouldn't do. Bryan died in March, and that following December I didn't want to put up a Christmas tree. We were going to do something different. But well-meaning people would say, "You need to remember you have another child at home. You should have a Christmas tree for Wayne." But Wayne could have cared less. Instead of putting up a tree, we were going snow skiing.

On the other hand, we have some friends who also lost a son in an accident, and the boy's mother didn't want to change a thing. She wanted everything just like it had always been.

Am I right or is she right? Answer: We're both right. You need to get real in the midst of the crisis. Be yourself. Do what you feel, do what you think, and don't worry about how other people react.

Steve: After the death of a child, one of the most vulnerable areas in the family is that one spouse expects the other one to snap out of it or to grieve in a certain way. It's kind of like: "I'm over this now, why can't you be over it?" Or, "You seem to be over this and handling it so well. You're back to work, and I'm here at home crying every single day. Didn't you love our daughter? Why don't you cry about it anymore?"

When the grieving styles are different, and we don't allow one another to grieve honestly and personally before God, then a serious problem will develop in the family.

■ **Jon: Bill, you mentioned your other children. How did Bryan's death affect your relationship with them?**

Bill: We decided to make every opportunity when we were together as a family the best we could. We lived each day so that when we went to bed that night we didn't have any regrets.

Ramona: Our other two children became even more precious to us after Bryan died; we showered them with love. Our son Wayne was gracious and understood that he was going to have to deal with some of our feelings, like when he wants to drive to the beach. Do we hamper him because of what happened to his older brother? Or do we allow him to go? Wayne is not Bryan, and we had to keep that in focus and let Wayne be Wayne. I had to pray a lot during that time, and I had to let God have control.

■ **Jon: In terms of giving the situation over to God, was there a point when even your thoughts needed to be taken captive for Christ?**

Malcolm: I've always tried to base my relationship with God on a kind of freedom. I allowed myself to take a hands-off approach. When I felt pain or accusation, I spent a lot of time in God's Word. There was desperation involved, but in searching, God showed me something I wasn't looking for—a sense of my place in this world, a sense of my family's place in this world, a sense that throughout history, He's always been there.

I related to King David's loss of a child and to other tragedies described throughout the Bible, and I knew I was no better than any of those people. There are families who've suffered much greater pain that I. My pain was real and theirs was real, and I tried to just keep a grip on where I was. At times, I felt a very personal kind of hugging love from God.

Ramona: As we approached the first anniversary of Bryan's death, not everyone understood why I still didn't have it together. "Where's your spiritual maturity?" they asked. But on the exact one-year anniversary of his death, we were at a conference led by author and pastor Vance Havner, and someone told him about our situation. He came over and asked us how we were.

"We lost a son a year ago," I replied.

"You mean you don't know where your son is?"

"I know exactly where my son is," I replied.

"Then he's not lost," he said, "He's just separated from you for a while. Death is not ceasing to be but separation from. Your son hasn't ceased to be. He's very much alive; you've just got a temporary span of being separated. Your family will one day be reunited."

That gave me such a relief knowing all of this is only temporary. I can handle anything if it's temporary. Now I have something to look forward to, and in eternity our family will be together.

Those were heavy, yet comforting, words. About five years later, our granddaughter developed bacterial spinal meningitis. When she was comatose, and the doctor said she'd never live through the night, I watched our daughter stay calm as she could be. I was amazed.

Later I asked her how she did it. She said, "I watched you and Dad go through Bryan's death, and I knew that if God could take our family through that, He could take me and my family through anything."

■ **Jon: What would you say to people who are currently struggling with the loss of a child? Will they ever get over it?**

Steve: Who wants to get over it?

Bill: I agree. Last year, we were asked to talk to a couple who'd lost their child in a car accident. I told them, "There's nothing I can say that's going to take away your hurt, not one thing, other than the fact that I'm a father who has been there. Yes, I can give you some consolation. I can pray with you. But no matter what I say, when I leave here, you're still going to hurt." I think it's important to be vulnerable and transparent around those in grief.

Ramona: The Scriptures say, "Blessed are those who mourn for they will be comforted" (Matt. 5:4). I think there's a comfort from God that's so special in the midst of this loss. It's a blessing, in a sense, because we've had the opportunity to feel God in a deeper way because we've had to mourn in a very deep way. The greater the mourning, the greater the presence of God in our lives. Bill and I have come to see the pain as a sign that we truly loved Bryan.

There was a magnificent love between God the Father and Christ the Son, so there must have been tremendous pain for the Father when the Son died. Did the Father ever forget the Son's pain? No, I don't think so. Are we ever going to forget the pain of our loss? No, and we've gone through half a box of tissues in this roundtable discussion. I don't want to forget the pain, but I'm no longer a prisoner of it.

■ Jon: What helped you and what hurt you?

Dee: People kept giving me books to read, and I finally quit looking at them. I didn't want another book or another solution. But I had one special friend who sent me cards about once a month. She kept asking, "How are you doing?" and she reminded me that she was praying for me.

Ramona: People gave us pictures of Bryan that they had taken, and we really appreciated those.

Steve: I would suggest people avoid religious clichés when talking to grieving parents. Don't say things like, "It must have been God's will," or "God's working this all for your good." That may be true, but that doesn't help in the moment, and I think often it's really just a way for us to comfort ourselves more than the people in grief.

Instead, be a good listener and don't come in with tools trying to fix the person or offer some explanation that will take the pain away. For instance, I will never say "I know exactly how you feel" because, even if I've had a similar loss, I really don't know how that other person feels.

Bill: One lady said to me, "I know exactly how you feel; I had a dog who was killed last week." Can you believe that? I tried to believe that she was speaking out of the depth of her experience. Some people mean well; they just don't know how to communicate it.

Bill: Eventually the experience, although painful, can become better. Sometimes I'll drive by the cemetery, and I'll think of Bryan and something he and I did together. Then I'll smile and think, *One of these days we'll be with you, Son.*

Deep down, I'm missing Bryan, but I still can say, "God, thank You for being so good."

The roundtable discussion was led by Jon Walker, editor-in-chief of HomeLife magazine, a Christian family publication. For information about subscribing, write HomeLife magazine, 127 Ninth Avenue, North, Nashville, TN 37234-0140, or call toll-free (800) 458-2772.

3

Growing Up in the Age of Choice

. . . .

■ Years ago—too many, I'm afraid to admit to—I was pregnant four times over a seven-year-period. Each time I was violently ill, but in those days, doctors didn't have more advice than "eat saltines" and stay off my feet as much as I could.

I'm about to become a grandmother for the first time, and my oldest daughter is in her second month of pregnancy— and hugging porcelain every hour. It distresses me to see her in that state, and doctors still don't have much more advice than to eat saltines and ride it out.

Jenni wants to know if there is any hope ahead of her. Some of her "friends" have even whispered that she may not be "cut out" for motherhood and should think about "ending" her pregnancy. Is there anything I can tell her to cheer her up and not waver from her pro-life stance?

It's hard—no, make that difficult—for mothers to stand by help-lessly while their daughters experience a problem pregnancy. Perhaps you can tell her about Karen Rehm, who is one of those women who probably never should have gotten pregnant in the first place. With each pregnancy (she has had three) she was vio-lently sick, not just in the morning and not just during the first trimester, but all day, every day, all nine months.

And not just a little queasy. Babies literally made Karen sick, from start to finish. She could keep nothing down, not even ice chips. Occasionally she did manage to keep down sherbet, a spoon-ful or two at a time, but even that was iffy. One day she begged her husband, Tony, to buy her some lime sherbet. When he finally returned, she ate the sherbet, then threw up.

Tony and Karen had spent nearly seven years trying unsuccess-fully to have a baby. Needless to say, in spite of all Karen endured during her first pregnancy, the Rehms were overjoyed when their daughter Emily was born.

■ Did they have any more children?

Karen had suspected pregnancy would be hard, but not this hard. Nevertheless, she and Tony did want more children. Thinking the severity of her first pregnancy was a fluke, the Rehms decided to try again. However, Karen's second pregnancy was as bad as the first.

What some people euphemistically refer to as "morning sick-ness," Karen's doctor now suspects was probably an allergic reaction to her own hormones. So severe was her reaction that she would actually jolt awake in the middle of the night, run to the bathroom, and throw up. She learned to carry plastic bags along with her in the car on her way to work or errands. It was a nightmarish ordeal but somehow she survived, and finally Clayton was born.

The Rehms had determined they probably wouldn't have any-more children, but after seven years of infertility, somehow steril-ization didn't seem right. As a result, they postponed their decision, and two years later Karen found herself pregnant once more. Knowing what lay ahead, she wept.

■ How could she bear it?

According to the World Health Organization (WHO), *maternal health* is defined as "a state of complete physical, mental, and social well-being and not merely the absence of disease or infirmity." Karen Rehm, who spent 90 percent of all three pregnancies kneeling over toilets, does not epitomize maternal health.

If anyone would be justified in choosing to abort this third pregnancy, using the politically acceptable notion of maternal health as her
excuse, surely she. But Karen and Tony could no more destroy their
unborn child than they could kill the two children they already had.
And so, once more, Karen suffered. Nine months of literally crawling
to the bathroom, only this time with two small children to care for.
Nine months of misery. Nine months . . . and then came Morgan.

In the age of choice, where the option to abort an unwanted,
inconvenient, or disagreeable pregnancy is virtually unrestricted,
Karen's actions seem foolhardy to pro-choice people. Of utmost
importance is the mother's health, many would say.

Karen doesn't agree. And if you could see her children—could
see Emily's brilliant blue eyes and her beguiling, mischievous grin
as she twirls and prances in a billowy gown; if you could observe
Clayton flying down a hill on a bike, face aglow with pure ecstasy;
if you could watch two-year-old Morgan's brows furrow as she
observes a grasshopper escape from a blue jay or feel her chubby
arms wrapped around your neck and a small, wet kiss planted
somewhere on your face—you wouldn't either.

Remind your daughter to keep her eyes on the future; the trials
of today will someday give way.

■ **Jenni was most disturbed when one of her college sorority
sisters said she thought she might be carrying a deformed
baby—that was why she was so sick. Do you have a story that
deals with deformed children?**

Yes, we sure do. When Kimber Edwards went in for her prenatal
checkup near the beginning of her fourth pregnancy, she wasn't
expecting anything unusual. She'd done this many times before.
She found it odd, however, when the technician was silent during
the ultrasound and then left the room. That's when Kimber began
to suspect something was amiss.

In the calm before the impending storm, Psalm 113:9 came to
mind: *He maketh the barren woman to dwell in a house, and to be a joyful
mother of children.* As though God Himself had uttered the words,
Kimber responded in prayer. "Lord," she whispered, "if there is
something wrong with this pregnancy, I'm going to be a joyful

mother, even of this baby."

The technician returned with her supervisor and conducted a more thorough ultrasound. Then Kimber was left alone again. Finally the nurse returned with the report. "There's a possibility," she said, "that your baby will be born without a major portion of her brain."

Kimber's heart sank. More details were given about her child's condition. *Anencephaly . . . neural tube defect . . . brain and skull not completely formed . . . won't survive outside the womb.* Kimber tried to concentrate, but it was too much data to process. She needed to go home, talk to her husband, pray. While she gathered her thoughts, the nurse then asked, "When would you like me to schedule your abortion?"

■ The nurse really said this?

Yes, these days many nurses—and other medical personnel—push abortion, and whether they know it or not, they are making a life-changing suggestion at a time when the pregnant mother (and father) are especially vulnerable.

When Kimber heard the suggestion, she stared at the nurse, dumbfounded. The thought hadn't entered her mind. When she began to object, it was the nurse's turn to be dumbfounded. "You realize," she told Kimber, "that this child has no possibility of life."

"Maybe I don't understand everything you've told me here today," Kimber replied, "and maybe I don't understand all the implications. All I know is abortion is not an option. God will decide whether this baby lives or dies." Thus began Kimber's battle to be a joyful mother of the child with "no possibility of life."

It was an uphill battle. Almost everyone, it seemed, felt carrying the baby to term was a mistake. Her mother, concerned for her daughter's well-being, started talking with obstetricians, who felt Kimber ought to abort immediately. Complete strangers castigated her for her decision. Once a woman, overhearing Kimber talking with her friends, became clearly agitated. Finally she interrupted the conversation.

"How can you be so cruel to that baby?" she said. "It's miserable—you should abort it." Just then Kimber felt her lively baby kick. With as much dignity as she could muster, she took the woman's hand and laid it on her belly. "You tell me," Kimber said quietly, "if this child seems miserable." Insulted, the woman yanked her hand away and left.

Despite Kimber's staunch pro-life convictions, the din of contrary voices began to take its toll. During previous pregnancies, Kimber, a fitness devotee, had always been careful not to overexert herself during athletic workouts. One day, however, while exercising at the gym, an insidious thought crept into her mind: *The baby's going to die anyway. Just go ahead and push yourself. What difference will it make?*

Suddenly she stopped short. "O Lord," she prayed, "I am so sorry." She packed her things and went home. That night she had a vivid dream in which she saw her child sitting beside the throne of God. *"Thank you, Mommy,"* the child said, *"for caring for me."* Kimber awoke sobbing. To her, the message was clear: Take care of this little baby—one day you'll see her again.

■ When the child was born, what happened?

Before the onset of labor, she and her husband, Danny, learned everything they could about anencephaly. They prepared themselves for their baby's birth and likely death. They were as ready as they could be, except for one thing. One thing they learned about anencephalic babies is that occasionally they can be deformed. How would they react when their baby finally came? Would they be repulsed, frightened, by their own child? There were no easy answers. All they could do was pray and wait.

Kimber's due date finally arrived, and after a long, difficult, and at one point, dangerous labor, their fourth child was born.

Sarah came into the world silent—an "awesome silence," is how Kimber describes it. Everyone in the room was awed, even Kimber's mother. The baby was placed in Kimber's arms. She looked at her daughter, perfectly formed and smiling. All her fears disappeared, and Kimber fell in love. Sarah's heart was beating, but once the umbilical cord was cut, her heartbeat slowly faded, then stopped. She lived ten minutes.

Danny spoke at Sarah's funeral. The hymn they had chosen, "Safe in the Arms of Jesus," formed the substance of his message. Sarah's life may have been brief, Danny said, but all her life she had known a safe place: a safe place inside Kimber, and now, a safe place with God.

■ **How touching. So what's the take-away value in all this?**

Karen Rehm and Kimber Edwards—and your grown children—
have come of age during the era of choice. From adolescence, they
have understood the essence of its philosophy: when faced with an
unwanted, inconvenient, or high-risk pregnancy, eliminate it.
Women have the legal right—and society's nod—to sidestep the
physical and emotional discomfort of childbearing and abort their
pregnancies, if they so choose.

But neither Karen nor Kimber made that choice. As Kimber
puts it, "It's not up to me to control when a child lives or dies. It's
in God's hands. I look at myself as the caretaker of something that
belongs to God."

Karen agrees. "The idea of abortion never once crossed my mind,
no matter how difficult things got," she says. When pressed to elaborate, she merely shrugs and smiles. "It's a privilege to carry a child."

Hopefully, your daughters and daughters-in-law will carry the
same attitude in their pregnancies.

This chapter is adapted from writings by Elaine Minamide of Escondido, California.

4

A Time of Recovery

Editor's note: Perhaps you came of age in the turbulent '60s, the decade of free love. Perhaps you were part of that "if it feels good, do it" movement. But then it happened: the pill failed, and you were pregnant. The pregnancy was unplanned, and you wondered what to do. But abortion was legal in your state, and it would soon be legal in all fifty states by 1973. So you went to the abortion table.

If so, you joined millions of women who have had an abortion since the procedure was legalized in the early 1970s. Patricia Bigliardi was one of those women who exercised "choice." In this chapter, she reflects on what that decision has meant in her life and how she dealt with it.

by Patricia A. Bigliardi

"Wake up, Pat. Wake up . . . ."

The incessant drone of a nurse's voice forced me into consciousness. *Why is she bothering me?* I wondered. *Oh, yes, I'm in the hospital.* I opened my eyes slowly. A small, heart-shaped red box gradually came into focus, then the smiling face of my eight-year-old son.

"Hi, Mom, I brought you a box of candy," he said.

"Thanks, champ," I mumbled, fighting sleep.

"Pat, they want you to stay awake," my husband said. I turned and noticed flowers in his hand.

"How nice of you to bring flowers," I said flatly, then closed my eyes and drifted into sleep. I had no desire to stay awake. It was Valentine's Day, 1976. I had just had an abortion.

My husband and I never mentioned the abortion after I returned home. We were like partners in a crime he had instigated months before. "I don't want this baby right now," he had said. Our marriage, which had been rocky, seemed to be stabilizing after a fifteen-month separation, so I followed through on the terrible implications of his remark.

The weeks and months after the abortion reaped a foul harvest. I was filled with shame and guilt, and I tried to bury my secret hurt. I had fooled myself into believing everything would be fine. Instead, my life fell apart.

Usually sociable, I became cynical and argumentative. Nothing met my approval. I seethed with a near uncontrollable rage. Drinking became my refuge from intense sadness and a feeling of helplessness. Nine months after the abortion, my marriage ended.

As a sense of total failure engulfed me, I thought about how far I had drifted from the religious values of my upbringing. In desperation, I called out, "Jesus, if You're real, please help me." After all I had done, how could I expect God to answer me?

Despite my doubt and sin, God graciously brought me the answer of His neverending love and forgiveness. Once I made Jesus the center of my life, I began a slow, but steady journey toward spiritual and emotional health.

A Moving Film

Along the road to recovery, the Lord taught me many things about myself and the abortion. A breakthrough in my healing came at church, eleven years after I had turned my life over to God. During a film presentation on abortion, a rising tide of grief welled up inside me.

Other similar occasions had moved me to gentle tears. This time, I quickly left the sanctuary, knowing if I allowed myself to sob deeply, a great burden would be lifted. On the way home, my grief came out in wrenching sobs. God was healing something in me only He could heal.

The next morning I tried to make sense of what had happened. "Lord, please help me understand last night. I know You've forgiven me," I prayed. Then the words of Matthew 5:4 came to mind: *Blessed are those who mourn, for they will be comforted.*

I have to mourn before I can be comforted, I realized. As long as I denied my grief, I couldn't receive the compassion and consolation God wanted to give. Acts 3:19 further nudged me into facing my loss: "Repent, then, and turn to God . . . that times of refreshing may come from the Lord." After all these years, I felt free to grieve.

I closed my eyes, thinking of my aborted daughter, trying to confirm the validity of her fragile, brief life. My baby girl was with the Lord, but I couldn't stand knowing that one day I would meet her face-to-face in heaven. "Please, God, tell her how sorry I am for what I did," I prayed. In this time of mourning, I wanted someone to hold me, but there was no one.

Coming to Terms

The act of facing my grief exposed a seething anger toward everyone involved with my abortion decision—my husband, the doctor, and most of all, myself. I had lived with unholy rage long enough, but I wasn't ready to come to terms with it.

I began to realize I needed others with whom to share my grief and shame. "I had two children—a boy and a girl," I wanted to tell the church, but the fear of rejection and judgment kept me silent.

A short time later, I was working with a small group of women on a church project. During a break, our conversation turned to abortion. "I just can't tolerate all this pro-choice talk," one young woman said sharply. "How could anyone kill her own baby? How self-centered can you get?"

Her blunt and insensitive words stunned me. "I've had an abortion," I said quietly, surprising myself. "And you're right. It was a selfish act, one I deeply regret. But haven't we all sinned and fallen short of God's glory?"

I'd finally said it: "I've had an abortion." While my admission was brave, even necessary, it intensified my sense of loss. In that moment of self-disclosure, I longed for someone to put her arms around me and say, "I understand what you've been through. I accept you, and affirm that God forgives and loves you. *And so do I.*" It didn't happen.

On another day, thinking about my abortion led to uncontrollable sobbing. A dear friend came to mind, and I phoned her. Her immediate response was a gentle prayer for my release from sorrow.

It was as if Jesus Himself had placed His arms around me, and was letting me know my grief was normal. The healing process was taking me through a range of feelings: denial, anger, depression, sadness, and acceptance, each appropriate in its own time.

Finding Help

As I began feeling stronger emotionally, I reached out to others with similar experiences. I joined a post-abortion support group where I could find comfort and understanding with other women. Gradually, as I studied God's Word and received encouragement from the group, I was able to forgive my ex-husband and the doctor. In the warmth of the group's love and acceptance, and, ultimately, divine love, I was at last able to forgive myself. This final act broke the yoke that had bound me for so many years.

Today, hundreds of women are sitting in church pews each Sunday with a secret shame locked deep inside. They will need great courage to emerge from the shadows of the past and admit to having had an abortion. Yet, true healing can begin only when they allow themselves to move past denial. This can happen as the church provides the framework of love and acceptance.

Looking back, I recognize that God has led me step by step to recovery. Being able to speak freely about my experience has been an important bridge in my gaining spiritual and emotional health. To accomplish this for me, Jesus provided others as instruments of release.

After Lazarus was raised from death, Jesus said to those standing around in awe, "Take off the grave clothes and let him go." It wasn't enough for Lazarus to be brought back from the dead. He needed to be released from the death wrappings by those around him.

Like Lazarus, I had been raised from death—although a spiritual one. But the emotional grave clothes of my past still bound me. Now, through the encouragement and love of others, those wrappings are falling off. As I reach out to those who've experienced similar agony, my complete recovery is closer to becoming a reality. I've finally realized I've been commissioned by the Lord to bring good news, the kind that binds up the brokenhearted, proclaims liberty to the captives, and releases those in prisons.

Patricia A. Bigliardi, who travels extensively as a speaker, lives in San Jose, California. She can be contacted at Face to Face Ministries, 1880 Meridan Ave., Suite 15, San Jose, CA 95125, or by calling (408) 269-1850.

5

Gentle Ways to Ease Depression

. . . .

■ **With a recent spate of sicknesses and death in the family, I have been in a long, low, lethargic mood. I have to force myself out of bed to begin my day. How can I break out of my depression?**

At one time or another everyone experiences depression. The author of the Psalms often gives vent and expression to feelings of depression. For example, the first two verses of Psalm 13 carries this lament: "How long, O Lord? Will you forget me forever? How long will you hide your face from me? How long must I wrestle with my thoughts and every day have sorrow in my heart?"

Interestingly, the same psalm ends on an upbeat note: "I will sing to the Lord, for he has been good to me" (v. 6). That is an important reminder that feelings come and go, that part of being human means experiencing both emotional highs and lows.

■ **What are some gentle ways to ease depression?**

Here are a handful of ideas:

▶ **Try walking away from depression.** An increasing number of psychologists use "walking therapy" as part of their treatment. Walks are especially good for those over fifty years of age since the exercise is not strenuous. Based on scientific research, these counselors know that regular walks can provide the following benefits:

- ▶ Help lift depression.
- ▶ Lessen tension.
- ▶ Increase optimism and hope.
- ▶ Boost self-esteem.
- ▶ Increase energy.

Another thing you can do is change your immediate environment. The simple act of moving furniture around can also move your attitude. So can hanging new curtains, switching lamp shades, buying a new bedspread, or rearranging pictures.

▶ **Be sure to feed your mind with healthy thoughts.** Remember Paul's advice to saturate the mind with higher thoughts: "Whatever is noble, whatever is right, whatever is pure, whatever is lovely, whatever is admirable—if anything is excellent or praiseworthy—think about such things" (Phil. 4:28). Indulge yourself in activities that are inspiring and uplifting. Concentrate on saying, "I can" rather than "I can't."

▶ **Don't forget to laugh.** Laughter helps balance the stress and strain of daily life. A low mood can be quickly transformed through a good chuckle. Increase your laughter quotient by going out to dinner with upbeat friends, renting a funny video, or glancing through a book of jokes. Looking for a humorous slant on an otherwise disturbing situation will also help.

▶ **Can you make a list of all the positives in your life?** When depressed, people tend to view everything in a highly negative light. Setbacks and letdowns become greatly magnified, while the positives are scarcely noted. Balance your perception by making a list of the many positives in your life.

▶ **Confront the source of persistent depressions.** Make an assessment of your depression source. Ask yourself if a particular person, condition, or circumstance is creating the stress that leads to depression. If possible, confront the source of such persistent depression. You can decide how long you are going to put up with such stresses. Seek counseling if necessary; lay your plans, and set an end to it.

▶ **Find the positive in your adversity.** Many depressions are the direct result of life's losses: the loss of a loved one to death or divorce, the loss of a job, the loss of health. If this is your situation, look closely at your adversity and try to find something positive in it. Allow your priorities to become clear so that the things that are most important in life shine out, and less important things fade away.

▶ **Do something nice for someone else.** Volunteering your time to help others is a natural way of alleviating depression because it takes the focus off yourself. Reaching out to someone in difficult circumstances also eases feelings of depression because the experience helps put your own problems into perspective.

▶ **Enjoy the arts.** It is difficult to remain depressed while studying a magnificent painting or listening to a moving piece of music. Try lifting depression by touring a museum of art, enjoying a musical concert, or listening to a tape of Gospel music.

WHEN TO SEEK PROFESSIONAL HELP

While most people experience blues, some individuals suffer from severe clinical depression, which differs from "the blues" in both duration and severity. According to the National Institute for Mental Health, the following are classical symptoms of severe depression. If you, or someone you know, suffers from a combination of these symptoms, seek professional help as soon as possible.

▶ Marked changes in sleep patterns.

▶ Appetite and/or weight loss or conversely, overeating and weight gain.

▶ Persistent sad, anxious, or "empty" moods.

▶ Feelings of hopelessness and pessimism.

▶ Feelings of guilt, worthlessness, or helplessness.

▶ Fatigue or decreased energy.

▶ Thoughts or talk of death or suicide.

▶ Suicide threats or attempts.

For further information, call the National Alliance for the Mentally Ill at (800) 950-NAMI (6264).

Finally, when depressive feelings come, be accepting of your emotional makeup. If there are changes you can make to ease the depression, then make them. If nothing can be done, then be patient. Like the clouds that give way to the sun, depressive feelings eventually give way to brighter, more hopeful days.

This material is adapted from writings by Victor M. Parachin of Claremont, California.

6

What If My Grandchild Is Gay?

. . . .

■ **Much has been made in recent years about treating boys and girls alike, that if you give a young girl a G.I. Joe set and a boy a Barbie doll, they'll learn to like them just the same. Now I know that's balderdash, but what should I be looking for to ease my mind when the grandchildren arrive?**

The advice can be summed up like this: Don't treat boys and girls alike. Little boys need to be encouraged to behave in masculine ways, and little girls to behave in feminine ways. For example, parents usually dress their daughters and sons differently as soon as they are born. A baby boy's baseball shirt says, both to the child and to those around him, that this child is male. A baby girl's frilly dress announces that this child is a female. Parents give little girls a purse "like Mommy's"; they don't do that for the little boy.

These behaviors may be arbitrary, yet they reinforce the roles our culture has assigned to males and females, and thus they help the young child identify with the proper sex.

■ **The last time we visited my four-year-old grandson, he took his little sister's tutu and ballet shoes and pranced** around the house. We all laughed, but deep down I shuddered. Should I have expressed my concern?

Grandparents and parents don't need to worry if small boys occasionally pretend they are girls or small girls pretend they are boys. Young children normally try out opposite-sex role behaviors as a way to learn and master what is masculine and feminine.

The key word here is *occasionally*. If a little boy dances around the house with Mommy's purses swaying from one side to another, there's no cause for worry. But if he starts compulsively wanting to hold a purse all the time, if he wants a dress like Mommy's, if he practices putting on lipstick in front of a mirror—and this behavior goes on and on—that's a strong signal of a sexual identity problem.

Most children, however, have no questions in their minds of their sexual identity. Normally a secure sexual identity develops very early in childhood. If you doubt this, try teasing your grandson by putting a girl's hat on him and saying, "Oh, you'd make such a pretty little girl!"

Even a two-year-old is likely to stomp his foot down and say, "No, I'm a boy! I'm just like Daddy!"

■ What about homosexuality? Why do children become homosexuals?

Family members need to differentiate between homosexuality and normal close relationships between two people of the same sex. During middle childhood, children go through a developmental phase where boys want to be only with other boys and girls want to be only with other girls. If a child of the other sex approaches, they're likely to exclaim, "Yuk! Get out of here!"

Children of this age are likely to have at least one deep, caring friendship with a person of the same sex. This is normal, and this is good. Having a close emotional bond with a person of the same sex is not the same as homosexuality. In fact it may help to prevent homosexuality by reaffirming the children's sexual identity. Family members must not jump to conclusions in this area.

■ So what causes homosexuality then?

Basically, there are three factors that contribute toward the development of homosexual behavior. The first factor, *family patterns*, seems to be the most significant. In spite of what you may have read in the mainstream press, no scientific research has ever turned up any biological condition that directly causes homosexual behavior. However, certain kinds of family patterns are repeatedly reported by people who are tempted by homosexuality. Some 80 percent of homosexual men, for example, describe their fathers as aloof, hostile, rejecting—or entirely absent from the home—during their growing-up years.

One large study found that only 13 percent of male homosexuals said they identified with their fathers, whereas the vast majority of the male heterosexuals in the study reported strong identification with their fathers. A young man who feels rejected by his father may seek male affirmation through homosexual behavior.

> **WHERE TO FIND HELP**
>
> Parents and grandparents of homosexuals may contact:
> **Spatula Ministries**
> P.O. Box 444
> La Habra, CA 90631
>
> For those seeking to leave the homosexual lifestyle, they should contact:
> **Exodus North America**
> P.O. Box 77652
> Seattle, WA 98177
> (206) 784-7799
> Fax: (206) 784-7872
> Internet: http://exodus.bse.org

The second factor, *homosexual seduction*, is widely feared by parents. Sometimes a perfectly normal child is approached by an older teenager or adult to initiate him into homosexual behavior. This is a real danger and should not be ignored, but most people are not seduced into homosexuality against their will.

A third factor is *homosexual pornography*. Some children who never would have thought about homosexuality come up with the idea by looking at pornographic photographs. This gets them started in unhealthy experimentation.

Obviously, parents and grandparents need to protect children from hurtful outside influences such as homosexual abduction and pornography. They also needed to be influenced by strong, caring male role models.

■ What should we do if we think our grandson could be a homosexual?

This is a grave question, and one that must be thought through before discussing it with the parents. Many time, homosexuals seek to keep their sexual nature from family members for various reasons, including guilt.

It is not a good idea to state to your grandson, "I suspect you are a homosexual," even if you think he will open up to you but not to the parents. It is better for you to wait for the proper time to raise the issue with the parents, but on more than a suspicion.

In the meantime, pray for your grandchild. Keep your eyes and ears open. If your questions persist and you do raise the subject with the parents, have the names of several good Christian counselors available. (Careful, however. Many people who call themselves Christian counselors these days endorse homosexual behavior, so you need to know where the counselor stands.)

This chapter is adapted from Parents and Children *(Chariot Victor).*

7

Forgiving a Difficult Dad

Editor's note: How can a son or daughter pardon a parent for years of abuse? If you find yourself in a position where it's difficult to forgive a difficult parent, then read closely this account by Ross Reinman.

In the autumn of 1988, I stared out the window of my room in the psychiatric ward. This was the place where I had visited *others* in my capacity as a youth minister. Now, at twenty-nine years of age, it was my turn to wonder if I would find the courage to face life.

Turning my face again into my soggy pillow, I cried myself to sleep, trying to shut out the childhood memories that rushed at me. Wild scenes punctuated my mind. I remembered an afternoon when I was in the fourth grade. My father, big and mean-looking, lost his patience and threw a twenty-five-pound tool chest at me from the balcony. It hurdled downward, narrowly missing my head.

Other times I climbed between him and my defenseless mother and three younger siblings, trying to protect them from his fits of rage. Then he'd turn on me. I remembered hiding in our dark basement after he'd chased me through the house at frenzied knife-point, threatening to kill me. Many times he'd pin me against the wall—high off the ground and suspended me only by his hands around my neck. It was an awful thing for a child to wonder if he's going to be killed by his own daddy.

But the worse pain came from my father's constant humiliation. When I was three or four, I accidentally urinated in the tub. My father washed me in the urine in a splashing tirade, telling me he was teaching me a lesson. When I was thirteen, he told me I needed to "become a man" and offered to take me to a prostitute. After I refused, he taunted me, saying I was less than male.

He often criticized me for things beyond my control. He'd ask why my nose was so big or why I had so many pimples. And every time he noticed my toed-in walk, he'd mimic it, waddling behind me in exaggerated turned-in steps, laughing hysterically.

Throughout my childhood I had to determine for myself right from wrong. Dad didn't have any regard for morals or the law. He encouraged me, along with my younger brothers and sister, to shoplift, even for our Christmas presents to each other! To my astonishment, when we were caught he punished us for tarnishing his "pillar-of-the-community" image. Once he even held up several shops in town, handling the clerks a note saying he'd blow their heads off if they made one wrong move. He bragged later about his daring.

When things got bad with lawsuits or other trouble, we'd move. We did that twelve times before I was in high school. The hardest part was not being able to tell our friends we were going. He was the one running from the police, but I was the one who felt like a fugitive.

Whenever I would object to his immoral lifestyle and ask him to change, he'd mock me and say, "What's the matter with you? Are you going to grow up and become a minister?" as if that would be the absolute worst thing I could do with my life. Much to my surprise—and his—the answer to that question turned out to be yes.

New Direction

Fueled by the pain and emptiness of years of abuse, I listened to the street preachers near the bank where I worked and read the tracts they thrust into my hands. At nineteen and without anyone to guide me in a "proper" prayer, I sat in the park and turned my life over to the Lord. Six months later I enrolled in Bible college and began preparing for the ministry.

A year after graduation I married Barbara, a young woman I met at the church where I served as a youth minister. When our daughter, Jordan, was born, I concentrated on putting my father's cruel domination behind me. But something was wrong. A volcano was brewing within me, waiting to erupt.

One of the older men on staff reminded me of my father in subtle ways, and I was finding it almost impossible to relate to males in authority. Gradually I developed what I thought was a little temper problem. I exploded over the smallest conflict and was overly critical of others.

Terrible anxiety filled my days; nightmares of failure and God's impending rejection disrupted my nights. Outwardly I continued my ministerial duties, but inwardly I rejected the idea that God really loved me. Soon I began to feel out of control, sinking into a severe depression that was accompanied by wild anxiety. I was at a loss to explain where it was coming from.

One Saturday night, after an especially intense week of juggling my normal duties as well as those of the vacationing pastor, the swirling pressures won, and I gave out. My depression deepening, I criticized Barbara about everything. She looked back at me, her eyes filled with hurt. In that moment, I realized I had become just like my father.

"I feel so out of control," I whispered. "I've got to get help."

Soon we were on our way to the local hospital where, as if in a bad dream, I checked myself into the psychiatric unit.

The Road Back

The next morning, a counselor talked to me about my work, my family, and my background. I answered his questions carefully, ashamed that I, a minister, was there. But I was looking for answers. What was it that was stopping me from being all that God had wanted for me as a husband, father, and Christian leader?

I stayed in the hospital for a week, but followed the counselor's recommendation that I go into therapy. He was blunt: "You're afraid to deal with your emotions because you're a minister. You think you should be above such pain."

I thought about that as I talked to the new counselor who saw me as an outpatient. When I answered his questions about my childhood, he looked at me in amazement.

"Have you ever talked about this with anyone?" he asked.

I shook my head. It did seem like an awful lot to have kept to myself. But that was the unspoken family rule: "Don't talk about what goes on here."

A few days into therapy, the counselor asked me another important question: "Have you forgiven your father?"

I averted my eyes and couldn't answer.

Oh, I knew the importance of forgiveness. After all, I'd often heard it preached from pulpits and even my own lips. Finally, out of desperation to salvage my sanity and my marriage, I acknowledged I had to work through the emotional chaos to forgive the man who had hurt me so deeply.

One Step at a Time

One afternoon I had the idea to ask him to forgive me for holding grudges and failing to show him love. I was certain he then would be so humbled that he would, in some sort of broken confession, ask me to forgive him.

Instead, while my jaw dropped in surprise, Dad agreed that I had wronged him. Then he added I had been a "problem" child and quite beyond his understanding. I cut short my visit, and, in the car, exploded into tears. Still, over the next couple of years, I continued to work at forgiving my dad. Each time I made some progress, it felt as though I was peeling away outer layers of hurt and resentment, getting closer to the core. But I always struggled: *Why did God put me in such an abusive family?*

Gradually it settled within my spirit that He had put me in a situation He knew I'd survive if I'd walk through it with Him. I had always looked at those tormenting childhood scenes through the eyes of the child I had been, but I began to look at them as the adult I had become. When the thoughts would swarm at me, I'd mentally walk into that long-ago room with Jesus by my side. Then in my imagination, I'd hug that sobbing, humiliated little boy and remind him that he wasn't alone.

Taking Action

Part of the process of letting go of my grudge was my trying to understand my father. I'd never thought of him as a victim of abuse, but it was true. His parents, Jewish immigrants from Poland, treated him cruelly. When he married a Sicilian "Gentile," they never spoke to him again. As I thought about his pain, it was easier for me to be somewhat sympathetic toward him.

Next I started a journal about my feelings toward him. On those pages I was able to uncork emotions that had been bottled up for many years. Those first months of working toward forgiveness were like riding a roller coaster. Just when I'd think, *I've done it! I've forgiven him!* the pain would resurface. I'd leave his house after an obligatory family gathering, feeling crippled by his cutting remarks. Then the cycle of anger would begin again.

The only way around that was to develop a strategy prior to visits with Dad. I learned to keep the interaction brief—setting some quiet limits as to where we would meet and for how long—and to guide the conversation to safe zones. I also quoted Scripture to myself and prayed inwardly. It was intense discipline, but I determined to win this battle.

One of the hardest disciplines, however, was what my counselor called "acting into feeling": to act as though we had reconciled. That meant greeting him with hugs, asking to also talk to him when my mother phoned, sending cards on special days—all the things I had refused to do during the years of my silent unforgiveness. It was a big step for me, but after doing those things, I did find my attitude toward him softening.

Once, to my amazement, the counselor asked me to list my dad's positive attributes. It took me a long time to think of any, but I eventually recalled his top sales ability and his hard work that kept us fed and clothed. Forcing myself to look for something positive helped me see something other than the painful, abusive aspects of his personality.

But while all these practical steps were important, I still had to depend on God for inner healing. Many times during prayer I broke down and sobbed, feeling overwhelmed by my inability to forgive the one who had been so cruel. But through prayer, I felt His Spirit changing me, giving me the strength to forgive and move closer to becoming whole. Gradually, as the painful memories came, I learned to lift them to heaven in prayer instead of reliving the details over and over.

I'd wanted the ability to forgive to come sweeping into my life in one dramatic moment. Instead it came ever so slowly, but it did come. I still remember the winter day when it hit me that I had finally reached my goal and had forgiven Dad.

In place of the anger that had brewed inside me was now a calming peace. I celebrated the realization by shouting over and over, "I forgive you! I forgive you!" A satisfied grin stretched across my face. Scars may never go away, but wounds can heal.

Several years ago, my father died from cancer. Recently I went back to his grave, clutching one red and one white carnation. The red symbolized the blood of Jesus that covers our sins. The white symbolized the new life that we can have in Him. As I straightened up from placing the flowers near the headstone, I felt as though a terrible burden had fallen from my shoulders. My forgiveness had made me truly free.

Ross Reinman and his family, including three children, live in Petaluma, California.

10

. . . .

*Ending
Note*

EPILOGUE

The Applause of Heaven

. . . .

by Max Lucado

You'll be home soon too. You may not have noticed it, but you are closer to home than ever before. Each moment is a step taken. Each breath is a page turned. Each day is a mile marked, a mountain climbed. You are closer to home that you've ever been.

Before you know it, your appointed arrival time will come; you'll descend the ramp and enter the City. You'll see faces that are waiting for you. And, maybe, just maybe—in the back, behind the crowds—the One who would rather die than live without you will remove His pierced hands from His heavenly robe and . . . applaud.

Other Cook titles
by Mike Yorkey

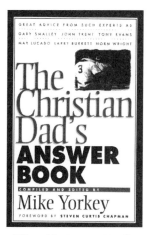

The Christian Dad's
Answer Book
ISBN: 0-78143-364-9
$13.99 (U.S.)

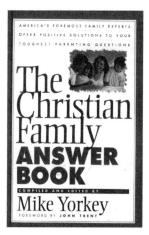

The Christian Family
Answer Book
ISBN: 0-78143-362-2
$13.99 (U.S.)

The Christian Mom's
Answer Book
ISBN: 0-78143-363-0
$13.99 (U.S.)